To Tony

With very best wishes,

Paul Codlis.

ABUSE OF TRUST

Frank Beck
and the Leicestershire
Children's Homes Scandal

Mark D'Arcy
and Paul Gosling

First published by The Bowerdean Publishing Co Ltd, 1998
This edition published by Canbury Press, 2016

Canbury Press,
Kingston upon Thames,
Surrey
www.canburypress.com

Printed and bound in Great Britain
by CPI Group (UK), Croydon CR0 4YY

ISBN: 978-0-9930407-8-8 (Hardback)

Contents

Note on sources

In the course of writing this book the authors have spoken to many victims of Beck, his co-accused Peter Jaynes and of his dead co-worker Colin Fiddaman. We have interviewed officials and politicians, lawyers and experts, and we have drawn on a vast body of documents from the case, and from Andrew Kirkwood QC's report on Leicestershire County Council's management of Beck. Some of the main protagonists – perhaps unsurprisingly – have refused to speak to us. Others have been prepared to speak only 'off the record'. In some cases we have quoted from interviews or court testimony, or statements made by people involved in the case who have not spoken to us directly, or who could not be traced.

Note on this edition

Abuse of Trust by Mark D'Arcy and Paul Gosling was first published in paperback by Bowerdean Publishing in 1998 (ISBN: 0906097304). It was widely praised by social work professionals for exploring the failures exposed, and lessons learnt, by Frank Beck's rampage through Leicestershire's care system in the 1970s and 1980s. By 2016, however, the binding of many copies had collapsed and the book had become hard to find in print. Canbury Press (www.canburypress.com) is reprinting *Abuse of Trust* in a limited run of hardbacks to ensure its survival as a permanent record of what happened. An epilogue examines significant new information about the behaviour of the Labour MP Greville Janner. The text has not otherwise been updated: contemporary references relate to the original publication date of 1998.

List of characters

Nasreen Akram: A residential social worker at The Beeches from March 1981 to January 1983. Made detailed complaints about the home, including excessive violence and possible sexual abuse to council managers, November 1982.

Peter Bastin: Convicted child abuser and murderer. Jailed for life 1979. Placed in The Poplars children's home in 1975. One of the earliest documented victims of sexual and psychological abuse by Beck and Fiddaman. Sued Leicestershire County Council for compensation in 1998.

Frank Beck: Employed by Leicestershire County Council 1973-86. Officer in charge of The Poplars children's home, 1973-75; The Ratcliffe Road Adolescent Unit, 1975-78; the Rosehill home (temporary officer-in-charge) 1978; The Beeches 1978-86. Subsequently worked for the London Borough of Brent and Hertfordshire County Council. Arrested 1990, imprisoned on five life sentences, 1991. Died May 1994.

John Cobb: Beck's immediate line manager. One of the principal assistants working under John Noblett (see below). Now retired. Criticised in the Kirkwood Report.

Anne Crumbie: Liberal Democrat county councillor in Leicestershire 1985-97. Spokesperson on social services. President of the East Midlands Region Liberal Democrats. Parliamentary candidate for Leicester South, 1992.

Henry Dunphy: Labour county councillor until 1977. Now a member of Leicester City Council. Grew concerned about Beck after receiving a tip-off about his therapeutic methods.

Dorothy Edwards: First Director of the newly created Leicestershire social services department, from 1973-1980. Believed Beck was getting excellent results' with his methods. Died in 1997.

Colin Fiddaman: Colleague of Beck from his earliest days at The Poplars home, having met him at the Highfields Centre in Northampton. Also worked at Ratcliffe Road. A serious child abuser in his own right. Committed suicide in Amsterdam while on the run, 1991.

Tim Harrison: County Secretary at Leicestershire County Council. Retired 1997. The in-house legal adviser to both Leicestershire County Council and the Leicestershire Constabulary. Advised both on what they could say during and after the criminal trial in 1991.

Ian Henning: former officer with Metropolitan Police. Circumstances of his discharge are disputed. Worked for Greene d'Sa on Beck defence. Convinced that Beck 'fitted-up' to cover guilt of Janner. Died in motor bike accident in 1995.

Masud Hoghughi: Consultant in clinical and forensic psychology. Gave evidence at the High Court action brought by Beck victims.

Greville Janner: Labour MP for Leicester North West and Leicester West 1970-97. Served as chairman of the Commons select committee on employment.

Peter Jaynes: Beck's deputy at The Poplars home, Market Harborough. Followed him to Ratcliffe Road. Convicted of assault and indecent assault of children in his care. Jailed for 3 years.

Mr Justice Jowitt: The High Court judge who presided over Beck's criminal trial in 1991. He also presided over the 1981 trial when Beck was acquitted of assaulting a ten year old boy.

Andrew Kirkwood QC: Chaired the inquiry into management failings during Beck's period at Leicestershire. His report was strongly critical of the management of Leicestershire social services in the 1970s and 80s, and of the conduct of several key managers. Now a judge.

George Lincoln: Deputy officer in charge at the Rosehill home, when Beck was temporarily in charge. Also worked at The Beeches. Convicted, in November 1991, of one count of assault against a child. Given a 12 month conditional discharge.

Sue Middleton: A Labour county councillor, influential in drawing up the childcare strategy which dramatically changed Leicestershire County Council's policy towards children's homes. She retired from the council in 1993.

Peter Naylor: The head of 'Care Branch', the section of the social services department which ran all residential care, including homes for the elderly, disabled and children. He was strongly criticised in the Kirkwood Report. Retired in 1988.

Terence Nelson: The senior assistant director of social services. He investigated claims of sexual abuse against staff, which led to Beck's resignation from Leicestershire social services. Retired in 1988.

Barrie Newell: Former assistant director, Nottinghamshire social services. He was called in to prepare an internal report on Leicestershire's management of Beck following his arrest in 1990.

John Noblett: The principal officer for residential care in Care Branch, working under Peter Naylor. He was John Cobb's line manager. Retired in 1988. Criticised in the Kirkwood Report.

Simon O'Donnell: Apparently killed himself aged 13 in 1977, while an inmate at the Ratcliffe Road Unit. Comments at his inquest led to an examination of Beck's methods. There are grounds now to doubt the official verdict about his death.

Robert Osborne: The Conservative leader on Leicestershire County Council. Returned to the council in 1981, just as his party lost its majority in that year's local elections.

Robert Pritchard: Leader of the Liberal Democrat group on Leicestershire County Council until April 1997. Emeritus Professor of Genetics at Leicester University. Attended much of Beck's criminal trial.

Brian Rice: Director of Social Services 1980-87, succeeding Dorothy Edwards. Now retired. He was the target of some of the harshest criticism from Kirkwood

Jim Roberts: Labour county councillor, elected 1981. Spokesperson on social services. Chairman of the county council 1996-7. A key figure in social services decision making at the time the Beck affair came to light.

Trevor Sturges: Beck's social work tutor at Stevenage College of Further Education. Had some disquiet about Beck and later took complaints from some of his students on placements at Beck's homes to officials at Leicestershire.

Billhar Singh Upall: Solicitor with the Leicester firm of Marron-Dodds. Represented most of the Beck victims seeking damages from Leicestershire County Council.

Brian Waller: Director of Leicestershire Social Services 1988-97, succeeding Brian Rice. In charge of the department when the Beck affair came to light. Later promised to resign if systematic child abuse was discovered at homes in the county under the monitoring systems he had put in place. As acting director of Cambridgeshire social services, he guided them through another major child care scandal, the Rikki Neave case, where a nine year old boy on the 'at risk' register was murdered.

Mick Wells: Acting director of Leicestershire social services 1997-98, succeeding Brian Waller. He was assistant director in charge of domiciliary (i.e. non-residential) services from 1974 and later became deputy director. He was the only serving social services official criticised by the Kirkwood Report still serving when the inquiry was published, but a subsequent internal inquiry praised his contribution to the county and he was not disciplined.

Acknowledgements

This book has only been possible because of the enormous help given by countless people – many of whom have had to keep their identities secret. The authors are indebted to everyone who co-operated in the research of this book, gave their time to be interviewed, and who provided copies of previously unpublished material.

We are especially grateful to Christian Wolmar and Tim Schadla-Hall for their valued assistance in reading the draft manuscript and suggesting improvements. Steve England and the staff at the *Leicester Mercury* library are sincerely thanked for their forbearance. Suzy Gibson's help with the chapter on the trial has been invaluable. The assistance of Allan Levy QC is also greatly appreciated.

To all the victims, the council officers, the politicians and the others whose painful memories were raked over for us to produce this book, we give our genuine thanks. We hope the re-opening of the wounds will prove to be worth it, if this book goes some way to preventing the vulnerable children of the future suffering the abuse inflicted on children in the past.

Introduction

'You rot in hell Becky!' The shout came from one of his victims, caught in the scrum of photographers and TV cameramen who jostled around the prison bus, struggling to capture the definitive image of a proven monster. Until then, the impassive, gaunt figure who was the object of their attention had ignored them, staring straight ahead as the cameras flashed and the TV lights glared in his eyes. Now he extended two defiant fingers and allowed himself a grim smile. It was an impressive display of self control by a man who had just been sentenced to five terms of life imprisonment. Then the bus was through the cordon of press photographers, the shouting died away, and that was the last glimpse the outside world ever had of Frank Beck, the most serious institutional child abuser in British criminal history.

Beck was indeed a remarkable man. For 13 years he committed acts of rape, violence and emotional abuse against vulnerable boys and girls who were sent by Leicestershire County Council to the children's homes where he was in charge. There is strong evidence to suggest that he killed one of them. That wasn't known – although it was suspected by a few – at the time of his trial. But the five life sentences, plus 24 years, he received for his crimes in 1991 were among the harshest punishments ordered by a British judge since the abolition of the death penalty.

The abuse was brutal, even bestial. The consequences for the victims were in many cases devastating. To this day, they live with a legacy of emotional problems and physical scars. Yet this was a man who enjoyed a high professional reputation as a committed, caring social worker. A man whose novel approach to therapy for troubled children was featured in articles in professional journals and on a TV documentary. A man whose abilities with children had come to be seen as indispensable to the child care system in Leicestershire.

What came to be called the Beck case combined all the elements seen separately in other cases. At the centre there was a charismatic abuser who had drawn lesser acolytes into his orbit. They practised a dangerous and damaging quack therapy on vulnerable children. There was systematic sexual abuse and terrifying violence – all accompanied by an almost unbelievable catalogue of negligence and failure by some managers and politicians. Even Beck's trial and conviction were not the end. They merely marked the start of a new phase of official investigations, press recrimination, and a long drawn out legal battle for compensation for the victims.

There are lessons to he drawn from every aspect of Frank Beck's career: about the survival of such a man in a position of trust for more than a decade; about attitudes toward delinquent, disturbed or simply unwanted children; and about the interplay between the council, the courts and the media as the full extent of the scandal emerged.

The extent of management failure in the Beck case is startling. It took complacency and ineptitude on an epic scale to ignore a string of credible and detailed complaints against Beck. They almost invariably disappeared into a bureaucratic limbo while he continued abusing children. Year after year, children ran away from Beck's children's homes, telling the police who caught them about the abuse

Beck was inflicting on them – but the allegations were usually ignored and the children returned to Beck's abusive care. If anyone had listened, Beck could have been caught many years before his eventual arrest.

These children were supposed to be 'in care', sent there by the courts, their families or social services. Some were out of control, engaged in crime, substance abuse or prostitution. Some were disturbed, often because they had already fallen victim to child abusers. Some were just unfortunate and had been placed with Beck because officialdom had nowhere else to put them. But in practice, council care gave them no effective protection from their council 'carers'. No one outside really knew what was happening to them – no one believed them if they talked. In the closed world of The Beeches and the other homes Beck managed, children could be raped or seduced, beaten senseless, or subjected to painful and humiliating 'treatments' which, one psychologist later said, amounted to torture. In cases like this the focus is on the sexual abuse, but the long term psychological damage inflicted by the systematic violence, including the terrifying restraint techniques used by Beck and others, could be just as serious.

Beck's crimes were well publicised at the time of his trial, in 1991. Leicestershire County Council's management failures were the subject of a major inquiry. Police mistakes were investigated by a second inquiry. But the specialised nature of a criminal trial and of the inquiries meant that the story of Beck in its entirety – of his co-abusers, of the aftermath of his trial and the sufferings of his victims – remained untold.

This book examines all these issues. It reveals problems that are still unresolved. With new abuse scandals emerging almost weekly, a clearer understanding of the nature of abuse and abusers, as well as of the management failings which allow such crimes to take place, is essential. Another theme is the political fallout from such cases. As long forgotten policy decisions, police investigations and management actions were scrutinised, there were careers to protect, as well as political and institutional interests. The Beck revelations posed a serious threat to a number of senior politicians and managers within Leicestershire County Council who stood accused of failing to stop him. Leicestershire's social services department had to rebuild shattered public confidence, and the county council itself faced the prospect of footing a multi-million pound compensation bill. On the margins, at times almost forgotten, were the victims, who wanted their day in court and retribution against those who had failed to protect them. They were to be sadly disillusioned by the legal process.

Some of the victims of Beck and the other Leicestershire abusers now live apparently normal, even successful lives. Others were shattered by their experiences, descending into substance abuse, self-mutilation and crime. Four Beck victims are convicted murderers. Others have killed themselves. Some are likely to spend their lives in prisons or mental hospitals. Some, perhaps, were always doomed to a miserable life. But they were supposed to be receiving help. Instead they were abused. It was as if a hospital casualty unit had begun torturing its patients.

The sheer misery they suffered is hard to imagine. The continuing distress many of them endure is painful to see. When the truth of what happened to them emerged, many found the battle for compensation more like an extension of their abuse. Care for difficult children had become an unfashionable backwater – a faraway country of which managers, policy makers, and ultimately voters, knew nothing. While that remains true – and it is still true – other Frank Becks will flourish.

CHAPTER ONE
Beck: the man, the career

'An unstable, macho, charismatic oddball.'
– **Brian Waller, Leicestershire's Director of Social Services, 1987-97.**

Frank Beck cut an unlikely figure for a social worker. He was tough, uncompromising and very, very strong. His arms were as thick as the thighs of the children in his care. If you did not know he had been a marine who had seen active service, you might have guessed. But if you were unaware that he was a social worker, then you were in for a shock.

Faced with resistance, Beck became extraordinarily awkward, sometimes to the point of threatening violence. He had a short fuse, and few people crossed him twice. Though Beck did not hit the people he worked with, he instilled an absolute fear in them – a terror based more on his capacity to dominate everyone in his orbit than on his physical strength.

Beck was not a tall man, but he kept himself very fit. A picture of him, taken at the height of his power and professional reputation, shows a burly figure in a sweater, exuding power and energy. He is posed outside The Beeches children's home, staring at the camera with a curiously menacing confidence. The picture captures something of his physical presence. Beck was broad across the shoulders, and had a thick set face, with a square chin. But the most striking feature was his eyes. Unruly children in his care were brought to order by a single piercing glance. Some later spoke of his eyes having a hypnotic effect – certainly they were a key element in his control over them.

A physical 'presence' was no disadvantage in dealing with these children. Some were there for no worse reason than their families had broken down, or their parents could no longer cope, and there was nowhere else to go to. Others, though, were hardened criminals and substance abusers before they had even become teenagers. These were tough nuts to crack, and only Frank Beck ever came close to cracking them.

Kids who had been regular runaways from Leicestershire children's homes became remarkably well-behaved in Frank Beck's care. Repeated criminal offending often ended when the youngsters were given to Frank Beck, and his bosses were very impressed. It became clear soon after Beck was employed by Leicestershire County Council in 1973 that this man had something special about him.

In short, Frank Beck was about as far away as it is possible to get from the society stereotype of a paedophile – this was no wimp who had never matured physically or mentally beyond adolescence. Lawrie Simpkin, a former Executive Editor of the *Leicester Mercury*, who knew most significant politicians in the county, was astonished at the sexual allegations against Beck: 'In some ways I wouldn't have been surprised if he had been accused of cruelty, or even raping a girl – but boys? I was utterly surprised. I had never had any inkling that he was a homosexual.'

Beck did not fit the stereotype of a gay man any more than he fitted that of the paedophile. There are, though, indications that he had sexual contact with men many years before working with boys in children's homes. He told the court during his trial that while in the marines he was regularly involved in group masturbation sessions with other servicemen. But in Beck's view there was nothing homosexual about this.

So what made Beck into a child abuser? One story, told by Beck to his friends, was that he had been abused by a stranger on a train, at the age of 12 or 13. He spoke on other occasions, more vaguely, of having been abused as a child, hinting at something more upsetting having been done by someone close to him. Certainly child abuse is most damaging when it continues over a long period of time and is perpetrated by a parent figure – the role that Beck himself adopted to children in his care – but abusers often falsely claim to have been victims as children in order to mitigate responsibility for their later behaviour.

Beck seduced and emotionally abused adult social workers, which does not suggest merely a sexual fixation on children – even if the social workers were mostly younger and junior to him. It suggests something much more complex – more concerned with power than sex. 'What he was really about,' one of the victims was to say years later, 'was the mind games. Forget the sex and the violence. Frank Beck really got his kicks from dominating those around him, from getting inside their heads.'

Dr Masud Hoghughi, a clinical and forensic psychologist who examined many of Beck's victims, said they reminded him of the Bosnian torture victims he had worked with. His interviews with the victims suggested that Beck was 'an aggressive psychopath, whose aim was to dominate others, who relished and revelled in inflicting hurt on others. It was systematic, purposive infliction of hurt, to master another person. That demands selecting a weak person and selecting their weakest point, and constantly assaulting it until they give in. To call the result a serious trauma underestimates it; they can never be put back together again'. Beck not only had a strong enough personality to do such things;

he was also capable of dominating weaker colleagues, luring some of them into abusing children, sexually and physically.

Beck's background offers few clues to his later behaviour. He was born in Salisbury and raised in Thornton Heath, South London, the son of a train driver. Beck was the youngest of five children, in a family that moved three times before he was five. According to his sister Mabel, the family member he was closest to, it was a happy childhood. He left school – a secondary modern – with no qualifications and spent three years working on a farm. Suddenly he announced he was joining the Royal Marines.

His nine years' service in the Marines was as apparently unremarkable as his childhood. He completed the gruelling Marine commando training course, served in Borneo and Aden and rose to the rank of Sergeant. According to his sister, he emerged with an honourable discharge and campaign medals and was offered officer training. A social worker at one of Beck's homes, Robert Erskine, was later to describe how Beck boasted of interrogating prisoners in Aden, and claimed that MI6 had wanted to recruit him when he left the Marines.

But his service career was not a straightforward tale of macho soldiering. Much later, Beck said he had been bullied because of a soft and effeminate manner or what passed for one in the Marines – and, bizarrely, for cross-dressing. He recalled that there had been frequent blatant sexual activity between men. Beck said that he chose what he saw as a 'masculine' occupation because he had been brought up in a female-dominated environment. It is possible that all this could indicate a confusion of sexuality, but most people who engage in such activities do not go on to become serial child abusers and rapists. Whatever made Frank Beck what he subsequently became, there was more to it than this.

There was a brief marriage, in the late 1960s, which his sister called a marriage of convenience, to Anna, a Czech woman; they were just good friends and it allowed her to stay in Britain. Years later, in 1987, there was a second marriage, as clinical as the first, to Alexandra Seale-Waithe, a black woman, who Beck first met as a social work student. Later she employed Beck at Brent council in North London at a time when Beck was under suspicion of being an abuser. If the first marriage was convenient for Anna from Czechoslovakia, the second was equally convenient for Beck, and helped to lift some of the doubts over his sexuality. But it was never something that Beck took seriously, and the couple separated after a few weeks, though they remained good friends. Seale-Waithe was subsequently to tell the police that Beck was gay, and not really interested in sex with her. The marriage does underline, though, Beck's ability as a charmer – something reported by his friends who say he could win over the people he wanted to.

Beck's second marriage highlights another contradiction of his life. He was capable of the crudest racist ranting against children and staff at his homes. One Asian woman was frequently and publicly described by Beck as 'a Paki', and black children were picked on by him. Yet two of his closest friendships were with people of African origin – Seale-Waithe and Nick Adjinka, who loyally worked with Beck, and who ran a business with Beck in 1987 between Beck's employment by Leicestershire and Brent councils. The best explanation is provided by Nasreen Akram, who was employed in one of Beck's homes as a social worker. Beck picked on any perceived weakness, she said, whether it was a stutter or racial difference, and used it to undermine a person, to humiliate and embarrass them, to reinforce his psychological advantage over everyone he knew.

Friends, though, were inspired to tremendous loyalty by Beck, despite his persistent cruelty to others. One of his regular visitors to prison, while on remand and after sentencing, was described by one of Beck's friends as his 'third wife', who visited him every week for years on end, and wanted to marry him. When Beck eventually died in prison she even extracted from the prison authorities the clothes he was wearing when he died, and put them to bed with her and slept with them.

Many other friends remained loyal to the end, and after. Pilar Munos was a Spanish woman who found herself alone and friendless in Leicester when she split from her husband in very unpleasant circumstances. She remembers Beck with respect. 'Frank Beck had a very strong need to help people,' explained Munos. 'He definitely did good for people.'

When her marriage finished, Ms Munos paid Beck £7 a week for several weeks to give her counselling sessions. She phoned him every day for advice. 'His behaviour with me was absolutely impeccable, and that was over three or four years,' she said. 'My younger brother died and while I was in Spain [sorting out family affairs] Frank Beck looked after my daughter. He was fine with her. He was not a father figure to me, or a friend, he was a bit of everything. He always portrayed himself to me as 100 per cent male, not interested sexually in men. He was a very strong man with a stubborn nature. He was very arrogant sometimes. You had to laugh at it. He knew more than anybody, he could see through anybody. The temptation to be God is big for everybody.' It was a temptation that Beck regularly yielded to.

'He always took the mickey out of me because I thought the answers were in books, and he thought the answers were in myself,' continued Ms Munos. 'He had thought so much about himself, inside himself.' Beck once told her that anyone was capable of committing appalling acts and he would not sit in judgement over people who did. It is interesting to speculate, with hindsight, how much his own experience informed that comment.

In prison, Beck regularly gave counselling sessions to other inmates. Just as he had been a social worker in the outside world, giving genuine support and advice to the many children he did not abuse, so, too, Beck became an unofficial social worker to those fellow prisoners who chose to socialise with him. Beck's defence solicitor, Oliver D'Sa, remembers the first time he met Beck. 'He made an immediate impression on me. I was struck that here was a very intelligent man. Even in prison, amongst rule 43s [convicted sex offenders], he began counselling other people in prison, in Whitemoor and Gartree.'

But if Beck was capable of charm, friendship and generosity, he was also capable of venomous hatred. He despised organised religion, and told his children to keep clear of the Church. He described the police as 'pigs and bastards', which went down well with the children in his care with a criminal record. Despite his marriages and close friendships with women, he was also an outrageous misogynist. On one occasion he told children 'women are only good in bed or in the kitchen'. Another time he said that children were in his care because of 'bad mothering', and that meant that only men should be involved in rearing them inside children's homes.

Beck the politician

Beck's politics were another mass of contradictions. He told the children they should become anarchists, that the Queen should be shot, that Maggie Thatcher was useless, and that the only good government was in the Soviet Union. Yet he rose to a powerful position within the Leicestershire Liberal Party, most of whose members believed none of these things.

In 1981 Beck joined the Liberals, and became active in local politics in Blaby, a suburb to the west of Leicester, which contained both The Beeches children's home, which he managed, and his own modest house in a quiet suburban close. In 1983 he won a seat on Blaby District Council, defending it successfully in 1987. While employed by Leicestershire County Council he was not allowed to stand for election to that council, though he regularly attended the Liberals' county group meetings as an informal social services advisor to their councillors. But after he left the county council's employment, he did stand for election in his home ward, Braunstone, in the 1989 county elections. At the time of his arrest, later in 1989, he was even being considered by the Liberal Democrats for nomination as a magistrate, according to a senior party figure.

Liberal Party colleagues remember him as a strong councillor who was influential on a number of occasions – once almost single-handedly forcing officials to change the route of a proposed road. He also kept his ward Liberal Party going. 'Frank Beck was the chairman and driving force in Braunstone branch,' recalled David Pollard, a long standing Blaby Liberal and Liberal Democrat councillor.

Top council officials were naturally uncomfortable about the political links between Beck and the county council's Liberal group – which at that time controlled the balance of power on a hung council – and clearly, embarrassing questions about his behaviour in children's homes were undesirable from the point of view of the fragile and unofficial Liberal/Labour coalition that effectively ran the county council.

Senior council officers are always worried about informal contact between officers and councillors, both because of the potential disciplinary implications, and because their policy advice might be second-guessed. Beck was a problem in both respects – his political links made his managers wary of him and made him even more confident and assertive in his dealings with the official hierarchy. In addition, by advising the Liberal group, he was helping to overturn policies supported by his bosses. Labour councillors were unhappy too, not least because some of them hated Beck on a personal basis, but were in no position to criticise him, as they were dependent on informal advice from other social services officers to keep a check on the actions of the most senior social services staff.

The reason that Beck grew so powerful is an everyday story of political rotten boroughs. No one else really wanted to be the Liberal candidate in Braunstone ward. Beck worked hard, recruited new members – including amongst his own staff – and spoke articulately and forcefully. When councillors discuss the minutiae of local politics, questions about broader beliefs may never arise. The Liberals at that time had no centralised system of candidate vetting – and even if they had, there would probably have been no reason to reject him as a candidate. As other child molesters such as Mark Trotter in the Hackney Labour Party have found, becoming influential in a political party can be a very useful form of protection when allegations are made.

Beck the social worker

Meanwhile, Beck had been rising high in his chosen career. After leaving the Marines, he stayed with sister Mabel and decided to take the plunge into social work. She says he thought it was a follow-up to the kind of work he had done in the Marines, handling people. He saw it as the kind of job he could cope with.

What followed was a rapid progression through social work training, with spells at children's homes in Northampton and Leicester. He started at Kirk Lodge in Leicester and then moved to Northampton. He said he left the home there after complaining about the way young people were treated. He was offered a job by Northamptonshire social services and went into a training course at Stevenage, where he acquired a Certificate of Qualification in Social Work and a Home Office Letter of Recognition in Child Care.

His tutor on the social work course at Stevenage College of Further Education, Trevor Sturges, said Beck completed the academic and residential requirements successfully. Sturges was surprised at how sharp Beck was, despite a limited educational background which revealed itself in his rather confused writing style. But Sturges had been left with a sense of 'unease' which he would like to have been able to pass on to future employers. His subsequent reference for Beck's application to head The Poplars home in Market Harborough, Leicestershire, shows traces of this disquiet. It hints that Beck could be destructive in his criticism and difficult to work with. And there is a comment that his success in the post would depend on his establishing 'a successful and consonant interaction with other staff in the establishment'. The reference did, though, praise Beck's sharp intelligence and critical ability, and his 'gifted understanding of emotional development'.

One crucial part of Beck's social work training was a spell at the Highfields Children's Centre in Northampton. This was a therapeutic unit caring for children aged from 5 to 12. The unit was run by Wendy Rowell, a disciple of the famous therapist Barbara Dockar-Drysdale, who used the technique of treating children as if they were babies at her Mulberry Bush School. This technique was imported to the Highfields Centre, where it was used on some children, under the direction of an educational psychologist. It was cynically distorted by Beck – with important and evil alterations – when he worked later in Leicestershire. The bottles and nappies that Beck was to use in his home-grown therapies were not used at Highfields. But it is clear that this was where he began to absorb the ideas which were later woven into his own 'regression therapy'.

Beck made his experience at Highfields a major plank of his application for his first important job in residential social work. He applied to become officer-in-charge of The Poplars, a children's home in Market Harborough, where up to 18 disturbed and difficult teenage boys were looked after by six staff. At the time, the newly created Leicestershire social services was trying to move away from the simple containment of problem children. The department wanted some kind of intervention strategy or treatment – but had little clear idea of what form it might take. Beck told them he wanted to 'develop a therapeutic community, where children and young persons can develop to their full emotional personalities'. Council officials were delighted – they saw him as quite a catch.

Wendy Rowell, a referee for Beck, had no idea he intended to set himself up as a therapist. If she had known, she would have pointed out that he had 'no therapeutic background, or knowledge, or training,' she said later. But on the basis of minimal experience at a therapeutic community, Beck had bluffed his way into a post which gave him a licence to rummage around children's minds. At best, he might have been experienced enough to assist a qualified person. But his job application was larded with psychological jargon, his references may have inadvertently made him sound more experienced than he was, and none of the managers in charge of selecting the next officer-in-charge of The Poplars had any detailed knowledge of the qualities or experience the successful candidate should possess. Leicestershire County Council's failure to check that the man they were appointing to create a therapeutic community was actually qualified for the job was to have disastrous long term consequences. It was the first link in a decade-long chain of management failure, and opened the way for everything that followed.

CHAPTER TWO
The Poplars, Market Harborough,
September 1973– March 1975

'I don't know quite what he's doing, but he's doing it very well.'
— Dorothy Edwards, Director of
Leicestershire social services 1973-80

The Poplars provided Beck's first real test as a therapist and a manager. Outwardly he was a success. But behind closed doors children were beaten and subjected to abusive therapies and staff were reduced to subservience. The pattern was set for crimes which were to be repeated for more than a decade and the key figures in the subsequent trail of child abuse began to assemble. Almost 20 years later, Peter Jaynes, the deputy officer-in-charge when Beck took over the home, was to stand next to Beck in the dock at Leicester Crown Court. Jaynes would be convicted of assault and indecent assault against children in his care. Although Jaynes preceded Beck to The Poplars, he was regarded as too young, untrained and inexperienced (he was 24) to run the home himself. Also on the staff was Colin Fiddaman, who had first met Beck at the Highfields Children's Home in

Northampton, where he took over Beck's post. He would later be revealed as a serial child abuser, and his association with Beck lasted until the mid-1980s. He too would have been in the dock if he had not killed himself while on the run.

The children who were sent there were mostly those who were seen as 'the hard cases'. Other parts of the care system had failed to cope with them. Typically, their files would recount unsuccessful placements in other children's homes, or failed fostering placements, or reveal that they had been on the probation service's books for some years. They were there to be contained and, if possible, helped to change their behaviour. Many acted in ways – violent, sexual or criminal – which are simply outside the experience of ordinary families and some were very seriously disturbed. Under the law at the time, these children were placed in homes through a care order or a place of safety order. These were issued by a court, usually at the request of the local social services authority – in this case Leicestershire County Council – which then took over parental responsibility. Other children might he sent there by voluntary arrangement with their families. None of Beck's homes were secure units where children were locked in. There might be restrictions imposed by the courts, for example limiting contact with particular people, but the main control on their movements were the home's own rules about such issues as bedtime and mealtimes. Runaways would usually be picked up and returned by the police, but they were no more breaking the law than a child that ran away from its own parents.

The Poplars was staffed by residential social workers – a job at the lower end of the social work pecking order. As the name suggests, they were based at the home, sometimes sleeping in to supervise the children overnight, so despite their low status they were in a position of considerable trust. Each child had a particular member of staff assigned to them as their 'key worker'.

Most children would also maintain contact with a field social worker from an area office. These were the people who helped decide to place them in a home. They would keep in touch, partly as a link with the child's family and partly to help them return to the community after their spell in care. This overlap in responsibility was a frequent source of friction between Beck and his staff, and the rest of the department. Over the years that followed, he would devote much effort to manoeuvring field social workers out of decisions about the children at his homes.

Very few women social workers were employed at The Poplars – Beck once explained that this was because many of the problems the boys suffered could be blamed on 'bad mothering'. None of the residential social workers at The Poplars had any psychiatric or social work training. Most had just a handful of 'O' Levels or CSEs, and did not dare question Beck's methods. Phrases like 'I assumed he knew what he was doing' feature prominently in their evidence about his treatment of children. Peter Jaynes' evidence at his trial gives a vivid picture of the pitfalls open to staff from Beck's therapy: 'We would have to go and challenge the child and just attempt to provoke the child in any way we possibly could.'

Jaynes said Beck co-ordinated the therapy and everyone else learned from him. This 'therapy' involved provocation in the form of constant tickling, or blowing in the child's ears, or discussing painful topics involving the child's family. The idea was to make the child lose control, to 'get their feelings out'. When they exploded, they were held down, often by several adults, until they subsided. Jaynes never questioned what they were doing, and thought at the time he was doing good. Some children, he said, did appear to respond and function better. His defence to the charge of indecently assaulting one girl – later in Ratcliffe Road – was that she misunderstood the therapy she was receiving. He admitted telling her that her father wouldn't help her because he didn't want her, and agreed he may have called her a lesbian. He said it to provoke a tantrum and get the anger out of her. He may have rubbed his body against hers while attempting to restrain her, but there was no sexual motive. If he had asked her if she was feeling randy, it would have been because he was taught that such questions were part of trying to understand their feelings, part of the therapy. The violence and physical restraint used against children were administered by Beck, Fiddaman and other members of the team. Jaynes told his trial: 'I did it because I saw my boss doing it, it was the ethos of the place. There was no way I wanted my boss to come on duty and find the place in chaos, so I used the same methods.'

Jaynes was probably the first of a series of adult social workers to be seduced and buggered by Beck. 'It terrified the life out of me,' Jaynes said. He submitted because he was scared of Beck. 'I was too frightened to tell him to stop. I was in a very vulnerable state. I used to dread hearing the lock on the door drop while I was watching TV.' He was at a low ebb when Beck arrived at The Poplars as the new officer-in-charge. Jaynes' marriage was breaking up and he was broke. 'Beck took both my hands in his and said 'It'll be all right Peter, we'll work it out together.' At the time it seemed very genuine, but the supervision sessions 'mostly happened between the sheets of his bed or mine'. He remembers Beck telling him the sessions were to free him, release his emotions and make him a better person.

Jaynes was simply too scared to tell Beck to stop: 'Mr Beck is a very powerful person, a very powerful personality. Mr Beck has a level of aggression in his voice, the way he treats me, that scared the life out of me on more than one occasion. He never hit me physically, but he knows how to hit you inside, he knows how to hit you in the brain and the emotions.'

He guessed that other staff were sexually intimate with Beck. Both Jaynes and Fiddaman suffered an irritation to their genitals during a holiday in Devon. 'We both went to seek out a chemist for ointment. I thought at the time it might have been passed by the hand of Mr Beck.' He was frightened and fed up with Beck's abuse. 'It was appalling and not a method I would use to supervise my staff.'

Another Poplars social worker was counselled by Beck after being 'rescued' by him, after a confrontation with a child. 'Frank said the child had confronted me on a sexual level. He said the children would always be able to manipulate me on the area of sex, because if I was not emotionally right they would find any skeleton in the cupboard and twist, and twist.' Beck gradually undressed the man, while telling him that sex was an area he had to work on. They began to have sex regularly. The social worker said he was aware that Beck was his boss and had his career in his hands. 'Frank always said to trust him, and at this stage I had no one else left to trust.'

Few accounts of child abuse have emerged from The Poplars. But in a 1998 compensation case Peter Bastin, now a convicted murderer, described how he was abused there while in his early teens. Bastin had already been abused before arriving at the home. He had been a persistent runaway and had worked as a rent boy in London. His key worker was Colin Fiddaman, who progressed from tucking him into bed to touching him. The boy would often wake up in the mornings to discover Fiddaman lurking by his bed. On one occasion Fiddaman accused him of sleeping in a provocative position to entice other boys. Bastin was also provoked into temper tantrums and then restrained, and subjected to 'regression therapy' in which he would be treated like a very young child – both forms of supposed treatment practised by Beck. This therapy would often be followed by sexual abuse by both Beck and Fiddaman, and years later it would have a horrific sequel.

Beck's bosses, meanwhile, had increasing faith in him, and all the indications they had at this time indicated that their trust was justified. Managers gave Beck enthusiastic reviews for his performance at The Poplars. Peter Naylor, the assistant director of social services in charge of Care Branch – the county council's residential homes – recommended his appointment should he confirmed at the end of the normal six months probation. 'From the outset he has set up a programme of therapy for each of the boys in the home, most of whom are severely disturbed and have suffered acute emotional deprivation', he wrote in a memo. 'There was praise for Beck's insight into the needs of individual boys and his management skills – his diligent attitude to the kind of routine paperwork that bored many colleagues was something his managers found very reassuring.

The new unit, with its novel therapeutic approach, became a talking point in social services circles. Dorothy Edwards, the then Director of Social Services, told friends that Beck was certainly unorthodox, but was getting 'marvellous results' with his regression therapy. If he came under fire from social workers and the probation service, it was because his thinking was so far ahead of theirs that they were 'jealous and nonplussed'. Although she was experienced in child care, she admitted that she was 'not quite au fait' with his therapeutic methods. 'I don't know quite what he's doing,' she told a friend, 'but he's doing it very well.'

Edwards' probity was legendary within her social services department; she had once sacked a home help for stealing a biscuit. It is inconceivable to those who knew her that she would have overlooked even 'minor' offences by Beck if they had come to her attention. It is hard to imagine she can have known the details of his therapeutic methods with all their obvious dangers. All she knew was that his approach was unorthodox and apparently successful. Children were contained, offending was reduced or eliminated. She should have known more. Beck's arrest and conviction were a terrible shock to her and left her very depressed. She died in 1997, never having recovered from the upset.

Another important Beck supporter was Norah Eady, later chair of the social services committee. She was the county councillor for Market Harborough, the small town where The Poplars was sited. Henry Dunphy, a Labour county councillor at the time, believes that Beck had become her protégé – 'her blue-eyed boy' – and that it was her influence that helped Beck to move on to the next important phase of his career – when in March 1975, the Poplars was transferred to new and bigger buildings at Ratcliffe Road in Leicester. This was an early example of what became an established pattern: building links with politicians bolstered Beck's influence through much of his career.

CHAPTER THREE
The Ratcliffe Road Adolescent Unit
March 1975 -June 1978

'Children did as they were told –
if not they were battered into submission.'
- Peter Jaynes, deputy officer-in-charge.

Beck's apparent success with his therapeutic approach to child-care was to have its reward at his new and bigger children's home. The new unit was sited next to an old people's home in a genteel Leicester district, in a new building composed of stubby brick-built hexagonal towers. A brochure set out its aims: to provide a stable environment for adolescents with severe emotional disturbances; provide specialised therapy and care; help children work through their inner conflicts and damaging experiences and prepare them for life outside. It seemed the very model of modern childcare. Beck would later be convicted of six serious sexual assaults on children there.

All staff were required to support Beck's methods and philosophy – he insisted that this was essential, if the home was going to work. This meant he would hand pick the three extra social workers who would be needed. The entire staff of The Poplars, including Jaynes and Fiddaman transferred with him to Ratcliffe Road. One major change at Ratcliffe Road was the arrival of girls – Beck said he was keen to introduce them into the previously 'monastic' home, although he did regard girls as more difficult to treat than boys.

As Beck later told his trial, the unit catered for the most difficult children. 'Anyone with anti-social behaviour in the extreme would be referred to us – 50 per cent of the children had been sexually abused. They were very aggressive, with a history of violence, normally with a weapon such as knives, a fairly extensive absconding rate and criminal records for offences such as ABH, GBH and robberies.' Beck regarded the children as difficult and demanding, but thought they could often be 'wonderful people'. He said his homes had less violence than most and blamed a quarter of the anti-social behaviour on the normal reaction of children to being placed in an institution.

As at The Poplars, the children sent to Ratcliffe Road could be uncontrollable, violent, self-mutilating, prostitutes, hardened criminals – or sometimes just unlucky, with no problems beyond the ordinary, but nowhere else to go. Some were referred to him, others were plucked from other parts of the childcare system in Leicestershire and occasionally beyond. By this time Beck was seen as more than a simple officer-in-charge; he had become a fully fledged childcare guru and could hand-pick children for his unit.

The regime at Ratcliffe Road had disturbing undertones for many of the children. A lot of the behaviour was the kind of thing they could not quite complain of – one girl who stayed at Ratcliffe Road remembers: 'Some of them were very clever at walking into the bedroom or the bathroom when you were there. He [Beck] would sit on the bed and read you a story, rubbing your back – he would come close but never actually touch where he shouldn't.' But a large number of adolescent children found they were being bathed by social workers – and many were uncomfortable with the kind of cuddling which Beck said they needed because they had been deprived of love.

A former Ratcliffe Road resident described the bizarre atmosphere at the home. 'You were allowed to smoke, the older kids sometimes had drinks in bottles with dummies – they would he walking around in pyjamas, holding bottles with dummies. I couldn't believe it at first, but then I was told that it was part of their therapy. The kids involved were in their early teens.' The bottles were part of Beck's home grown 'regression therapy' – an attempt to dig down to the supposed roots of children's problems, by returning them to a state of infancy. Younger children might be dressed in nappies and fed from bottles. Social workers might cut up the food on their plates, as if feeding infants. Children would be given toys designed for much younger children. There was a lot of cuddling and bodily contact. Regression is a legitimate element of psychology and psychoanalysis but Beck had no qualification to impose his own variation of it on vulnerable children. It was as if someone with a City and Guilds in carpentry had started performing brain surgery.

Beck believed emotions should not be bottled up – so children were deliberately provoked into violent temper tantrums, physically restrained, often by several social workers, and sometimes choked around the neck with a towel. Beck trained his staff to use a special 'paddy hold' in which arms were placed across the child and legs wrapped around them from behind. It was supposed to cause the least damage and make the child feel safe. This procedure was called 'having a paddy'. For young children it was terrifying. 'The first time I saw one, I was horrified; it was totally scary,' a Ratcliffe Road resident recalls. 'If you had a disagreement with staff, they would grab you – several would hold you down and they'd hold on no matter how you kicked, until you either stopped or became hysterical – some kids would be carried out in distress.'

Another girl in care at Ratcliffe Road had similar experiences. 'I was pinned down and provoked into a temper tantrum several times. Peter Jaynes, the deputy, would do it and then put me on someone's knee. Jaynes was a very big man, especially compared to a small young girl. When he was on top of you, that was frightening. You wondered if he was getting his kicks, but it was something you never talked about. It was totally taboo. I've never seen 'owt like it in my life. There was something round my neck, they said it was a towel. Next day I was all bloodshot round my neck. I ran away to see my dad, and he went round to my mother's and kicked down the door to show her; she just sent me back. I had to wear a polo-neck sweater afterwards. When I went to school, I never said anything.' This was a fairly typical tale. Often parents simply didn't believe the stories their children told them, and were in any case reluctant to take on the system.

'Jaynes brutalised children. He was a big Liverpool supporter, and I can't stand Liverpool to this day,' another former resident said. 'Particular children were picked on. One kid, Mark, was a favourite victim. He was put on bottle and dummy aged 13-14. I've never seen anyone so scared in all my life. He was mainly afraid of Colin Fiddaman, who was his key worker. I saw him being dragged around by the hair. I can still see his face. He used to curl up in a corner, shrieking like a small child. Now I have a better idea of what he must have been frightened of. I remember one particular time seeing him being dragged towards the social worker's flat, screaming 'No! No!''

A boy at the home recalls being dragged upstairs by Fiddaman. 'Colin got hold of a towel and started to twist and flick it at me,' he said. 'The result was the towel was used very much like a whip. This continued for about 15 minutes as Colin kept on goading me. He then got hold of me and put the towel around my neck and began pulling on it. He was strangling me with the towel. He would tighten the towel round my neck until I began to panic and then he would loosen its grip. The more I struggled, the tighter the towel became. This continued for quite some time and on each occasion that Colin would tighten the towel, he would tighten it for a much longer period. I remember thinking, just a few moments before the incident stopped, that these were my last few moments of life. Colin had tightened the towel to such a point that I could not breathe. I was exhausted and just simply gave up.'

Jaynes himself said children were broken down by the regime at Ratcliffe Road. 'Children did as they were told. If they didn't, things happened – physical violence that was unnecessary.' Children were 'battered into submission'. The aim was to 'overpower them and then reduce their own opinions and views, not necessarily to make them into a clone, but along those lines'.

'I can remember laying in bed and hearing kids cry,' one resident recalled. 'There were always staff coming in and checking you were sleeping, mainly the suspect ones. There was a lot of shouting from the bathrooms. I think a lot used to happen there. They would be locked, so you could never get in and see.' Some of the taunting by staff was vicious: 'There was one particular girl who was there when I first arrived. This was about a year after the case of Simon O'Donnell, (*see Chapter 16*) the lad who killed himself; he was one of her friends, so she was taunted with his death. Another girl was taunted about her mother's death. You were treated worse if you had no back-up from others. My mum was banned from visiting, because she was supposed to be a bad influence, and they told me she didn't care about me, and nobody wanted me.'

One resident was Pat Holyland, who was later to play a crucial role in bringing the Beck affair to light. She was fairly typical of the kind of child sent to Ratcliffe Road. She had already been on the social services' books for some years and went into the home at the age of 14, because she was beyond her mother's control and was stealing. 'She was beating me a lot at the time,' Holyland said. 'Maybe without that I wouldn't have behaved as I did, but back then, strict discipline was the thing to do, so I can't blame her one hundred per cent.

'First I went into The Holt [another Leicestershire children's home] for about six months assessment when I was about 11. There were no rules, or very few – I loved it, I went nuts because there was so much freedom. So when I went into Ratcliffe Road a few years later, after being back with my mother for a while, I was very prejudiced in favour of children's homes, because of my time at The Holt. I don't know exactly how it came about that I went to Ratcliffe Road – it was unusual to be taken straight there, normally you were sent there from another home. Frank Beck came to my house to see me before I went in. He said my mum couldn't cope with me and that I was a bad kid. I think he knew my mother was hitting me the moment he walked in.'

She, too, found the home odd: 'When I first got there I saw children walking around in the daytime in pyjamas. Most of the interaction was between kids and staff rather than between the kids – I saw kids being cuddled on adults' knees and I didn't think the kids were normal, but what did I know about normal? Early on, I walked in on a temper tantrum, and that was a shock.'

After about four months, Holyland's mother went to court to try and get her back. She was worried because her daughter was putting on weight and being encouraged to dissociate from her parents. But her attempt to regain custody failed.

'I have this memory of walking through the small lounge near the office and Frank Beck and Peter Jaynes came into the building,' Holyland said. 'They were very cheerful and said I would never go home again, they had a care order until I was

18. It was a taunt because I had been telling them how she would come and fetch me and sort them out.

'I ran away when I was 14, because my mum had written saying that she hadn't got a bed for me at her house. She was saying she just didn't have the room, which was reasonable enough, but they twisted it round and said that what she really meant was that she didn't want me at all, and would never have a bed for me – and that was easy for me to believe because I knew that my mother had never really wanted me and would have had an abortion if she wasn't a Catholic. I was unhappy, because I'd been hoping she would come and take me home, but after a year in there I was beginning to get a sense that no one wanted me anyway. It was another smack in the mouth, and eventually, in there, you learn to accept every smack that comes along.'

Holyland was subjected to Beck's regression therapy and temper tantrums for more than three years. She still recalls the terror it inspired. 'Every child at Ratcliffe Road had the temper tantrum treatment,' she said. 'You would be taken into your room, or into another room with no other children, and they would taunt you about your childhood, your parents, your sexuality, anything they could think of to get at you. Eventually you would start reacting, shouting – and at the first flicker of emotion they would pounce on you. They would lie down beside you, you would be on your back, they would be on their side, facing you, one of their legs under you, one over you, one arm across you, the other free to dig you in the ribs or whatever.

'They would put towels round your neck, or pillows over your face to choke you – they did it whether you were resisting or not, it was just part of the procedure. In fact, if you didn't resist, they would use the towels and pillows to make you fight back, because otherwise you couldn't breathe. It wasn't a case of being broken down, it was a case of life preservation; if you did what they wanted, they would stop, so I would scream and shout about my mother or whatever, because that was what they wanted me to do. When they were doing this to me I was about 4' 6' tall and weighed seven stone; I was tiny, they were big fully-grown men.

'Sometimes when they were doing it in the lounge, kids would come walking by – I saw it happening to two kids, but you didn't stop to watch, because they might decide to do it to you. It was very frightening, horrific. You were petrified before it happened and when it was over you felt good, because you knew you were safe, at least for a couple of days. I was terrified most of the time – for a while I managed to avoid tantrums by going to my key worker and bawling on her shoulder and saying I was feeling bad. But after about four weeks they [Beck and other staff at the unit] wanted to know why I was feeling bad all the time, and I had a major session.'

The regression therapy went on in conjunction with the tantrums; when Holyland first went to Ratcliffe Road, she was feeding herself. But suddenly she was no longer allowed to eat or bathe unaided. 'First I was given a baby's cup, then a bottle – and if you resisted, that was when you would he taken away for a temper tantrum. You could just be sat at the dinner table, and they would accuse you of chucking angry feelings out. They would use other children, particularly the older boys against you. You were on your own in that home, you couldn't count on anyone – if you told other children anything, they could use it against you. It happened even when they took us on holiday. I remember once we were taken to Rhyl in Wales – another girl knew she was in for a temper tantrum, so she told Peter Jaynes I had tried to touch her – although she did warn me, I'll give her that.

'I was off – I squeezed through this tiny window and ran away, and managed to hide for most of the day. They sent the older boys off to find me, but luckily that day I had had my first period, and I used that to get me out of trouble – I think my key worker was pleased to have an excuse not to do anything. But God only knows what people must have thought of us on that holiday – you had 14 year olds expected to play on the beach like little kids, making sand castles and playing games much younger kids would play, even in front of the public.'

The treatment stopped when Holyland was 15. She was told she had gone through her regressive cycle and it was time to start growing up again. But she was given no help to 'mature' again, and after two years of regression this was not easy. Beck and his colleagues, with no psycho-therapeutic training, demanded for years that she act younger than her age, and then simply demanded that she grew up overnight. 'You can't just turn round and start acting mature – I didn't really get my head together until I was about 30,' she said. 'I think the real reason it stopped was that I was being sent to school – Sir Jonathan North Community College – I was erratic at school and bullied by some of the older kids, and it was impossible to make friends, because by then I didn't trust anybody.'

Holyland remembers Jaynes and George Lincoln – who was also tried alongside Beck, convicted of common assault and conditionally discharged – as men with tempers, but she does not believe they would have hit children the way they did, but for meeting Beck. But Colin Fiddaman, who was away on a training course when she arrived, was different. 'He was cruel and calculating and knew how to inflict pain without leaving marks – although he did bite my ear during a temper tantrum. All the kids were petrified of Fiddaman, and they warned me what it would be like when he came back – there was never anything said about sexual abuse of the boys – but you kept yourself to yourself in that home.'

She recalls one serious beating, which came after some of the girls were discovered with a group of boys. 'Jaynes went nuts and dragged me upstairs and laid into me, punching and kicking and smashing me into walls,' she remembers. 'I was petrified and I still don't know why he did it – it was well over the top. They made all the girls take pregnancy tests, to make sure that we weren't. And I'm pretty certain that they used one of the members of staff who was pregnant so that they could deliberately show us positive results – I went round for three or four months thinking I must be pregnant – then I slowly realised that I couldn't be because I was still having my period. Remember I was only 14 or so at the time.'

The effects lasted well into her adult life. 'I will never, never forget what happened in that kids' home. I'm aware of some of the effects. I'm less likely to act rationally, I can be very impulsive and I have to watch my temper. The only reason I'm sane now is that I have learned to detach it from my life.'

Another Ratcliffe Road resident was Jenny L, who was later to receive the biggest compensation pay-out of any of the victims. She was a severely disturbed teenage girl, who had already spent time in a mental hospital. Years later, when she applied for compensation for the abuse she had suffered at Beck's hands, Jenny L had to describe the other aspects of her childhood which contributed to her problems. She told the court that her mother had been mentally ill and once threatened to cut out her daughter's tongue. Jenny went to Ratcliffe Road after Beck came to visit her in the mental hospital, and promised that she would receive plenty of love and care. She was one of the first arrivals at the new Ratcliffe Road Unit – placed there ten days after it opened – and her experiences indicate that the abusive therapy regime at the home was already well developed and that Beck was already sexually abusing children. It is unlikely that such behaviour started at the inception of the new unit; it is far more probable that it was a continuation of the established pattern of behaviour at The Poplars.

Jenny L was repeatedly raped by Beck over several months, the first time after an incident where she found him on a sofa with a half-undressed boy. 'I had been in school and there was a test,' she recalled. 'It was easy. I ran to tell him I had done well. He was in his sitting room with a boy. Beck's trousers and shirt were undone, as were the boy's. The boy was crying – I think he was about 12 or 13. I knew something was going on, but I didn't realise what. Frank Beck came to my room and told me to put my nightie and dressing gown on. He took me to his flat. He told me that I was supposed to knock before I went into his room. The boy was having problems with his sexuality. He went on about me needing a man. He said he was going to show me what I had been missing. He said that women were put on this earth to have babies because we were whores and sluts. He pulled me about. He shook me by the hair so that I fell. He pushed me, lifted up my nightie, and raped me. He said I wouldn't need another woman after this, this was what I was missing.' He told her that he loved her and would care for her.

Adult social workers were also victims. Beck bolstered his domination of many of his male staff by sexual abuse. The seduction process started under the guise of professional counselling. Beck would be alone with a member of staff and would put his hand on the man's thigh, asking if he was uncomfortable with that. If the answer was yes, the man would be criticised on a professional level. 'How can you expect to relate to these children if you're shy about physical contact?' If the approach was not rejected, the touching became progressively more intimate. One worker recalled: 'He got me to touch his chest, then his genitals, then over a period of time moved on to sustained oral sex. Every time I was put into that position I cried.'

Another male social worker recalled using a pillow to muffle his screams during sex with Beck, who told him he needed to redress an imbalance in his sexuality. He says Beck encouraged him to seek sexual contact with other men on the staff, and threatened to engineer his dismissal. Abuse of mostly unwilling social workers, often at a time when they were vulnerable, was a regular feature in Beck's career in Leicestershire. One social worker recalls being interviewed by Beck. He had sent in what he thought was a very poor application and was surprised to be offered an interview. His performance during the interview was also uninspired – he was 'at a low ebb' at the time. So he was amazed to be offered a job. Now he speculates that Beck may have seen him as a target for abuse.

Some of Beck's social worker victims had their careers threatened. Most said they believed his aim was to dominate them, or 'get inside people's heads'. The experience left many of his victims dependent on him – and certainly too ashamed to challenge him. He was able to tell them what was right and what was wrong, and in some cases play a significant role in their lives years after they had stopped working with him. Peter Jaynes was a classic example – Beck was the best man at his wedding and seemed to dominate him when he visited Ratcliffe Road (where Jaynes remained as deputy officer-in-charge after Beck moved on to his next children's home). At least one child at Ratcliffe Road was abused there by Beck after Beck had formally left the home.

From the start, the regime at Ratcliffe Road was Beck's creation. In sometimes purple prose, he told social services managers he wanted an environment where children were 'free from the compulsive constriction of suppressive rules and routines, narrowed by a programmeless exposive [sic] to boredom, sprinkled with the overstimulations coming from seductive contagion-initiators in the child's peer group. Thus for us to succeed in creating a therapeutic community, which I believe is now possible, it could not be divided into those who tell others how to create and others who are supposed to do so, as they are told. The therapeutic community is a continuous creation of and by all members and there could be none who 'also serve".

Managers may not have been very clear what all this meant, but the right buzzwords about open, safe and free communication, and avoiding undemocratic hierarchical structures were used. An expert would have questioned the cocktail of psychological thinking Beck used to explain his approach. But his methods were never vetted by a real expert. He used what he called the 'Warrendale system', based on Canadian experience, provoking children to violent tantrums to release their emotions – the 'paddy attacks' – and he would cite Freud (a developmentalist) and Balint (a behaviouralist) as his key influences – a bit like basing economic policy on the works of Friedman and Marx. Indeed one of the visiting psychologists at Ratcliffe Road, Dr Bhate, did challenge his methods, but Beck dismissed his views, saying he was not an analyst, and his Indian background meant he had cultural problems with the idea of cuddling teenage girls in therapy. The visiting psychiatrists were there to minister to the staff, rather than the children – to ensure that the social workers were coping with the demands of working closely with disturbed children. They did not have any direct contact with the children themselves, but their presence does seem to have given at least the impression that Beck was being monitored by qualified professionals. It does seem strange, however, that they were not more aware of what was going on.

Otherwise, Beck's work went on almost unquestioned. One exception was in 1975, when Henry Dunphy, a Labour councillor from Leicester, received an anonymous phone call – he now believes one of Beck's close colleagues prompted the person to ring him. 'The caller asked me if I knew what was going on at the Ratcliffe Road children's home. I said I had no idea. They said children were being held down on the floor, screaming their heads off, with their arms twisted behind their backs – children were jumping out of windows to get away from it. They said it was bedlam, and cruelty to the children. I asked who was speaking but they wouldn't say – they just insisted that I passed the information on.'

The next day, Dunphy phoned Dorothy Edwards, then Director of Social Services, and recounted the story to her. Soon after, he was visited at home by two social services officials, including John Noblett, the principal residential care officer. They reassured him that they were aware of what was going on – it was all part of the therapy operating there. Dunphy might have accepted that, but for an irate phone call from Frank Beck. Dunphy describes his call as 'threatening'. This was hardly the normal way in which council employees dealt with politicians who had access to their bosses. 'He told me I was slandering him, and he was prepared to take me to court, and his final comment was that I was afraid to face him personally.'

Dunphy, a heavily-built man who does not duck away from challenges, responded by driving straight round to Ratcliffe Road. His first impression of Beck, who he had never met or even heard of before his phone call, was of a very threatening presence. Again, it was hardly the normal way for a council officer to behave towards a politician. 'I remember thinking I would have a job holding off this bloke if it came to blows,' he said. 'He looked reasonably fit, and his manner was what I can only call controlled aggression, never going too far, but trying to keep me off-balance and provoke me into doing something stupid.'

In the discussion that followed Beck explained he was using the Canadian 'Warrendale system', which relied on making children 'explode' into temper tantrums. His staff were trained in physical containment. Dunphy was not convinced by Beck's answers, and his alarm grew when he consulted Father Michael Ingram, a Dominican priest at Leicester's

Holy Cross Priory, who was also a trained child psychologist. Father Ingram's advice was that the Warrendale method was completely discredited. He told Dunphy: 'If you know someone who's practising this, stop them.' He added the treatment would probably not harm nine children out of ten – but it could totally destroy the tenth.

Again Dunphy raised his concerns with the Director, Dorothy Edwards. But at about that time, Beck gave a presentation to the social services committee about his work – and came away with an official seal of approval. Dunphy came off the county council soon afterwards. He now believes the net result of his complaint was simply to add to Beck's aura of invincibility – Beck had taken on a councillor and won.

By the late 1970s Beck was a senior and trusted figure in Leicestershire social services. He was not only respected for his work at The Poplars and Ratcliffe Road, he was also regarded as an authoritative figure within the department, who could be turned to for practical advice. As chair of a departmental working party on childcare practice, he helped steer through a new recommendation that no corporal punishment, defined as punishment to the body by hand or instrument, should be used in Leicestershire children's homes. The working party also said that physical restraint was acceptable only in reasonable circumstances. Beck did not practise what his working party preached.

An interlude: the Rosehill home, Market Harborough, 1978

Another sign of Beck's standing in the social service department was his use as a trouble-shooter when the Rosehill children's home in Market Harborough ran into difficulties. The children were out of control and the staff were disaffected. While remaining in charge at Ratcliffe Road, Beck was chosen to act also as Rosehill's temporary officer-in-charge, to try and deal with the problems. A change in management and approach in Rosehill had caused unrest with children and staff. Beck's remit was to restore order. Almost his first action was to deploy his now familiar seduction technique on George Lincoln, the deputy officer-in-charge. Lincoln (then aged 26) was in a very vulnerable state, having failed to manage the home effectively himself. At first Beck was very sympathetic, and drank a bottle of wine with Lincoln as they discussed his problems. Later he turned up in Lincoln's bedroom and got into bed with him. Lincoln rejected Beck's advances, but he was frightened by the incident. 'Somehow he seemed to know my secret, that I was, perhaps, homosexual. I felt very confused and frightened of who he might tell, because he had mentioned his closeness to the Director of Social Services and that he'd been given the authority to sack me.'

Beck was acting officer-in-charge at Rosehill for eight weeks: it was a revealing period. He brought with him one of the girls in care at Ratcliffe Road, who acted as an assistant. Staff were not told that she was a child in care, and it wasn't until Beck handed out some case files from Ratcliffe Road, to demonstrate the effectiveness of his methods, that the Rosehill staff realised she was one of the children in the files. His methods began to be employed at Rosehill – his 'assistant' was found using the 'paddy hold' to restrain one of the children and sometimes slapped them. She read the children's files and gave out confidential information on one girl. Even more alarmingly, she started conducting treatment sessions with Rosehill children, which seemed to be based on a consumer's experiences of the therapy Beck practised at Ratcliffe Road: clumsy attempts at provocation were mixed with violence.

Lincoln, too, seems to have started using Beck's therapies: he was accused of making a teenage boy repeat the words 'I hate

Daddy' over and over again, in a Beck-style provocation session. On another occasion, he made a girl re-enact abuse by her father – with Lincoln taking the father's role and shouting the words: 'I want your body. Where is your bra?'

Beck's brief intervention at Rosehill was an illuminating demonstration of his prowess: it showed him establishing dominance over another vulnerable young social worker, who began to employ Beck's methods uncritically. And he introduced an acolyte who should never have been working with children. The sheer confidence with which he moved in and introduced his methods, and the vigour with which he beat off outside criticism, highlight the powerful position he now enjoyed within the Leicestershire social services. Unsettled children were calmed, staff were given firm direction, and social services managers breathed more easily. What was apparent to social services managers – despite what was happening within the home – was that Rosehill had quietened down. Beck was awarded a £500 special payment for his efforts.

When complaints about some of the incidents at Rosehill – including Lincoln's provocation session with the teenage boy – began to filter out, an investigation was ordered by Dorothy Edwards. Beck, who had been congratulated by the management for restoring order at Rosehill, sprang to Lincoln's defence, condemning the 'unjust and heartless' treatment of a 'sincere young social worker'. 'It is clear that young residential workers are expected to take risks by dealing with damaged young people, without any support or understanding of the children in care, who in this affair are clearly seen to be angels,' he wrote, in a memo to Edwards. Such was his disgust, he added, that he planned to move out of Leicestershire as soon as he could. Edwards blamed the threats on the stress of managing a centre like Ratcliffe Road.

But even while he threatened to leave, Beck was applying to head another children's home, The Beeches, in the suburb of Leicester Forest East, close to the service station on the M1. This was another home with a troubled recent past and now social services wanted to convert it into an 'assessment centre', a specialised unit which would work on children's problems and then help them re-enter the community. Beck's application suggested The Beeches should provide short-term treatment for children. He said too many were 'sentenced' to long periods in institutions. In an interview panel chaired by Dorothy Edwards, Beck emerged as the only serious candidate for officer-in-charge at The Beeches.

CHAPTER FOUR
The Beeches
1978-1986

'Beck had a kind of aura: you could feel him like static.'
– Beeches resident.

The Beeches sat on a main road out of Leicester. A solid Edwardian mini-mansion, ivy covered, with trees all around and a huge glass conservatory at one side, it looked like an ideal environment for troubled children. A place where they could play and feel secure, while skilled social workers helped them deal with their problems. This was the image Beck cultivated with visiting politicians and journalists. His brief when he took over in 1978, was to create something new, an observation and assessment centre which would provide short term, intensive treatment for troubled children, so that after a short stay they could return to their families and the outside world.

With his reputation as an advanced child care practitioner, Beck had seemed the ideal man to head the new-look unit. He was officer-in-charge, with a staff of 19 residential social workers looking after up to 26 children – although he exceeded this limit. His ability to 'get results' with even the most difficult children meant he had huge discretion over what went on inside his homes. Managers had done little detailed thinking about how the home would function in its new role. Dorothy Edwards had told Beck that she did not believe his regression therapy would be appropriate in a home where most children would be staying no more than three months – although bodily contact might be needed to reassure some children. Otherwise, Beck was left to decide what treatment was needed for children. He continued to use regression therapy occasionally – 'to crack the really hard nuts'. And paddies continued to be used. Children were frequently hit – the daily log in which events at the home were recorded, is littered with references to clipped ears and slaps.

As at his earlier homes, Beck personally chose most of the residents – sometimes marching into a case conference about a child and announcing that he was taking over, sometimes moving them into The Beeches without consulting anyone. The social services high command at County Hall often had little idea which children were there – despite repeated attempts to chivvy him into working through the normal channels. Frequently, more children were crammed into The Beeches than was officially permitted. Managers noted that the home was over capacity even while other homes had empty beds. Often, extra children slept on mattresses on the floor. Some staff remember having to sleep on sofas when they were on duty overnight, because the designated sleeping-in room was filled with children – they would often see rats skittering through the room in search of food.

Children were there because they had committed serious criminal offences, or were on remand from local courts, or because a fostering arrangement had broken down. Others were outside The Beeches' normal remit – one boy was taken in because he was the cousin of an official Beeches resident and had nowhere else to go. He seems never to have been on the books at County Hall – though it is impossible to be certain given the pathetic nature of the county council's own records of the children in its care. But the boy became a useful unofficial helper for Beck, and was encouraged to bully the other children.

To outsiders, The Beeches seemed chaotic – often kids would be running round, screaming their heads off with no apparent control, or they might be slouched on the sofas talking to the care workers, or scrawling something on the designated graffiti wall where they could write whatever they wanted – although swear words were strictly forbidden. Staff might be in the office typing notes, Frank Beck would bustle round dealing with social workers and children, the phone rang constantly. The overall impression was of benign, child-centred chaos. Unlike his previous homes, The Beeches had an in-house school with its own teaching staff.

There was plenty of open space, the grounds were lined with trees and there was a menagerie of pets and farm animals including ferrets, geese and ducks, which delighted visitors but caused council officials to worry about a possible health hazard. Residents particularly remember the goat, which was castrated too late, and stank as a result. It would come into the house and eat the fag-ends out of the overflowing ashtrays.

For all the fine words that were used to describe a relaxed and child-friendly home, the truth was that it was in a terrible state. The efforts of its cleaners were overwhelmed by the activities of the children and by the animals – whose excreta plastered the rear courtyard and was trodden around the main building. Beck refused to make the children do much cleaning, saying they were 'not being trained for domestic service'. Several staff recall suffering lice and stomach bugs while working there. One social worker, John Hartshorne, remembers being particularly revolted by the state of a small lounge known as the green room, which was greasy with a 'gooey, sticky mess' left by the accumulated remnants of the children's food. The cooks kept the kitchen clean, but their efforts ended at the kitchen door.

A leaflet called *The Beeches Booklet* told the children's parents or relatives what to expect. It promised that the children 'will be looked after by skilled and friendly people in small house groups'. Parents were welcome to come and meet the staff, but by appointment. A child would be allowed home leave, but not for the first two weekends, 'to allow your child to settle in'. The normal stay would be for six to eight weeks, after which a case conference would be held to decide what to do next.

The children had little respect for their carers. Only Frank Beck had any real authority. One staff member, Nasreen Akram, remembers: 'We were just one step above the kids, each staff member had their role – the sex symbol, the father figure, the mother figure, the wimp – and you were ridiculed along those lines. You were on duty a long time, isolated and controlled by him.'

The children would run wild when Beck was away – playing favourite pranks like putting the home's ferrets into a tumble drier. The pranks could go horribly wrong. On June 4, 1981, two teenage boys at The Beeches decided to ride the home's resident donkey around the building. After several circuits a dog belonging to one of the other children began to bark and snap at the donkey's legs. A well aimed kick only increased the dog's determination and the donkey, now riderless, bolted into the main road, straight into the path of a car. It was badly injured and died shortly afterwards. The car was damaged too, and the incident prompted questions from councillors, but everything was blamed on the dog.

The Beeches' log provides a flavour of life in the home; the tantrums, fights, wet beds, clipped ears, thefts, vandalism, sexual experiments, and punishments. All children's homes were required to keep a log of daily events, but entries to The

Beeches' log do not amount to a systematic record of events – often they were not even signed. What was recorded and the level of detail given, depended on the person writing the entry. Even so, the log shows the kind of chaotic behaviour the home was intended to contain, and the methods some of the social workers used. John Cobb, the social services manager who oversaw The Beeches, signed the log on June 10, 1980.

Extracts from the log also show the high emotional temperature of The Beeches children. 'MD received a phone call from home was very upset, went upstairs and I followed him, he had a paddy, eventually he told me that dad had told him that his hamster had died and then dad had started to moan at him about offences he is going to be charged for. Quite a lot of guilt/ self hate came out.'

'M only giving away little bits, anger at mother for not caring and hate of The Beeches but refusing to let herself go. Crying, but with no real feeling, feeling very sorry for herself as she has forced herself into a corner. Said she doesn't want to live in a children's home but a mental home as she is mental. I have tried to talk it out with her, her feelings over mother, father, Christmas, school, guilt over everything she has done.'

'Kevin especially warm and cuddly on his return from dad's. Got a little silly later on and was sent to bed by Frank (thanks!). Mardy with me, then seductive, then mardy, then lovely! O giving out lots of sex talk this evening, especially after in bed. Some ribbing of M about being gay.'

The log is full of entries like: 'Chris had a temper tantrum re torn photos, so I sat on him.' and: 'Found Ron holding onto Chris in the corridor. Chris was dressed, said that he was running away and was going to kill himself. Ron was screaming if Chris was going, he was too. I grabbed Ron and Chris ran past me. Steve caught him, and after half an hour in the office with him, got him back to bed. I sat with him. He was talking about suicide, so I slapped him and he quietened down and was asleep by about 11.30.'

Later that night the log records: 'Ron and Eric fighting. Ron had been generally stirring all night and Eric said he had thumped him for tearing his shirt. Pete came in at 11 and reduced him to tears and also stayed till Ron was asleep. Thanks Pete!!'

Slapping, thumping and clipped ears were regularly recorded in the log. One intriguing entry reads: 'Kevin slapped me round the face at tea time, because I made a smelling sound as per Mick's instructions. Put in the TV room.'

The log – which the police were told had been 'lost', but then was 'found' by the county council after Beck's trial was completed – has frequent references to children 'throwing out sex' or being 'very sexy'.

For example, on May 2, 1982: 'Karl throwing out sex to me after tea. Pretended to make a pass at him and he ran out of the room and then came back in – RL.' 'Sara very sexual – scared most of the older lads to death.' One entry records a new arrival being 'somewhat bewildered by the older boys kissing and cuddling... a number of sex maniacs in the house at the moment... all of it kept on a reasonably light hearted level and treated in that manner'.

Nights were particularly busy, according to the log: 'Screams heard after 11.00 pm, went upstairs. D said he had had a bad dream and dreamt that his mother was stabbing him to death, rewarded for telling me.' 'Partition room beds all changed and little boys' room – not enough sheets for the rest. Andy's bed had been wee'd on.'

'Ian caught with a lighted match under the bed clothes reading Steve a story, pulled him from the bed and smacked his bottom...' The log also reports more serious incidents of violence by workers on the children – despite its contravention of the council's policy, and despite its periodic inspection by social services managers.

A more sinister picture comes from the children placed in Beck's homes: years on, they are still fascinated by the array of manipulative tricks he used to dominate those around him. One boy recalls meeting Beck for the first time and saying he must really care about the children: 'He turned and looked at me, his face changed in a couple of seconds to this very intense, almost drilling look, his eyebrows rose. It was quite frightening for a young kid. He replied 'fuck off'. He said it in a very, very intense fashion, he wasn't laughing it off, he was very focused. If he came into the room, you wouldn't have to look round to know it was him; he wouldn't have to speak; he had a kind of aura, you could feel him like static. He was charismatic. There was this real sense of authority, as if he had the power of life or death over you. Even if you weren't in the home, he still had that authority over you. I met him a few years afterwards and he tried to exert authority over me. I was dumbfounded, this was [years later after Beck had left The Beeches] when he was working as a security guard.'

Another Beeches resident said: 'He was a very snidey kind of person, he had a way of trying to slide into your personal fears. Other social workers and carers at The Beeches tried to be quite professional, but he operated on a more personal level, arm on shoulder, very touchy-feely. He had a way of twisting words. He knew how to play with your emotions and your mind – a very sleazy kind of guy. At mealtimes there were a lot of separate tables and Beck would pick and choose where, and with who, he sat.'

'If he was working with someone in particular, he would be close by, but not right next to them, just close enough to impose his presence. If he was talking and wanted quiet, he could silence anyone with a look. He had this tone, it was some kind of acting technique, and these little touches – like if he was talking and got interrupted, he'd lower his voice and emphasise his syllables.'

The bedrooms at The Beeches were partitioned into smaller units with walls that went up to head height. At night, Beck would wander into the bedrooms, treading very lightly. 'He would say one or two words at the end of an aisle, to someone out of sight, people would hold their breath,' one Beeches resident recalled. 'There would be a rustle of clothing, a creak of floor-boards he'd say something routine like 'school tomorrow, make sure you're in time'. The voice would be very, very menacing, then he'd add something like 'your mother rang today, but I didn't think it would be wise for you to speak to her,' something that would really get under someone's skin. If Frank heard from the staff that someone was getting a bit out of hand, they might not even know he'd come into the room, there'd just be a sudden clap around the head. You would be called into the office and told that you were nothing to society and had no dad, you were a bastard, slag, whore.'

Beck's phobias and prejudices were an unpredictable feature of Beeches life. Women members of staff were dismissed as neurotic females and fat cows. Some kids had been prostitutes and Beck, 'had this nutty thing about prostitutes,' according to one ex-resident. Slag and whore were among his favourite terms of abuse. Others recalled a morbid hatred of the Church and priests – dismissed as 'the devil's spawn'. He said only idiots believed in God. As in his earlier homes, life at the Beeches revolved around Beck and the regime reflected his personality. Beck could justify many of its more unusual features in terms of his therapeutic techniques, and it seemed to be tacitly accepted that a higher than usual level of physical discipline was needed to control such difficult children. Far from providing the stable boundaries between acceptable and unacceptable behaviour called for in orthodox child care practice, Beck's approach to discipline was frighteningly unpredictable. Children would wait, terrified, for Beck to return and deal with some major breach of the rules, only for him to be all smiles and understanding. But on another occasion he might fly into a rage over something trivial. Liz Clarke, a social worker at The Beeches, remembers seeing Beck lift a boy up by the throat and bang him against a wall, as children cowered around him. A few moments later, he was cuddling a couple of boys on his knee.

Several entries in The Beeches' log show Beck being used as a kind of ultimate threat against unruly children: 'L and D together in the upstairs for ages at lunchtime. Smoking definitely, what else I can only hazard a guess at. Told them to come out about five times, wouldn't until I threatened to get Frank to yank them out. Looked sheepish when they emerged and sick when told they had been reported.' And sometimes they show Beck issuing rather arbitrary and dangerous instructions: 'Ken spent the whole evening with breathing problems. Frank has banned further use of the inhaler as it is being overused and is addictive. To be taken to the doctors for asthma tablets. Used Vick to ease breathing.' There are several instances of Beck, who had no medical qualifications, arbitrarily stopping children from using medicines prescribed by their doctors.

Beck used carrots as well as sticks. As officer-in-charge, he controlled the clothing allowances for the children, and this gave him substantial scope to reward favourites. Girls would seldom get anything spent on them – even for basic necessities like new knickers. Many of the children became very unkempt during their stay at The Beeches. But some boys would have money showered on them. Clarke recalls one large tattooed skinhead who was bought expensive trainers and a tracksuit out of the clothing allowances, much to the envy of the other children.

The psychological dominance games helped to stifle criticism of some of the other things that went on at the Beeches, and the children found they had little chance to tell the outside world. When managers or councillors came round, everyone was on their best behaviour. There was seldom a chance for the children actually to say something to them. Even if they did say something, Beck would be there to explain it away. There was a sexual undertone to a lot of the care. One girl recalls: 'On Friday nights it was horror night – all the kids gathered to watch the Friday night horror film – adult social workers with kids gathered round, stroking their bodies, getting off on it. I can remember sitting on one social worker's knee, feeling that he had a hard-on.'

Sexual abuse was a taboo subject, although the children sometimes gossiped about which of the staff might be gay or lesbian. But the whole issue of staff having sex with children was 'kind of in wraps'. Beck was known to be close to one boy at The Beeches, Dale Elkington, who was openly gay and was to die of an AIDS-related illness. 'You drew your own conclusions, especially if Frank had made a move on you himself and knowing Dale was gay and spending a lot of time with him,' a Beeches resident said. His own sexual contact with Beck was, he thought, not as serious as others suffered. 'He would sit on the bed and read stories – there would be wandering hands, but active resistance was very unusual.'

Boys were raped in their bedrooms or at bath-time, or in Beck's quarters. Some boys were taken to his home – sometimes sleeping three-in-a-bed with Beck and another youth. One boy described how Beck would make him have a shower when he had been glue sniffing. He would be undressed and washed by Beck in the shower, and on one occasion he was raped there. He was also abused in his bedroom, after Beck caught him kissing a girl. Another boy, who was 14 when he arrived at The Beeches, recalls being allocated a bed in a big empty dormitory. He was quite frightened to be in such a large room on his own. Beck would come and tell him ghost stories – he would never switch the light on, preferring to bring a candle. One night the boy awoke to find Beck trying to climb on top of him. He was raped on two occasions, but was too afraid and ashamed to tell anyone.

'When I was allowed to go home for good from The Beeches, I used to sleep with the light on,' he said. 'My mum used to sneak in and turn the light off, but if ever I knew what she was doing, I would freak out and jump out of bed screaming. My mum got a bedside lamp in the end, to solve the problem. To this day I sleep with the light on.'

Beck's preference for boys over girls was striking and with hindsight several children from his homes say they should have realised its significance. 'Certain lads would go and stay with him or go on holidays with him; there were never any girls, it was almost always boys. But people didn't really realise at the time. If you went to his home at the weekend you would get treats. He would buy you something, toys or something like that. I remember the girls thought they were missing out; we would ask why we were never allowed to go,' said one girl.

He could react furiously if boys and girls in his care started relationships – lesbian or gay relationships seemed acceptable, but he didn't like heterosexual contact. One boy recalled Beck's fury when he was caught with a girl: 'It was just before I got out, I was involved in an incident, a sexual incident, with a girl. He threatened me with a mental institution unless I did exactly what he said. I was terrified: he told me, 'if you go in, I'm going to have you for the rest of your life'. It was all my nightmares rolled into one. Forget *Friday 13th*, forget *Aliens*, forget *Predators*, here comes Frank Beck.'

One girl resident of The Beeches, Farida Hakim, claims that not only was she raped by Beck while she lived there, but that she was to go on to give birth to his daughter. She says she was repeatedly sexually abused and raped by Beck after she discovered him raping a boy while on a Beeches' holiday in Devon. Farida says that she was addicted to solvents while at

The Beeches, and spent much of her time there 'high' from glue sniffing. Under pressure from Beck, she says, she falsely stated at the time that the baby's father was a fellow glue-sniffer, even though she never had sex with the boy, and the child was very physically different from him. The daughter, Gemma, was born in May, 1984, but fell victim to cot-death syndrome at the age of five months. Beck paid for the funeral costs in return for her silence, says Farida, having threatened to kill her if she told anyone the truth. She was thrown out of The Beeches by Beck when her pregnancy became obvious.

At The Beeches, 'paddies' – the induced temper tantrums – were so commonplace that children would be allowed to carry on watching TV while they happened around them. The Beeches' log records regular use of the technique: 'Ron had a super temper tantrum with me after crying a lot. He reacted well with a good cry and accepted a cuddle afterwards.' In February 1979, the log records: 'Breakthrough with M. Mourning the loss of his mother after very disruptive early evening. Taken upstairs by Frank Beck very forcibly. M was very angry, tried to stop himself. Attacked bedroom. Broke down after mum was talked about. Helped clean up room. Had coffee, very nice. Told could lay in if still tired.'

Beck's regression therapy was used at The Beeches, but not as much as it had been at Ratcliffe Road: 'E much nicer at bedtime and allowed herself to regress. At one point had a sit-down protest outside her room because she didn't want to be left but was coaxed back in... worried about Frank's reaction to her paddies.'

Sometimes the paddies would develop into beatings; sometimes there were just straightforward beatings, which, according to the children, were all the more painful because Beck had learned how to hurt them without leaving marks during his time in the Marines. 'His military training came across, he was a bit of an old soldier,' one resident remembers. 'Sometimes he would take someone into a side room and give them a beating like they'd never had in their lives. He was careful not to break bones. He'd do something like kick their calf muscles repeatedly. There was a core of three social workers, led by Beck, who did most of the beatings. Others had lines they didn't cross.'

Leicestershire social services did not completely ban physical punishment until 1982, when the council decided that staff should rely on 'good personal relationships' to control the children. Before that, it was permitted to slap children on the hand, arm or leg, where the circumstances justified it – such punishments had to be recorded in a log book. But what Beck and his co-workers were doing – and recording in the log book – clearly went far beyond what the county council permitted.

To outsiders, managers, politicians and even the occasional journalist, Beck presented the structure at The Beeches as relaxed and deliberately loose, a place where the children could feel at home. This was noted by Nicholas Murray, a reporter from *Community Care* magazine, in an article about The Beeches in 1983:

> *'The young people are obviously relaxed, unhampered by rigid rules, able to say what they feel like, but never disrespectful. The sort of trust clearly exists where the young people are free but do not take liberties. 'We appear to be liberal but we are not,' says Frank Beck, implying that there is an underlying firmness to the open and tolerant atmosphere.'*

The article also reported that Beck saw his approach as 'a major step forward in revitalising social work procedure'. This kind of coverage, and an item on The Beeches on BBC2's *Brass Tacks* programme, sent his prestige soaring. Councillors who visited The Beeches also came away impressed. One such visitor was Anne Crumbie, a Liberal, and an experienced social worker herself: 'The Beeches was in a terrible, terrible state, it desperately needed money spent on it,' Crumbie recalls. 'Frank asked me to visit alone, so I could see the state of the place, the condition of the building, for myself. Whilst I was there, a young man came in, who was out of his mind on drugs, so I stood back and observed Frank Beck dealing with him. My impression was that here was a very gifted and caring social worker.' Another liberal councillor, Jeff Kaufman, remembers complaining to the Director of Social Services about the 'dirty, unkempt state' of The Beeches. At that time all councillors had a list of council facilities they were supposed to visit, to check on the quality of the service. The Beeches was on Kaufman's list, and he and his wife would look in from time to time. He never saw 'the slightest hint' of anything wrong. He recalls thinking what a marvellous man Beck was, to devote his whole life to children.

Managers also saw Beck as a success. Beck presented monthly figures that stressed the success he was having with children, helping them to be 'rehabilitated' into society. On July 18, 1979, for example, he sent Peter Naylor, the head of Care Branch – the arm of the county council which ran residential homes – a short note which he hoped would 'lighten the gloom around the latest departmental spending cuts'. In it, he said that out of 102 children referred to The Beeches in the previous 11 months, 53 were now back at home, 25 in care and 10 were in the observation and assessment system. Four families were still being worked with and 10 children had been 'processed into the system'. Turnover at The Beeches had increased by 50 per cent, he said. 'The obvious savings go without saying,' he added.

In a later report, Beck produced figures on the savings. They showed that between April 1978 and October 1979, 123 children had been admitted to The Beeches, 73 had been discharged, 25 had been taken into care and 25 were still there. This was a substantially greater throughput than achieved by the home in its previous incarnation. He claimed he had saved social services £100,000 by reducing the time children needed to spend in care. Beck also produced lengthy reports for his managers, extolling the ground breaking approach he had introduced to The Beeches. These seemed designed to show him as a progressive expert in the child care field, who was forced to train the old-fashioned staff around him in his new thinking. In one such paper, *The Beeches Family Centre – a fully integrated flexible method of social work intervention*, he said the home was a 'major step forward in revitalising social work procedure,' at a time when sending a child to residential care was seen as 'tantamount to an admission of failure'. But he warned that the methods at The Beeches were so new that staff had to be 're-educated' out of their previous experience in children's homes. 'There is no place for the old fashioned and restricted housemothering, or auntie and uncle titles normally associated with residential care, but a clear undertaking to develop a genuine therapeutic system, based on the individual needs, both of the family and of the child in care,' he wrote.

Beck said he was using limited regression therapy, family therapy, behaviour modification and group work, and the approach was proving helpful with children who had suffered non-accidental injuries, were not attending school, or were beyond their parents' control 'By its intensity of work, and early intervention, a number of children have been diverted from their path into delinquency and admission into care,' he wrote. His managers appear to have been impressed by this barrage of jargon.

There was no reliable analysis of Beck's methods, so his line managers had no basis for understanding his so-called 'therapy'. They allowed Beck to forbid unannounced inspections of his homes, on the pretext that such visits might interfere with the children's therapy, and he ensured that everyone was on their best behaviour for scheduled visits. Field social workers dealing with particular children also found their access limited – something which concerned their immediate bosses in the area offices. Beck spurned help and advice from his managers and reacted furiously against any incursion into his domain, or any criticism from outside.

Beck had won extra favour with his managers by defying an admissions ban by his union, NALGO, which had been imposed as part of a dispute over the pay of residential staff, in September 1983. His highly publicised break with the union involved a particular boy whose mother was dying of cancer and who could not be admitted to The Beeches because of the ban. He was quoted in the *Leicester Mercury* denouncing the ban as 'criminal, heartless and appalling', and insisted that the boy would be admitted. This infuriated NALGO officials, who expelled him from the union. They said his public criticism had brought the organisation into disrepute – the local paper had used Beck's comments to attack the union. But Beck's action had endeared him to his managers, who saw him as having put the service first.

Beck's contempt for the management hierarchy above him may have been shaped by the ease with which they accepted his jargon. But his dismissive attitude towards 'County Hall bureaucrats' was not unusual amongst front line social services staff, and it was something the politicians rather admired. They tended to respect people on the front line, rather than the officials in desk jobs.

With visitors and even managers arriving mostly by appointment, the abuse and violence were kept well out of sight. Children were not believed, even by the police who retrieved the absconders, and any complaints were explained away by Beck and his co-workers. Staff remember how Beck's more scathing letters to his managers would be casually left lying around the office, where they could he read. They contained phrases like 'what a naughty boy I've been – slap my wrist'. The sight of his often withering rejoinders and the letters from County Hall accepting his explanations, helped discourage staff and children from complaining themselves.

CHAPTER FIVE
Confusion at County Hall

'A Cinderella service going through an identity crisis.'
**- A senior Leicestershire County Council
manager, on the social services department.**

Both local government and the child care system were being
thoroughly reformed when Beck joined Leicestershire County
Council. His later career coincided with shifts in the conven-
tional wisdom about child care and changes in the political
control and direction of the council which employed him. These
factors helped Beck build an unchallenged position, and helped
him get away with abuse for so many years.

Beck's appointment as officer-in-charge of The Poplars home
in Market Harborough coincided with one of the childcare
world's periodic revolutions. The old approved school system,
which contained difficult children in large institutions, usually
in remote countryside locations, was being phased out and
replaced. It was regarded as a failed system which demonstrably
did not reform delinquent children. In its place the 1969
Children and Young Person's Act had introduced a new system,
which included the concept of intermediate treatment (IT) as

a compromise between supervising troubled children in the community and locking them up away from it. Children in trouble with the police and the courts would now be housed in smaller council-run community homes, usually in suburbs or small towns, where they would be rehabilitated and contained.

Local authorities were still setting up these new style homes in the early 1970s, and in Leicestershire there was only a very general idea of how they should function and what kind of treatment, if any, they should deliver. According to Professor Phillip Bean, of the Midlands Centre for Criminology at Loughborough University, this was not untypical. There was no tested, established therapy which could 'cure' delinquent children. The 'treatment' called for by the 1969 Act simply did not exist.

Many therapeutic approaches were being tried. Bean recalls that in one residential home the head would welcome new children by sitting them on his knee and handing them a flower. This, it was explained, would create a 'warm area'. This may have been harmless enough, but the naïveté it reflected was an open door which dedicated abusers like Beck walked straight through. Treatments which later came to be seen as abusive or dangerous were not uncommon in residential homes.

Bean points to the lack of a central orthodoxy against which techniques could be judged. In surgery, there is established good practice, based on research into which operations are effective and which are not. In psychiatry, psychology and psycho-analysis there are competing – often mutually exclusive – theoretical frameworks. Each individual is subject to a wide range of external influences, most of which will be unknown to the practitioner, and it is far harder to judge whether a treatment is delivering a cure. This was not well understood by lay people – including councillors and managers. Someone who used scientific sounding jargon, talked the language of compassion, promised solutions and perhaps made the right political noises, could win undeserved credibility with their political and professional masters.

Another immediate problem in putting the 1969 Act into effect was finding appropriate people to run the new homes. Approved schools had fallen into disfavour, and their managers were seen as tainted by a failed system which many believed had brutalised children. Those in charge of 'normal' children's homes at the time were often married couples – usually called uncle' and 'auntie' – with no special training, who had begun by fostering children, and moved to running small homes. Many lacked the skills to deal with more difficult cases. Traditionally council homes had been isolated and independent, and managers who tried to reform them following the 1969 Act found themselves encountering resistance when offered new advice and guidance.

Compared to these old guard staff, Beck was a rarity. He was a social worker with a Certificate of Qualification in Social Work (CQSW), who wanted to enter the field of residential care at a time when it was the 'Cinderella' end of the service, and the high flyers went into fieldwork. Not only was he willing to do residential work, his claimed experience indicated to his managers that he was qualified to operate a therapeutic community, bringing with him clear ideas about how it should function.

Over several years he built a reputation for bringing uncontrollable children under control. There was positive comment about his effect on the behaviour of troubled children from staff and parents. In later years, Beck's reputation was not confined to Leicestershire. He received flattering coverage in the specialist press and in a TV documentary. He was an advisor to Trent Polytechnic (now Nottingham Trent University) on the childcare elements of its social work courses. He assisted in training at the Hendon Police College and advised the Greater Manchester Police on how officers should deal with child protection issues. Beck had gained a national reputation as a childcare expert. In Leicestershire, he seemed a one man solution to the problems of setting up the new homes.

In the 1970s, people working in residential care were seen as highly dedicated staff who worked long hours for a very poor salary. 'Wonderful people doing a thankless job,' according to one senior social services manager. Some who became quasi-professionals with higher salaries often 'made waves' by trying to provide a better experience for the children, and Beck was a recognisable example of this sub-species. Many were indeed wonderful people and their motives were seldom questioned. Certainly, at the time, people's sexual history was not an issue.' Basically you had to turn up to the interview in a dirty mac before people started to get anxious,' a senior manager recalled.

According to Sue Middleton, a leading Labour councillor and one of the architects of a major reform of Leicestershire's child care services, the new approach to troubled children introduced in the 1970s did not go far enough. 'There was a culture – that we spent a lot of time fighting against – that you did not believe children. All the evidence about the child abuse was there. Not that members ever got to hear about it. The attitude was that if a child was in residential care it was inevitably criminal and delinquent – which was not necessarily true – and that children are congenital liars, so you don't believe anything they say.'

The organisation which employed Beck was itself a new creation. The local government reorganisation of 1974 made Leicestershire County Council into a new super-authority, operating a social services department, which brought together social services from various smaller councils and from the National Health Service. At the head of the new department was Dorothy Edwards, an acknowledged expert in child care, who had been the children's officer in charge of children's homes and other services in the old, pre-reform county council. Anne Crumbie, later a Liberal county councillor and spokesperson on social services, was a manager in the department at the time. She remembers Edwards throwing 'the most marvellous parties'. Some were attended by senior council officials, including the chief executive, Sam Jones – others were for more junior staff. Edwards maintained close links with the local media, dining regularly with Lawrie Simpkin, the Executive Editor of the *Leicester Mercury*.

The team around Edwards included several people who were administrators first, and social services professionals second. Terence Nelson, the senior assistant director, was a highly respected figure, but his background was as a politically astute administrator, rather than in social work. Peter Naylor, the assistant director in the chain of command which managed Beck, had been a social worker, but had worked with elderly and physically disabled people, not with children. He was the head of Care Branch, the arm of social services which provided all Leicestershire's residential and day-care services. This was an important role, because Leicestershire social services started with a strong residential focus, running more homes and conducting less fieldwork than its neighbours. In all, Naylor was in charge of about 120 residential units with around 2,500 staff. He made a practice of visiting three homes every Wednesday, and expected to visit each home at least once a year. Anne Crumbie knew Naylor well, and believed he had been over-promoted. 'It was far too big a job for him, and he clearly didn't have the qualities needed to deal with it,' she said.

Next in line was John Noblett, who was in charge of the residential side of Care Branch – including homes for elderly people. He had started in clerical and administrative work, but had gained a CQSW in 1972, and now administered a mixed bag of more than 100 residential units, including 30 or so children's homes. After his retirement, he became a Conservative candidate in the 1987 elections for Hinckley and Bosworth council.

These senior managers worked together in offices along a drab, grey-walled, brown carpeted corridor on the fourth floor of County Hall – an ugly concrete building whose main redeeming feature is that it provides a beautiful view of the nearby Bradgate Park. These senior officers ruled in a relaxed fashion, with a lot of informal consultation as heads popped round doors, and senior managers nipped in and out of each other's offices. It also made for fewer formal, minuted meetings, and occasional confusion as to what had been decided.

Beck's immediate manager for much of his career was John Cobb, a former carpenter who had moved into social work. Cobb was one of three principal assistants to Noblett, responsible for all the homes in a particular section of the county. He believed that he was given neither the manpower nor the authority to oversee the homes in his charge: 'There were 80 or 90 homes I was responsible for, with two members of staff to assist. They kept chopping and chopping money from the budget. The council would not allow me to be paid as much as Beck. You would go to Beck to tell him to do something and he says: 'Boil your head. I will go to the Director and he will tell you what to do. You earn less than me.' The pay differential was important as a status symbol for officers in charge, and it remained a bone of contention for many years. Edwards' successor, Brian Rice, did ask for a review of the salary structure, but councillors refused to approve it.

John Wilmott, another of the three principal assistants, recalled that Naylor and Noblett had different approaches to problems. Naylor preferred to be non-confrontational, Noblett would try to meet problems at source. An example was that if a senior officer was found to be working a shift pattern that suited his needs, rather than those of his home, a general memo would be sent to all homes rather than a specific memo to the person concerned. Officials would sometimes he left bemused by detailed discussion of something that was not a problem for them.

It is noticeable that only Dorothy Edwards, in the chain of command above Beck, had any real experience of child care. As Director she had such a wide range of responsibilities that she could not possibly supervise Beck: none of the others was sufficiently qualified to challenge the legend that he was a qualified therapist and all-round child-care guru. Dr Masud Hoghughi, a genuine expert, who was later asked to examine Beck's approach, is contemptuous of what he found. A detailed description of Beck's treatment methods 'shows the grossest and most primitive and spurious brand of folksy psychopathology about the relationship of guilt and loss to disruptive behaviour', Hoghughi said.

Dorothy Edwards was seen at the time as an inspirational leader of the social services department. With hindsight, senior County Hall officials came to regard her as a weak manager, who lacked strategic vision and allowed a comfortable culture to develop, without proper controls over what went on within children's homes. She was criticised for tolerating too many weak links in her management team and for failing to ensure that there was sufficient child care expertise among her top managers.

If Edwards seemed a strong leader, her successor, Brian Rice, appointed in 1980, soon acquired the opposite reputation. One of his fellow senior council officers says he was resented by the team assembled by Edwards, who thought one of them should have become Director. Rice was 50 when he arrived at Leicestershire County Council. He had spent most of his career with Gloucestershire County Council, where he had been the county's mental health officer. He eventually rose to become assistant director of social services and also spent seven years lecturing in social administration and local government studies. During his national service, he spent two years in the

Intelligence Corps. With hindsight, one councillor thought the panel which had appointed him Director should have taken more notice of his failure to obtain that post in Gloucestershire. Crumbie remembers Rice as 'perfectly gentlemanly', but says many councillors quickly began to suspect that he was not up to the job. She recalls an incident where he was questioned in committee, and a senior colleague walked out in disgust at Rice's inability to answer – a remarkable incident in the staid environment of a County Hall meeting, where stoicism was the normal official response to blunders.

Rice was also a mason – a member of the Temperantia 4088 Lodge, which also included the county treasurer, Ray Hale, and the chief personnel officer, Jack Wymont. At the time, there was a substantial number of masons at all levels of the County Hall bureaucracy, including the chief executive Sam Jones, who went on to become chief executive at the City of London Corporation, where being a mason has never been a handicap. Many Conservative politicians were also masons, including the then leader, Robert Angrave, and the social services spokesperson Neville Hanger. Leicestershire's Chief Constable, Michael Hirst, was another mason. Terence Nelson, too, had been a mason from 1962 to 1978. Even some leading Conservatives were privately critical of a 'masonic mafia' at the top of the council, and Labour politicians went to town when an old masonic year book was found at a car boot sale revealing the extent of masonic influence at County Hall. The Kirkwood Inquiry investigated the membership of masons by senior county council officers and councillors, and were advised by the United Grand Lodge, the foremost body of freemasons in England, that Beck had never been a mason, nor had most of the other social services managers. The inquiry concluded that 'speculation that freemasonry played any part in management failures in relation to Mr Beck is, therefore, without foundation'.

But senior council officers who were not masons were privately very critical of the masonic influence, and believed it was a key factor in the poor management of the county council. 'People were put into positions who weren't capable of holding them – Brian Rice was the prime example of that,' said one very senior manager. 'Leicestershire was full of masons among the members and at chief officer and deputy chief officer level at that time, and you do have to ask questions about how they got there. People were not appointed on merit, and the relationship between officers and members who were not masons was different. Rice was not appointed on merit and didn't prove to he a competent officer.' This was not an isolated view.

Barrie Newell, a retired assistant director of social services from neighbouring Nottinghamshire, who compiled a private report on behalf of Leicestershire council on the Beck affair, was highly critical of Rice. 'I think he was weak and a bit aimless and didn't give any sense of direction. One sign was that he was disinclined to take decisive action on nasty issues, unless forced to do so.'

Newell attaches some importance to a formative incident in the early part of Rice's tenure. Rice had taken a staff member to committee for disciplinary reasons, but, to Rice's amazement, councillors criticised him and seemed to take sides with the staff member. After that, Rice was unconfident that members would support him if he disciplined staff. It was only years later that anyone thought of sacking Frank Beck, but even then Rice believed that the committee would resist dismissing a high profile figure like Beck, and would be more inclined to over-rule him instead.

Junior staff remember the social services department at that time operating as 'a rigid hierarchy' in which they were discouraged from speaking to anyone but their immediate line manager. One social worker recalls being taken aside and told not to speak directly to the Director when he visited their office. But a wave of change was about to break over the department. The Conservative defeat in the 1981 council elections heralded a cultural revolution at County Hall. The council became hung, hut it was soon clear that there was a majority in favour of substantial change in social services, and in childcare practices in particular.

No overall control meant a pivotal role for the five Liberals who were elected that year. Neither the Conservatives nor Labour could implement policies without negotiating with the Liberals. Their support had to be won for each decision. Jeff Kaufman, one of the five, recalls Lawrie Simpkin, the Conservative-leaning number two on the *Leicester Mercury*, informing him, between puffs of thick cigar smoke, that the future of the county was in his hands. Before long the *Mercury* was lambasting the Liberal group's decisions.

There was also substantial change in the Labour group. In the party at large, the Bennite revolution was in full swing, and in the city of Leicester (which at that time elected councillors to Leicestershire County Council) new left wing candidates had been chosen, who won seats lost to the Tories during Labour's slump in the late 1970s. The Leicestershire Labour group soon installed a new leadership with its own ideas about how the county council should be run.

None of the five Liberals had been county councillors before, and the range of services and size of budgets they had to deal with were of an order of magnitude greater than anything experienced by those who had sat on district councils. Initially, they allowed the Conservatives to stay in power and retain the chairs of committees. But after a year they switched their support to Labour, which wanted major reforms to the childcare system. The result of this political change was that relatively junior, or even newly-elected, Labour and Liberal councillors were making policy. In the old days, such junior figures would never have attained such positions. Previously, before becoming a committee 'chairman' (or 'chair' as it soon became) councillors had to make a stately progress up the ladder of seniority, gaining experience, and perhaps losing their appetite for reform, on the way.

Brian Rice, his officers and the politicians were conscious that the Conservatives might well regain power after the next elections in 1985. Labour and Liberal politicians wanted to push through change quickly: officials were unhappy about reforms which they expected to be reversed after the next election.

CHAPTER SIX
The child care strategy

'We were regarded as lunatics for doing these things.'
– county councillor, Sue Middleton

The child care strategy introduced by Leicestershire County Council in the early 1980s was one of Labour's key policy commitments from the 1981 election. It rested on a simple principle: too many troubled kids were dumped in institutions, and more of them should be fostered, or looked after in other ways.

To this day Jim Roberts, then one of Labour's most able county councillors, believes the child care strategy was the only major strategic change driven by councillors rather than officials during his 16 years at County Hall. It was a classic product of the kind of new thinking generated by the fresh intake of Labour councillors, who came in as the Conservatives lost control. Bob Osborne, later the Conservative leader, still remembers the 'real culture shock' caused by an influx of 'vociferous, articulate new councillors, many of them women, who actually knew something about social services'.

For many months the Conservatives were shell-shocked from their fall from power – suddenly they were not in control and the political environment at County Hall became much less congenial. 'We were very much on the defensive. We found ourselves being taunted as racist and geriatric,' Osborne remembers. The architects of the new strategy included Ian Whitehead ('a social worker through and through,' according to Roberts) who went on to become an assistant director of social services at Leicester City Council, and Sue Middleton, an experienced social work researcher who had been an advisor to the Department of Health and Social Security, and had considerable knowledge of the latest child care thinking in the United States.

The strategy's essence was, first, don't take children into care, and instead find ways of supporting them with their families; second, if you have to take them into care, don't use residential homes, find other forms of provision like fostering; third, if you have to use residential care, don't lock them up if they run away. In particular, Labour and Liberal councillors thought it was absurd to lock young people in secure units when they were remanded into care for crimes such as car theft, for which a court would not imprison them. Except in extreme circumstances, they preferred to see children remanded to homes like Beck's, which were not secure units, but which had a track record of exercising control over difficult children. Their policy was shaped in part by experience in Warwickshire, which had done away with its children's homes completely but then found it still needed some. Some children had to be put in care homes, if only as a place of safety.

The strategy implied shifting millions of pounds away from residential care, and therefore closing many, perhaps most, county council children's homes – only a small core of homes were to remain, to cater for children for whom residential care seemed the only option. The money once spent on homes would be shifted into intermediate treatment. The term had a less precise meaning in Leicestershire than in some other authorities, where it was used to describe very specific kinds of treatment for children. In Leicestershire it referred to pretty well anything which happened outside residential care.

It was a huge upheaval for the department, and the ramifications of closing homes, finding new posts for hundreds of staff and establishing new mechanisms for dealing with the children came close to swamping senior management. The first phase involved moving £3,000,000 of spending. It ran into criticism even within the Labour Party. Roberts recalls having to prepare for county party meetings with chapter and verse on where the money was going, to fend off critics who thought he was closing homes to save money. There was also dissent within his party's group, with some councillors saying secure accommodation was a good thing. Between 1980 and 1986, 17 homes with 306 beds were closed and more than 200 staff were made redundant.

One unintended result of the new policy was to reduce the status of the residential care which remained. Staff saw themselves as the last resort. Children sent to the homes now tended to be the more difficult cases – but staff did not receive extra training to deal with them. In the mid-1980s less than half had even in-service training and there were long waiting lists for places on training courses. Each home had been promised a written statement of its aims and objectives, but these did not appear for some years. A Social Services Inspectorate report on a children's home in Leicestershire in the mid-1980s noted: 'a lack of a clear strategy for residential care and its fit within the broader strategy of child care and a lack of a specific role within each of the homes within an overall strategy'. This, the report said, undermined the effectiveness and performance of the homes.

The new approach was based on 'gate-keeping' – a mechanism for ensuring that children going into care were placed in the most appropriate setting, whether a residential home or a foster family. It also created a new post of complaints officer, to give the children a route by which to appeal if they were unhappy with their treatment. 'The whole idea was to close children's homes, to release resources to provide properly funded foster care, and other provision in the community,' said Middleton. 'If you put more money into child care all you do is put more children into the system. All of these things now sound reasonable and respectable, but we were regarded as equivalent to the Militant Tendency on Liverpool council, and regarded as lunatics for doing these things, and the Director of Social Services regarded us as that too.'

Relationships between the labour and Liberal groups grew stronger, and, generally, more trusting. 'Once we had convinced Kaufman [the Liberal chief whip and social services spokesperson] that we knew what we were doing, and it was not just ideological, he was a tremendous supporter,' recalls Middleton. 'We were very concerned at Beck attending their group meetings – it seemed to us a blur of roles, but we had no idea of what was going on, and we thought we could hardly talk because we were seeing officers privately, and if it kept Kaufman on board it seemed all right. What mattered to us was getting the strategy in place. 1,000 kids were in care; 30 kids a year going through secure accommodation, costing God knows what. The committee putting kids in care was like a rubber stamp.'

The five Liberals had to learn fast, particularly about social services. They quickly became embroiled in the crucial battle to introduce the childcare strategy. The issue was whether or not to open a newly-completed secure unit at Polebrook House, the former Desford Boys Approved School in the countryside to the west of Leicester. It had been a flagship policy of the council when under Conservative control, paid for with the aid of a Home Office grant. The unit was brand new and purpose-built to contain the most difficult children. But it didn't fit into the new strategy, and Labour councillors in particular were determined that it should not be opened. Conservative councillors argued that it was only intended for the most damaged children, not just in Leicestershire, but across the East Midlands. Labour retorted that if the home was there, children would be sent to it, whether secure accommodation was the best option for them, or not.

At this point Beck, who until then had no known political persuasion, suddenly swung the debate. He phoned the Liberal chief whip, Jeff Kaufman, who at that time had never even heard of him. Beck urged the Liberals not to allow the unit to open. 'You can't lock kids up like that, it would be much better to give me the resources to deal with them,' Beck said. Kaufman's response was to invite Beck to address a meeting of the Liberal Group, along with Sydney Jones, the head of Polebrook House. 'Jones argued that if you could contain a child, you could help them,' remembers Kaufman. 'Beck said that if you had to lock a child up, there was no way you could help that child – he could do a better job. There's no doubt that Frank Beck was instrumental in swinging the group behind the closure of Polebrook House. And the guy was so impressed with the Liberal group that he became a Liberal and was later elected as a councillor.'

An alternative explanation is that Beck spotted a very inexperienced set of local politicians, who had suddenly acquired considerable political power, and were open to his influence. Either way, it was an important connection at a time when child care policy in Leicestershire was being thoroughly reformed, and Beck's advice informed Liberal and later Liberal Democrat policy on child care issues.

Eventually, the decision was made. The Polebrook House secure unit was never opened, the property sold and the government grant which financed it was repaid. 'We spent a mint on it and sold it for a song,' Trevor Griffiths, the Conservative councillor for the area, recalls bitterly.

A risk in closing Polebrook House was that some children would now have to be sent to another residential home where they would be disruptive. One of the main reasons councillors were satisfied the policy could work was The Beeches. The home was described by the senior assistant director of social services, Terence Nelson, as achieving 'extraordinary successes' with the most difficult young people. Thus under the new strategy, The Beeches became even more essential to the department. The only alternatives were DHSS Youth Treatment Centres – 'extraordinarily expensive' according to Nelson – or out of county placements, or youth custody, both of which ran counter to the basic thinking behind the new policy.

The decision was bitterly criticised in the local press. Kaufman found himself in a war of words with the *Leicester Mercury* after remarking in a council meeting that *Pravda* meant truth in Russian, and he wondered what *Leicester Mercury* meant in the same language. Alongside spats with local journalists, the war of attrition over the implementation of the child care strategy continued, Labour councillors complained that the policy had to be pushed through in the teeth of officer resistance, led by the Director, Brian Rice. In some cases there was downright obstructionism, says Sue Middleton. She and other councillors were frustrated by officers writing reports that only argued for the opposing position. Labour members ended up writing their own reports and presenting them to committee – something unprecedented at County Hall. Some officials gave unofficial advice to Labour members. 'We would have meetings in people's houses and officers turned up virtually in scarves and dark glasses, because if Rice knew they were there they would be in serious trouble,' says Middleton.

The Director, Brian Rice, was at the eye of the storm. He opposed the child care strategy, particularly the closure of Polebrook House. The Conservatives, who appointed him, rallied round. 'He had some kind of skin complaint, clearly stress related, and it really flared up at that point,' Osborne recalls. Rice lacked the political and diplomatic skills needed to operate on a hung council, where every major policy decision has to be thrashed out between the parties. And without those skills, he floundered at the centre of Leicestershire's main political row in the early 1980s.

'There existed a strong division of opinion between members on the direction child care should take, particularly for those juveniles on remand, or those who had committed offences,' Rice wrote later. 'These differences occasionally spilt over into council chamber debates, and were not helpful to senior management.' Trevor Griffiths, by then the Conservative whip at County Hall, believes Rice knew that Beck, one of his junior officers, had swung the council against his advice to keep Polebrook House open: 'He was in a very difficult position, but he didn't feel he could do anything about it.'

Beck slips the leash

Whatever the arguments around the child care strategy – and its supporters continue to believe it was the right policy – it served to strengthen Beck's position. The county had a declining number of children's homes and Beck would take almost any child. His 'success' was a great bonus for the department and he became indispensable to its functioning on a day to day level. 'You earn a lot of house points for doing that,' commented Barrie Newell, who conducted the first investigation into the Beck affair. 'Heads of homes don't have a veto, they can be instructed to take children, but departments don't like to get into that situation of over-riding someone. Beck set himself up as a therapist and found that everyone gave his methods great credibility. That was one reason Rice was reluctant to act against him: he would be in a jam without Beck there. Another was that a badly run home would normally have large numbers of children absconding or being expelled and, especially given the children he was taking, Beck had a good record in that respect. Also, when he was dealing with the most difficult kids, managers might be more tolerant about stories of – say – violence. If the kids moan, you can say that they've had similar problems before; it could prevent you asking what he was actually doing with them.'

It is hard to overstate the problems that children running out of control caused for social services managers. The county council had parental responsibility if crimes were committed, neighbours annoyed or property vandalised. If children absconded, there would be worries about their safety, the crimes they might commit, the need to liaise with the police and worried parents, and the comments of irate magistrates to address. Beck's ability to keep even very difficult children under control does much to explain the esteem in which his managers held him. Years later Jim Roberts – Labour's social services spokesman when the Beck affair came to light – was to comment: 'You can control children through affection and respect, or through fear: what was apparent was that they were being controlled.' There may have been suspicions that Beck used violence to control the children, but many were known to be extremely difficult and he was given more latitude than others might have been allowed. It would have taken a much closer inspection to discover exactly how abusive his methods really were.

Beck certainly created headaches for his managers by his refusal to work with other arms of the department. The Beeches had been intended as a short-stay home, where children were sent for a few months at a time. Their case workers would continue to work with them during their stay, and when they were returned to their families or to the community. So even when a child was staying at the home, field social workers from area offices were supposed to maintain their links with the child and share in any major decisions about their future. Beck preferred to run things his way and expected unconditional support for whatever he did.

In one case in 1982, a teenage girl was pulled out of a job social workers had found for her in the Leicestershire Family Service Unit, which provided various community care support services. This was because managers there would not agree to pay her salary to The Beeches – Beck said he was concerned that the girl would use the money to abscond. The area office which had placed her at The Beeches in the first place, and which was supposed to oversee her case, was not informed, let alone consulted. Nor were they alerted when the girl's glue-sniffing problem began to escalate, and she began to abscond, or when Beck decided she should be withdrawn from college. Later, a planned Christmas holiday with relatives in Portsmouth was cancelled, and then re-scheduled for the new year by Beeches staff, leaving the field workers to smooth over the changes with the girl's relatives. Later the same girl was to allege privately that she had been abused and raped by Beck.

Complaints about Beck's unilateral actions began to reach senior managers. Beck's attitude at meetings with social workers from the area office was described as 'domineering and ill-mannered'. He was quoted as saying he didn't have the time to 'track down bloody social workers and keep having meetings'.

A more extreme case involved a 13 year old boy who Beck was later convicted of buggering and indecently assaulting. The boy had a history of glue sniffing and was considered very disturbed. When he began to attend the school based at The Beeches in May 1984, he was in trouble with the law and the courts were soon to consider how he should be dealt with. A case conference had suggested he should have 'intermediate treatment' with a youth group, to try and address his offending behaviour, but The Beeches began to dissent from the agreed approach.

Paul Bardsley, the boy's social worker, was worried that Beck's regression therapy would conflict with the youth group's approach which tried to encourage more adult behaviour, and he thought Beeches staff were trying to turn the boy against him. 'The Beeches' staff seem to be setting themselves up against me, with themselves as the good guys and me – and it seems the rest of social services – as the bad guys,' he wrote. The disagreement became open dissent when Beeches staff broke ranks during a court hearing on the boy's future and advised magistrates against the agreed intermediate treatment plan. The effect was a month's delay in starting work with the boy, while further reports on him were prepared. Memos with phrases like 'unprofessional conduct' began to fly, and demands were made for an inquiry into The Beeches' role in the case.

Even after the court had agreed to send the boy to the youth group, The Beeches' staff continued to be obstructive, prompting further complaints. Eventually, it was decided that the boy should spend more time at the Beeches. Then quite suddenly, relations between the boy and the home broke down. The Beeches refused to take him until his attitude changed, and the boy refused to go there. In both cases, Beck and his staff spurned the department's normal procedures and overturned joint decisions. Beck already had a reputation for this kind of behaviour and the two cases simply highlighted his contempt for the judgement of his colleagues and his refusal to act inside the normal framework for deciding a child's future. He was out of control, but his managers were unable to make him conform.

The downfall of Brian Rice

At the time, the Director, Brian Rice, had larger issues than such demarcation squabbles to deal with. His rearguard action against the child care strategy had made him enemies. He was seen as obstructive to the new policies Labour and the Liberals wanted to push through.

Some who were then critical now believe they were over-harsh on Rice. Chief officers had been used to the old Conservative-led council's culture, which expected them to be 'wise advisors' on policy, not just implementers of politicians' decisions. Tim Swift, then leader of the Liberal group and forthright critic of Rice, now believed that the behaviour he saw as obstructive was an attempt to give honest, if unwelcome advice.

Others disagree. One chief officer from this period thought his opposition 'went beyond what might have been considered acceptable'. Rice is still remembered with venom by some Labour politicians.

Roberts recalls taking an instant dislike to Rice on becoming Labour's spokesperson on social services. (By this time Leicestershire had settled into an arrangement whereby, instead of having a chairman for each committee, there would be three 'spokespersons' from the parties, who would be consulted together on urgent matters and briefed by chief officers.) Senior Labour councillors told him his first task should be removing Rice.

Roberts believed Rice was 'no bloody good,' and began a campaign to remove him. 'He never seemed to actually do anything – an officer once told me Rice's desk was always clear because anything that landed on it was instantly referred to someone else,' Roberts said. Roberts didn't believe Rice was really committed to Leicestershire, because he kept his home in Gloucester and sometimes worked from there. And Roberts also thought his weakness as a director imposed a tremendous burden on his subordinate officers, particularly Rice's deputy, Mick Wells.

Sam Jones, the council's chief executive, was now confronted with concerns about Rice by two of the most senior county councillors – Swift for the Liberals and Roberts for Labour. Jones responded by conducting a straw poll of Rice's management team. They agreed with the politicians, and Rice was told he would have to go. He negotiated a package worth about £100,000, and retired early. Roberts recalls bringing a letter confirming his departure to a Labour election rally in 1987: the news delighted his colleagues.

CHAPTER SEVEN
Regression therapy
...the truth and the lies

---

*'Regression therapy was the veil behind
which the perverts took their pleasure.'*
– Peter Joyce QC, prosecuting counsel, November 1991.

Frank Beck brought together the respected psychoanalytic ideas of Sigmund Freud, Michael Balint, Bruno Bettelheim and Barbara Dockar-Drysdale, together with the practices of the Warrendale home in Canada, into a theoretical hotchpotch which provided him with a cover for the sexual abuse of children. It allowed him to justify treatment of children which should have been unacceptable, and even to explain away some of the complaints of his victims. The credulity and complacency of his political and professional masters meant no one penetrated his veneer of psychoanalytic respectability.

It is impossible to know whether Beck began as a man of good intentions, who fell victim to warped temptation, or whether he planned from the outset to use psychotherapy as a cover for abuse. Given the evidence from psychiatrists and psychologists that Beck was a psychopath, able to convince himself of his own goodness even when he was committing evil, perhaps in the end any examination of intent is futile.

Beck's supposedly therapeutic practice, though, was devastatingly bad for the children in his care. He physically abused them, hit them, throttled them with towels, held them down to suppress them and sexually abused them. Meanwhile, Beck's co-worker and co-abuser Colin Fiddaman, used 'regression therapy' for other ends by maintaining a regime of deliberate cruelty and torture. Children were told it was for their own good.

What is also true is that when Beck was challenged at his trial by prosecution counsel, Peter Joyce, he was unable to explain his theory of childcare therapy. It became clear in court that Beck understood little of the ideas of the therapists and authors he so freely quoted. By a few days' reading, Joyce had become more of an expert on 'regression therapy' than Beck himself was after 13 years of practising it. The question as to why Beck's bosses were so much less thorough than his prosecuting counsel remains unanswered.

'Regression therapy' was given credibility by Beck's use of phrases and practices that were current in psychotherapy in the early 1970s, while Beck was training. He first came into contact with them when he worked at the Highfields Children's Home in Northampton, immediately after he trained. Highfields' manager, Wendy Rowell, had seen the work of child psychotherapist Barbara Dockar-Drysdale put into action at the Mulberry Bush School for disturbed children, and believed it had a major beneficial impact on the children. Dockar-Drysdale's approach focused on the Freudian concept of regression.

The word 'regression' was frequently used by Sigmund Freud, the architect of psychoanalysis. He used it to describe the inner process by which a person reaches back to an earlier stage in their life, to re-think and re-live that period. When discussed by Freud, the analyst is a bystander, viewing the process. The analyst is then able to assist the patient in confronting the root of current traumas, which have their origins in the period to which the patient has voluntarily regressed.

Barbara Dockar-Drysdale, a German born psychotherapist, leaned heavily on the works of the 'Austrian school', which is to say Freud and Carl Jung. But she departed from them in her belief that the psychotherapist should not be a mere passive observer of regression, and she became keen, in later years of practice, to encourage children in care to regress to periods of trauma. Dockar-Drysdale spelt out her evolving ideas most cogently in *Therapy in Child Care*, and to a lesser extent in the companion volume, *Consultation in Child Care*.

Beck read Dockar-Drysdale's theoretical work carefully, having seen her ideas in practice, as did Colin Fiddaman, while working at the Highfields Centre. Most of Dockar-Drysdale's writing dates back to the 1960s, a period when the social environment was very different from the 1980s and 90s. Sex, for instance, was hardly referred to by Dockar-Drysdale in her writing. According to figures quoted by Leicestershire County Council at one point, something in the region of 90 per cent of children allocated to Beck's care had been sexually abused before entering care. Sex abuse was probably as common in Dockar-Drysdale's day, but it was not recognised as such, and was seldom spoken about. By failing to confront sexual problems among the children in her care, Dockar-Drysdale can be seen, in retrospect, unwittingly to have assisted in creating an environment in which Beck could abuse children in care. A more worldly analyst might have recognised the risk that her ideas might be exploited by a potential child abuser – it would certainly he recognised as a danger today.

But Dockar-Drysdale cannot be blamed for much of Beck's behaviour – the child care practices that she advocated were far removed from those used by Beck. It is merely tragic that the words she used to explain her ideas were open to manipulation by Beck, who used legitimate ideas for distorted ends. Dockar-Drysdale stressed the benefits of using kindness, persuasion and reassurance to achieve change among difficult children. While Beck sometimes used this approach, he also did the opposite, with threats, violence and humiliation, when it helped him achieve what he wanted.

So, for Dockar-Drysdale, regression was a way of re-creating a healthy outlook in which a regressed mind was taken forward through a process of mental re-building. But her writing concentrated on the nature of the regression, and it was seized on by Beck to give an apparent theoretical under-pinning for his own 'therapies', which used regression, but without any attempt at psychological repair. There was much else that Dockar-Drysdale wrote that could have been misused by Beck and shown to his bosses to justify what he and his staff were doing, cloaking their actions with an appearance of legitimacy. We know that Beck warned his managers in advance that children would claim to have been abused – and that this method of preparing lines of defence in advance is a classic paedophile tactic. Beck even referred his managers to psychotherapy handbooks, which spelt out the risks that legitimate practitioners faced of being falsely accused. Dockar-Drysdale wrote, for example, of the need to take a regressed child – she dealt with children, mostly boys, between the ages of eight and 14 – and put him on a care worker's knee, and spoon feed him, recognising that in the child's own mind he had returned to infancy.

She said that in the Mulberry Bush, a worker might give a child a bath, which she compared favourably to a school environment where a teacher would not 'give a child a meal, put him to bed, or take him out alone'. She wrote also of sitting up all night with a child in regression, by the child's bed, holding his hand, allowing the child to regress into being a baby again, to be dressed, cleaned, washed and changed every hour or so (though she did not envisage the use of nappies). These were all ideas that Beck willingly took on board, and used for his own ends.

While recognising that Dockar-Drysdale was writing in the 1960s, it is still necessary, even in the context of the 1990s, to criticise her for failing to realise the potential for child care workers with the wrong motives to misuse her ideas. Yet Dockar-Drysdale was aware of the risk, at least as others saw it. She complained that unsympathetic care workers might argue: 'There's something kinky about a man looking after a boy as though he were a baby'. She also explained: 'It is easy too for involvement to he seen as perverse. A man accepting a maternal role created by a small boy may look after the child in a maternal way. The fact that he is quite aware of what he is doing, discusses his work in detail, and so on, may not save him from suggestions that he is homosexual. There is nothing more vulnerable than a therapeutic involvement...' It is easy to contemplate how these words might have been used by Beck to fight off any allegation made against him by the boys in his care.

Although Beck was a qualified social worker, he was not in any way trained to conduct psychotherapy. This should have warned his management against his use of therapy, but even here he had a defence from Dockar-Drysdale. She claimed that therapy was an important part of child care, adding that 'child care workers, although not psycho-therapists, can nevertheless do valuable therapeutic work of a special kind'. If she meant that this should only be undertaken under the close supervision of a qualified psychotherapist or psychiatrist, she failed to spell this out. Again we return to a key issue – Beck's managers lacked the knowledge to debunk his half-baked ideas.

Another of Beck's major influences was the Warrendale film, produced in Canada in 1967 by Allan King. This film was used as justification for Beck's regime of physical restraint of children in care, and his claim that this could be used to 'regress' a child. While Dockar-Drysdale is critical of the film, for being 'indiscriminate' in its use of restraint, she also expresses her approval for 'holding' children, which can, she said, 'prove valuable if used with discretion and in an appropriate context'. Unfortunately she fails to suggest how much force might he legitimate to restrain a child as part of a 'holding' exercise.

Dr Masud Hoghughi, a consultant in clinical and forensic psychology, who gave evidence to the first compensation hearing brought by Beck victims, was appalled by the contents of the Warrendale film. The film was not only used by Beck as a model for much of his work, but was also shown to visitors in council training sessions and to county councillors, to explain the intent and practice of the work at Ratcliffe Road. 'In the 1970s, because of the general lack of rigour and consensus in determining what was best for children, a number of questionable practices found currency for a time,' wrote Hoghughi.

'An example of these was the 'Warrendale method.' Hoghughi said it presented 'a bleak and contentious form of provoking confrontations with children. It does this through forceful and unnecessary physical contact, and other acts which generate angry reactions in children...'

Beck's other major theoretical influence was Michael Balint, a leading psychoanalyst. Beck told people that Balint's work was 'the handbook' for his 'regression therapy' at Ratcliffe Road. However, the expression 'regression therapy' was not one used by Balint himself.

There is a striking paradox in Beck's use of both Balint and Dockar-Drysdale as his theoretical building blocks. It is one that should have been understood at least by the consultant psychiatrists who attended Ratcliffe Road, and is a measure of how distant was the supervision of Beck's hack psychotherapies.

While Dockar-Drysdale was an uncritical supporter of Freud, Balint based his work much more on the ideas of Sandor Ferenczi, whose schism with Freud was, in Balint's own words, 'a trauma on the psychoanalytic world'. Balint was a student of Ferenzci, and the executor of his estate, and although he was capable of criticising his mentor, fundamentally he shared his outlook. Freud, Balint believed, saw things too narrowly, and failed to recognise the impact of the wider environment on a person's emotional development. At one point Balint wrote that psychological problems were more likely to be caused by environmental damage than by an Oedipus complex, penis envy or breast envy – a stinging implied rebuke of Freud's approach.

Balint's most important work was *The Basic Fault*, which spelled out his approach to psychoanalysis, including that for children. All disturbed people, believed Balint, had a fundamental flaw in their character, a basic fault, which had been caused by the inter-relationship between the individual and their environment, dating from a trauma earlier in their life. It was only by allowing a patient to regress to the point in their life where this basic fault had originated, that it could be overcome. The trauma may have been a single event, or a series of events, which the analyst needed to reveal through effective therapy sessions.

A flawed individual could have 'a new beginning' if their basic fault could be uncovered and confronted. Balint was clear that this could only be a partial solution, as the basic fault would still lie within the patient, because the basic fault could not be 'removed, resolved or undone'. What could be achieved, by confronting the root of the problem, was development of a more appropriate way of relating to other people, including loved ones.

For Beck, one of the advantages of Balint's work was that it had a clear application to children who had already been sexually abused. Where Dockar-Drysdale and Freud saw children as having been in want of sufficient care, Balint recognised that a person may have been treated hideously badly, and that this may cause a severe personality disorder. Nowhere in Balint's writings is there anything to justify Beck's use of force, supposedly to 'regress' a child in his care, nor physically to recreate a situation to remind a person of an earlier period of their life – as Beck did, with his use of bottles and nappies. Indeed, Balint is very clear that the psychoanalyst should remain detached from the patient, who should be lying on a couch while the analyst sits in a chair.

Balint even criticised his mentor, Ferenczi, for extending the psychoanalyst's role, by offering more comprehensive therapy to a patient with a severe problem, providing weekend treatment sessions, and even taking the patient on holiday to maintain regular therapy sessions. The result, pointed out Balint, was excessive dependence by the patient on the therapist, a point graphically illustrated when the analyst, Ferenczi, died before the treatment was completed. Many of Beck's victims were left highly dependent on him – and it is clear that he did not maintain the kind of detachment Balint suggests.

There is no sign from Balint's writing that he would have approved of Beck acting as a therapist to children who were in his full-time care. This would clearly have breached the separation that Balint insisted on between therapist and patient. One of Balint's persistent concerns was that if this separation were breached, the role of the analyst was fatally compromised, with the patient becoming too aware of the mood of the analyst and understanding the analyst too well.

Where Balint agreed with Dockar-Drysdale, and where Beck departed from them both, was on the whole reason for a patient's regression. To a reputable psychotherapist, the only point of a patient going through regression was for them to re-build their lives and their emotional development from that point on – the so-called maturation process. Balint explicitly warns against the bad therapist, who regresses a patient back to the point of trauma, and then fails to assist them to deal with it better. Instead, the bad therapist incurs the risk of 'pathological regression' – re-opening the wound destructively, leading subsequently to pathologically bad behaviour. Beck, though, made no effort to re-build children, to mature them. On the contrary, the result of his 'treatment' was to make them permanently vulnerable, and more open to abuse by him and others.

There were things that Balint wrote that might have been misused by Beck to justify some of his activities, especially as most of Beck's managers had little understanding of child care, and even less of psychotherapy. Balint wrote, for instance, that 'during the treatment of a child of 3-4 years old, no analyst can avoid being called upon to help the child with his excrementary function' – without making it clear whether he meant literally assisting them, or helping them over-come psychological problems attached to toilet functions.

Balint also warned of the vulnerability of the patient. The analyst might be seen as omnipotent, while the child undergoing analysis who has been a past victim of trauma, and now has symptoms of neurosis, may be prone to sexual seduction. One can only speculate what effect reading this might have had on Beck. In any case, it was exactly this type of patient, suggested Balint, that might least be able to create a 'new beginning', and would be the most difficult to work with. Even if Beck had been a man of good intentions, his lack of any psychotherapeutic qualification, and his years of practice based on superficial reading of highly complex and often very contentious text books, would have left him singularly ill-equipped to work with disturbed children.

In his prospectus for The Beeches, Beck wrote that the centre would be 'a fully integrated flexible method of social work intervention' that would use 'limited regression therapies' based on the ideas of Bruno Bettelheim.

Bettelheim was a prolific writer, a psychoanalyst of the Freudian school, who has been described as one of the leading child psychologists of his generation. He was a Jewish survivor of German concentration camps, who wrote on the kibbutz experiments in Israel, and campaigned against racism – which is ironic given that Beck not only championed Bettelheim's work, but also used racist terms against children in care while doing so.

Bettelheim wrote of his experience in dealing with autistic children, as well as other children who are emotionally disturbed. Much of his writing, especially in the influential book *Love is Not Enough*, focused on the need to give children affection to help them recover from earlier neglect or abuse. This affection would include physical cuddling, bathing and washing them, drying them, and reading them 'simple and non-threatening' bed time stories. In *The Empty Fortress* he also wrote of the concept of 'regression as progress'. He placed great importance on the use of the baby bottle, even for older children if they were regressed. Bettelheim did not argue, like Beck, that children could be induced to regress through the use of early childhood props, such as the baby bottle, merely that children who were comforted would regress, and would use a baby's bottle.

'The value of enjoyment of such regressive behaviour [as a baby bottle], when correctly used, is now widely recognised,' wrote Bettelheim about his therapeutic school. 'But it is much easier to make good use of such a device and to dose it correctly, in a setting where the total behaviour of the children is known, and where we can take best advantage of all of it, than in a treatment situation which remains apart from the rest of the child's life.' However, Bettelheim was very aware of the risk of using baby bottles as a regressive device in the wrong circumstances. 'While its use is a valuable aid in a well-established relationship (which is a maturing experience), returning to the baby bottle outside of such a relationship may bring undesirable withdrawal from the world, may further regression into autistic isolation,' he wrote. Beck's use of the baby bottle clearly ignored this warning.

Beck might have claimed justification for sitting children on his lap from Bettelheim's work. Children in early stages of regression might, wrote Bettelheim, begin 'curling up in the adult's lap while they suck out of a baby's bottle'. In later stages of treatment, children will begin to mature again, and replace inappropriate behaviour, such as violence, with a more responsible attitude.

Bettelheim did not refer to the use of nappies to assist regression, nor did he write about the use of provocation or restraint to induce regression in a child. He was also very wary about the use of physical expressions of affection between therapist and child. 'We avoid back rubbing or other direct physical skin contact, although many children request it at first,' he wrote. 'We have found that such contacts usually provide too much erotic stimulation, and with it, fresh anxieties.'

Some words and phrases from Bettelheim's work might have helped Beck satisfy the casual observer looking at Ratcliffe Road and The Beeches. But there was nothing that should have reassured the expert or anyone who made the effort to examine properly the source material that Beck so glibly quoted from. Freud's concept of patient regression was hideously distorted by Beck, in breach of every tenet of therapy. He shouted at children, reminding them of the worst experiences of their young lives.

One girl in Beck's care, for instance, was told, while being held on a child care worker's knee, that her mother had never wanted her. 'It must be something about you, she did not want you,' the worker said. The whole regime exercised by Beck and Fiddaman was a pretext for bullying vulnerable children, to destroy their fragile self-confidence, to make them emotionally empty vessels that could be re-filled in any way that Beck and Fiddaman wanted.

To make them even more vulnerable, the children were dressed as infants, supposedly to take them back to a period in their lives before they were first abused, before their lives went wrong, before their 'basic fault' developed, as Balint would have expressed it. This was outlined in the rules for Ratcliffe Road, published in 1977, which described the supposed therapy that Beck and his staff were implementing. The rules could have been challenged by management, who might also have sought expert advice on what they meant, and what effects they might have had on the children. But management did not see the potential dangers in the treatment described in the rules – indeed the Ratcliffe Road rules were signed by Dorothy Edwards herself.

Beck wrote that 'All children are to be individually assessed, and a personal treatment programme worked out, based on Development/Regression Therapy. As part of this treatment children may need to regress to an early stage of development. Within the unit, the staff, will, in dealing with the regressed child, interact as the mother would with a child under five years old, creating a warm emotional envelopment. This will include dressing the child daily, and when necessary, bathing, and/or washing him.

'At meals it may be necessary to assist the child by cutting his food into more manageable sizes and spoon-feeding when needed. Many regressed children demand what one would expect of the very young child, which includes baby bottles or feeders, particularly at bed-times. Dummies become useful as they reduce the number of toys eaten. Most children, however, revert to their thumbs or fingers. The staff will he expected to maintain close physical contact with the children by having them sitting on their laps, holding hands, cuddling and giving pick-a-backs.'

Each child would, said the rules, be given 15 minutes to an hour each evening of close attention while being put to bed, with a story, and 'a good night cuddle'. 'As part of the treatment programme it may be necessary sometimes for children to be provoked', but no details were given about when or how this might be done. Evidence from staff indicated that provocation included blowing in children's ears, rubbing their ribs with knuckles, tickling their feet, as well as restraint by means of a strong embrace from behind, and taunts about the child's personal life and their relationships with parents. At worst, children were throttled by towels in the pretence that this assisted them to release their feelings.

The rules did, though, say that 'corporal punishment' was not permitted. It later emerged that Beck claimed this merely prevented staff hitting children with canes and the like, and did not prevent them using their hands to inflict pain. However, as Beck chaired the committee that defined the rules, he should have known perfectly well what they were and what they meant.

Hoghughi said of the Ratcliffe Road prospectus: 'This bears correction marks by a senior officer and should have struck horror in the heart of anyone with even an uneducated understanding of damaged children. It seems instead to have been accepted with equanimity.'

Children at Ratcliffe Road were dressed and undressed by members of staff, who put nappies on them, and sometimes kept them in pyjamas for days. They were spoon fed, put on staff members' laps, read bed time stories suitable for children of three or four. These were, though, adolescent boys and girls of 14 and 15 who might spend several years in the home. Mr Justice Potts, in giving his judgement in the compensation case brought by several Beck victims in 1996, described the kind of experiences one of these adolescents encountered. 'On a typical day she was encouraged to play with toys and watch children's programmes on television whilst sitting on the knee of a male member of staff.

She was required to listen to nursery rhymes. She was twice beaten for failing to carry the Honey Monster toy.'

It is not surprising that this so-called 'therapy' had effects that seemed, at least to the distant County Hall managers, to have beneficial effects. Children were too closely watched, too bullied and too cowed to cause as much trouble as in the past, and the managers were so relieved that they failed to look closely. The compensation hearing was told that Beck's regression therapy had no legitimate psycho-therapeutic base to it. This was the view of the expert witness for the plaintiffs, Dr Masud Hoghughi, ironically himself director of an institution criticised in a subsequent report. Dr Hoghughi is an acknowledged expert in deviant children's behaviour, and was Director of the Aycliffe Centre for Children in Durham. Aycliffe was itself investigated by the Social Services Inspectorate after a critical television programme. The SSI investigation found that staff – not including the Director – had used force to restrain violent children. The report added that the Director had often referred to the 'dangerousness' of residents which must be 'confronted', and that junior staff may have misunderstood a 'sophisticated philosophy', too often relying on 'power relations' to enforce children's good behaviour.

'The description of the plaintiff's [of regression therapy] bore no relationship to any recognised form of therapy...,' Dr Hoghughi told the court. 'As I heard the plaintiff's unrebutted comments, it appeared to me that what was happening was torture and not abuse. We were not dealing with passive reactive forms of abuse, but rather as a psychological and physical hurt intended to subjugate the plaintiffs and gain mastery over them so that the children had to become dependent.'

Hoghughi was particularly critical of the use of the Warrendale film as the basis for any treatment in Leicestershire. 'Mr Beck's allusions to this 'method' as a model for his own practice were partial but powerful in creating a smokescreen for a gullible management staff of a social services department who did not check it out. The film does not present a rationale or show any coherent means of achieving 'regression' beyond some forms of perceived care appropriate to infants, such as the use of feeding bottles.'

Leicestershire's managers, argued Hoghughi, should have recognised as a warning sign the fact that its staff were using a form of treatment that had not been adopted in neighbouring, or any other, local authorities. 'The major reason why responsible and well qualified heads of facilities for troubled children did not adopt 'the Warrendale method' was the knowledge that it would provide a cover for improper and indecent behaviour towards the young people,' said Hoghughi. 'If Leicestershire social services department had acted with due diligence, they would have perceived Mr Beck's ambitions, his frequent references to bodily contact, comments regarding 'undressing' in the Ratcliffe Road prospectus and his own reported behaviour, as a cover for 'grooming' and otherwise setting up the context in which he could carry out his physically, emotionally and sexually abusive behaviour. As is evident in his finding of guilt, there is little doubt that pretensions of 'regression therapy' were no more than cover for sexual abuse.'

Psychologist Peter Wilson was also strongly critical of the supposed therapy. In evidence to the Kirkwood Inquiry he wrote: 'To my knowledge, regression therapy as such does not stand in professional circles as a distinct and credible therapy... The undertaking of psychotherapeutic work that involves a significant regressive component is an ambitious and potentially dangerous one. It can lead to very primitive and dangerous behaviour emerging in troubled children, especially adolescents, whose newly developed energy and strength is still precariously under control.'

But Beck had a good write-up in some of the specialist press about his use of 'regression therapy', and was publicly praised by the then Director of Social Services, Dorothy Edwards. He also claimed the support, in his use of the therapy, of two consultant psychiatrists, Surjakant Bhate and Ivan Carter, who were regular visitors, first to Ratcliffe Road and then The Beeches. Dr Carter has since died, but Dr Bhate has disputed that he supported Beck's use of regression therapy. 'My own opinion was at best cynical,' he told the 1992 inquiry into the Beck case. 'I could not and still cannot accept that there is not at least some danger in the practice that, for instance, allows a 15 year old girl to be sat upon a member of staff's knee and cuddled. I expressed this cynicism in the context of the staff group meetings, saying I felt it was somewhat bizarre. Beck and his staff would retort that I was not an analyst. Beck considered it my lack of training in the therapy which led me to question the rationale behind it. He also felt that I had problems with it because of cultural differences arising due to my having been born in India.'

It is surprising that his predecessor psychiatrists did not do more to challenge Beck's use of the 'therapy', says Dr Chris Lewis, who replaced Carter as consultant psychiatrist to The Beeches and later played an important role in Beck's departure. 'I expressed the view that I could not go along with any type of regressive therapy – it was not a therapeutic base I could agree with. I tend to maturation not regression. I had worked in several social services departments elsewhere and I had not come across it. I had read about it. It is a very dubious therapy. You are trying to jump 'N' number of steps. You must have somebody who really knows what they are doing, or else you don't have the basis to deal with any of the problems. It is not legitimate.

'In some of the discussions about clients – my role was not to interfere in processes – we did have discussions about 'regressive therapy'. Beck was very keen on that. There was not the use of regressive therapy at The Beeches as there had been at Ratcliffe Road. I expressed the view that I could not go along with any type of regressive therapy – it was not a therapeutic base I could agree with.'

According to Dr Lewis, Leicestershire County Council had discreetly withdrawn its support for Beck's use of regression therapy after the nature of the treatment came to light during the inquest into the death of a 13 year old Ratcliffe Road resident, Simon O'Donnell, in 1977 (*see Chapter 16*). The coroner had condemned regression therapy – not for opening up children to abuse, but because even then it was clear to him that it had no psychotherapeutic legitimacy, and was what he described as 'fumbling in the dark'.

However, Beck carried on using the treatment throughout the remaining period that he was employed in Leicestershire – and the involvement of qualified psychiatrists in his homes was clearly a factor in reassuring managers about his approach. His prospectus at Ratcliffe Road was published two years after the death of O'Donnell. Almost 20 years later, the judge in a High Court compensation action brought by Beck's victims was told that this document went to senior social services managers, who apparently approved it, even though the limitations it imposed on parental visits and the provocation process it described, amounted to intrusions on the children's rights. While they instructed Beck not to pursue it at The Beeches, their instructions were not enforced and on several occasions managers took no action on complaints which made clear that it was continuing to he used.

There was an obvious attraction to regression therapy for Beck, because it heightened his position of power and influence over the children in care. 'You are putting a child in a very vulnerable position,' explained Dr Lewis. 'You are almost brain washing them.' By creating a new trauma, which in itself was redolent for many of the children of the sexual abuse which led them to be taken into care, Beck was able to ensure that there was little chance that the children would lodge complaints against him. 'Things do get done and said, and people won't want to remember,' suggested Dr Lewis. And if any child had complained, there was zero chance of their word being believed against Beck's.

If there was a psycho-therapeutic base to what Beck claimed to be doing, it had been so distorted that, even leaving aside the sexual abuse, it was counter-productive. The ideas of Freud, Dockar-Drysdale and Balint were to touch the past in order to relieve its pain, and create a new way of dealing with it. What Beck did was to plunge a child back into its old trauma, and leave the child there.

'There seemed to be a concentration on the regression, not on the maturation,' explained Dr Lewis. 'You take them back to the traumatic events. You infantilise them, you engineer that, and you must then move them on. One is always very dubious about people who are not specifically trained in procedures who use them. If a child regresses naturally, you work with that. The difficulty is forcing it. You are short-circuiting a process. That was the worst type of abuse. Any abuse is evil, but you have vulnerable children in care of a local authority, to be looked after, then they are abused again. Self-esteem, their lack of confidence, are all mucked up. They will have major problems with self-esteem, and trusting people, and in forming relationships. A lot went on unseen for a long time, and the victims had no counselling. You can't change what has happened, you can just minimise the effect of the abuse on later life, their post-traumatic stress, and the effects of that.'

Not surprisingly, the children who suffered a regime that was supposed to make them better, have never got over its dreadful effects.

CHAPTER EIGHT
A charmed life?

'What seems to me amazing is that nobody actually did anything about Frank Beck until 1986.'
– **Barrie Newell.**

Frank Beck got away with extraordinary breaches of Leicestershire social services rules almost from the day he began working for the department in September, 1973. Complaints against Beck from reliable witnesses rained down on his bosses. Some involved allegations of serious violence and sexual abuse; others seemed less serious, but had disturbing overtones. Other council officers might have been suspended or at least investigated, but Beck seemed to have a Teflon coating. nothing stuck.

The more he got away with, the worse it became. Many people in social services thought something was seriously wrong in Beck's homes, but believed complaints were pointless, because Beck was untouchable. Accusations were made by children, social workers, parents, teachers and police officers. One boy died in suspicious circumstances, and Beck was found not guilty in a criminal trial of assaulting another. In every case, even where they did stumble across disturbing evidence, managers had been incapable of investigating effectively or taking action.

There were few major complaints during the early phase of Beck's career, at The Poplars. But at least one former resident has sought compensation for sexual and physical abuse inflicted there. Beck was certainly abusing his junior staff, and he seems to have been a habitual – indeed practised – abuser of children by the time he took over Ratcliffe Road. So it is highly likely that he began abusing children very soon after arriving at The Poplars, if indeed he had not abused them during his earlier social work employment. The first major complaints about Beck and his methods surfaced after his move to Ratcliffe Road – in one incident, Beck called a girl being transferred from another home a 'slag' and a 'whore' and staff from the other home complained to John Noblett, a senior manager in charge of care homes. He did nothing.

In 1975, Trevor Sturges, one of Beck's referees for his original appointment to The Poplars, arranged a meeting with Peter Naylor, the head of Care Branch, the section of the social services department which ran residential homes. Sturges wanted to pass on the concerns of two of his students who were placed with Beck at The Poplars and Ratcliffe Road. They had seen Beck's regression therapy in action and were horrified by what seemed to them to be the systematic torment and humiliation of children – with other children often encouraged to join in. It was a credible complaint from an informed professional source, but it was never investigated, and the two students were never contacted.

Two years later, Beck admitted to the police 'sexual contact' with a I5 year old boy – and insisted it was a necessary part of his therapy. The boy, who had been sent to Ratcliffe Road because of his increasingly disturbed behaviour, had told his mother that he had been sexually assaulted by Beck and by his deputy Peter

Jaynes. She complained to the police. Beck was interviewed by the police, and explained the complaint away: 'Well certainly I have had sexual contact with him, but you must realise that this boy came to us in a very regressed state and the staff dealing with him have to do everything for him, from seeing to his toilet activities to spoon-feeding him.'

Beck denied any sexual interference with the boy, and explained what he meant by sexual contact: 'I go into the dormitory and wake him, and I would undress him. If he had an erection I would most likely tell him to go into the toilet and masturbate. He is going through a sexual stage at his age and we do encourage him to talk freely about any sexual problems he has. We encourage close physical contact between staff and children and they sit on our knees and things like that. When he feels randy and has been sitting on my knee, he has made a grab for me, but that is immediately stopped and I would tell him to leave the room and go and masturbate. It's quite possible I did make a remark about him being a rotten rapist and telling him to go and masturbate. He has got sexual problems and I felt it was necessary to talk to him like that to help him out.'

Beck did not allow the children at Ratcliffe Road to be interviewed without a member of his staff in the room. Police found no evidence to back up the boy's complaint, and no action was taken. To social services managers, that meant the matter was closed for them as well – without making any further investigations or considering whether the department's own rules had been breached. If the police could not find sufficient evidence, the reasoning went, managers would not be able to find enough to bring internal disciplinary proceedings. This was a poor argument. In criminal cases proof is required 'beyond reasonable doubt'. An internal disciplinary hearing requires a lower standard, the balance of probability.

Clearly, social services managers had to avoid interfering with a criminal investigation, so they could not investigate Beck and Jaynes while the police were still on the case – but there was nothing to stop them investigating when the police had finished, whether or not a prosecution was to follow. This blind spot was a regular feature of the council's handling of complaints against Beck – an inconclusive police inquiry was used on several occasions as an excuse for dropping an investigation into a complaint or concern about Beck or his staff. In this case, Naylor did not interview Beck or Jaynes, and did not attempt to find out the details of the allegation or look at the evidence the police had obtained. It was a serious mistake; Beck's comments at his police interview were enough to warrant disciplinary proceedings.

A year later, the investigation into Beck's brief spell as acting officer-in-charge at the Rosehill home (*see Chapter 3*) produced alarming evidence about Beck's methods. It followed a complaint that George Lincoln, Beck's deputy, had used provocation techniques on a 14 year old boy, forcing him to shout 'I hate daddy'. There were stories of children being grabbed around the neck or beaten about the shoulders – all familiar Beck techniques and there were also claims that the boy was later bribed to drop his complaint and say he had lied, in order to get a day off school.

Even more disturbingly, staff at Rosehill described how Beck had brought in one of the children from Ratcliffe Road as a volunteer, and that she had used the temper tantrum technique on other children, telling one girl that her mother did not love her. It found evidence that Lincoln and the 'volunteer' had hit children, and that Beck had pulled a girl's hair and called her a 'bitch'. Once again, nothing happened. The evidence of ham-fisted 'treatment' being administered to children in an ordinary home, rather than a special adolescent unit and, worse, being administered by another child, does not appear to have disturbed the social services high command. Nor did it lead to questions being asked about the methods used at Ratcliffe Road. There was no formal report and no discussion of disciplinary action. Beck was paid a £500 bonus for his work at Rosehill, and applied for the post of officer-in-charge of The Beeches.

Beck wrote to the then Director, Dorothy Edwards, to express his disgust with the handling of the Rosehill investigation and the allegations against Lincoln. He said he planned to leave Leicestershire. Edwards' reply was conciliatory. She suggested Beck's anger was the product of stress, brought on by pressures of his job at Ratcliffe Road. 'I will be sorry if you decide to go elsewhere, since I value your work,' she wrote. 'But I think you may be right and might in fact be better to try to do something quite different for a while. If you want to talk to me I should be glad to do so.'

Beck continued with his application for The Beeches job, and took over as head of the home in July 1978. Complaints about the behaviour of the children and the state of the home soon began to surface, but again they were brushed aside. The first formal, documented complaint, early in 1980, came from a teacher whose pupils included a teenage boy at The Beeches. He wrote to the department about children being drunk and teenage couples 'disappearing into the darkness' at a Christmas party, and about nude pin-ups in the boys' rooms – Beck dismissed this as simple prudery. A few months later, there was an incident in which a 15 year old girl was hit in the face by a social worker, suffering a bruise and a cut lip. Some staff were unhappy that the incident was part of a pattern of heavy-handed behaviour and appeared to have been swept under the carpet. In both cases, Beck was left to deal with the issue himself. His managers did not see any need to question what was going on at the home.

A more substantial complaint came from Jenny Whitehead, an experienced foster mother. In 1980, The Beeches was helping her to look after two disturbed children in her care, a nine year old boy and an 11 year old girl. The girl's reaction to counselling sessions with Beck was alarming; she begged to be protected from him and began to have nightmares. Whitehead, a gentle former nurse, who cared for children in a beautiful old house in a village just outside Leicester, was caught in what became the classic dilemma for those alarmed by Beck's activities. On the one hand, she was horrified by the things she was seeing and hearing; on the other, Beck was a very plausible person and those in authority insisted he knew what he was doing, and that his methods worked.

Whitehead thought the sessions with her foster daughter could not be doing much good as if they reduced the child to hysteria. The hour long sessions were conducted in an upstairs bedroom in her home, and she had been told that under no circumstances could she come upstairs. But from the ground floor she could hear the child's screams. 'She would scream the house down, you could hear her from the road,' Whitehead said. 'I would get very upset because I didn't think getting a child hysterical did any good. She used to come into my room at night, and years later she told me that Frank Beck made her hate her own bedroom.'

But Whitehead was told by a Beeches social worker, in a classic example of 'Beckspeak', that the outbursts were a good sign and that they showed the girl was losing her 'iron control on the bad feelings she had inside'. For a time, Whitehead managed to avoid the sessions, by taking the children out of the house if she knew that Beck or one of his helpers was due to visit. But as her foster daughter's problems began to worsen again, Beck was allowed back and the traumatic therapy sessions resumed. Soon, Whitehead found her worries about the treatment resurfacing as well. Still unconvinced about regression therapy, Whitehead took her concerns directly to Dorothy Edwards, turning up at the Director's office without an appointment and demanding to see her. Edwards told her that the screams were a normal reaction to the treatment and that Beck was one of the best and most experienced practitioners in the country. She was clearly so confident about Beck's methods that she dismissed the complaint out of hand.

The first trial

Two years later, social services officials gave a much more substantial demonstration of their confidence in Beck by giving him absolute support when he was arrested by the police. Beck was charged with actual bodily harm against a ten year old boy, who had been left severely bruised across the buttocks, after Beck had spanked him. The boy was not in council care, but he stayed at The Beeches at weekends under an informal arrangement with his family – as was quite common. When his mother saw the bruising, she went to the police. Beck was charged with causing actual bodily harm, and social services officials then had to decide whether he should he suspended from duty until his trial.

By then, Beck had almost ten years service with Leicestershire, and Brian Rice – who had taken over as Director from Dorothy Edwards – was advised by the personnel department that there was no need to suspend him, because he was a long serving member of staff and did not pose a danger to children.

Rice also received a letter from The Beeches staff – orchestrated by Beck – supporting their officer-in-charge. 'All of us feel the need to express our backing of him, in his child care work, especially now at this time, as his methods are being questioned at such a serious level.' Rice may also have been influenced by the length of the possible suspension – the case did not come to court until the following February – and the prospect of doing without Beck's ability to control difficult children for several months.

At the trial Beck admitted smacking the boy. The main legal issue was whether the boy was Beck's guest at the home, in which case he was allowed to use reasonable chastisement, or whether the boy was in the care of the county council, in which case regulations banning anything more than a slap would apply. The court ruled that the boy was Beck's guest and that the chastisement was reasonable and Beck was acquitted. As far as social services were concerned, the trial verdict was the end of the matter. Despite the growing list of incidents, they did not see any reason to question the level of physical force being used against children in The Beeches, even when it emerged that Beck was now seeking written permission from parents to 'chastise and restrain' children as necessary.

Another revealing aspect of the trial was the barrage of character references supporting Beck. It showed how highly he was regarded by politicians, colleagues and managers. Ian Whitehead, then a Labour councillor and vice-chairman of the social services committee, and later assistant director of social services at Leicester City Council, praised Beck's 'outstanding skill in relating to young people'. John Noblett wrote that 'within the department there has never been any doubt about Mr Beck's intentions toward any child in his care. Whatever he has done has always been for the benefit of the children.' And Ivan Carter, the visiting psychiatrist at The Beeches, wrote that: 'Mr Beck is the most outstanding child care worker in Leicestershire.'

John Cobb, Beck's immediate superior, rang The Beeches on February 23, 1983, to ask about the trial verdict. He spoke to Ann Midgeley, the deputy, and later wrote down a memo of the conversation: 'She said Frank had been acquitted but they did not know what they were going to do now, as they had had their sanction taken away from them. They did not know how they were going to control the children. I said if the only sanction they had was chastisation [sic] I was disappointed. She said that if they had a child they could not control could they bring him/her to County Hall. I said no...' At the very least, this conversation should have raised questions over the apparently routine use of physical punishment at The Beeches. It certainly implied levels well in excess of the county council's guidelines.

At the time Beck was awaiting trial, in the summer of 1982, Irene Shimeld, a Trent Polytechnic social work student on placement at The Beeches, complained about the use of provocation against a 14 year old girl she was working with, who stayed at The Beeches a few days a week. Shimeld had already been told about the technique – deliberate provocation, followed by physical restraint – and she was uncomfortable with it. One day, she found a member of The Beeches staff, in the garden, dragging the girl around the grass and into the rose bushes. Shimeld retreated into the house and the child, who by now was very upset, broke away and joined her inside. The other member of staff followed her and continued the provocation, hitting the girl around the head and calling her names. Finally, the girl admitted to feeling jealous of her brothers. This story was relayed to John Cobb, who simply did not know which children at The Beeches were receiving therapy, what methods were being used, which staff were conducting the treatment and what supervision they had. In short, he had little idea what was going on inside a home he was supposed to be supervising.

Meanwhile, the girl's father had sent a letter of complaint about the use of physical force against his daughter to the Director, Brian Rice. Rice asked John Noblett to investigate, and Noblett interviewed Beck and Ann Midley, his then deputy. The interview focused on the similarity between this case and the allegations which had emerged from Rosehill, about deliberate provocation. As before, Beck denied that children were ever deliberately provoked; staff would use any tantrums which blew up to try to make children talk about issues and feelings that were normally locked away.

He claimed the incident with the girl had started as a game of hide and seek in the garden. The girl had a tantrum and was taken inside the home and restrained on a sofa. At one point her face was slapped. Eventually she talked about her family and her feelings about her parents and calmed down.

The two people Noblett didn't speak to were the girl at the centre of the incident and Irene Shimeld. He accepted the explanation he was given and informed the girl's family that: 'This matter has now been fully investigated and all appropriate action taken.' The girl herself was expelled from The Beeches.

The only other tangible result was a warning to Beck that any course of treatment which involved deliberate provocation of a child was 'unacceptable'. Beck responded in a letter by denying that there was any deliberate taunting or provocation of children at The Beeches. But he added: 'I would also like to point out that the higher degree of damaged children also equals the higher degree of risk, therefore such allegations and misinterpretations will no doubt occur from time to time. Those of us taking the risks can only hope for your understanding and hope for your support.' Once again an incident with serious ramifications faded painlessly away.

Noblett's warning to Beck seems to suggest that he wasn't convinced by the denials of deliberate provocation, and previous complaints along these lines must surely have left their mark. But because both Shimeld and the girl were no longer at The Beeches, there was no pressure for further action.

Even so, Beck was on the defensive. When, in September 1983, a 16 year old boy at the Beeches complained, through his solicitors, that he had been hit by Richard Loweth, one of the residential care workers, Beck launched a pre-emptive strike against the complaint. The boy had refused to get out of bed to go to work, saying he was poorly. The Beeches' log records that he was 'thumped by Richard and told to get up and go to work'. When the boy returned, later that day, he was sent for by Beck and wrote a statement saying the incident was as much his fault as Loweth's. He later explained that Beck had asked him to drop the complaint in return for being allowed to stay with his sister during the week, and for Loweth being removed as his key worker.

Beck wrote to the Director to try to defuse the complaint before it arrived on his desk – pointing out that the boy had assaulted his teachers in the past, and that he was now backing off from his original complaint. Loweth had wanted to bring assault charges of his own over the scuffle, Beck added. The letter had an uncharacteristically humble tone. Early on, Beck wrote: 'I feel it is important that you should have some information so that you do not think that this is a reoccurrence [sic] of previous instances,' and he concluded: 'I respectfully suggest that this incident should not be allowed to be seen out of proportion.'

Meanwhile, Loweth prepared a statement of his own, describing how he had pulled the boy from his bed and ended up fighting with him on the floor. Loweth also described how he tried to trap the boy in a 'paddy hold' which, past experience had shown, usually calmed him down. Loweth was later interviewed by Noblett, but no connection was made to previous incidents and the use of the 'paddy hold' was not questioned.

A much more wide-ranging and serious complaint about The Beeches landed on officials' desks on November 22, 1982, while Beck was awaiting trial for beating the ten year old boy. It was from Nasreen Akram, a junior social worker with a psychology degree, who had worked at the Beeches for 18 months. She appeared at the Director's office, intent on making her complaint directly to him, because she had heard that Beck had friends among the senior management. Eventually, she was referred to John Noblett – the principal officer for residential care – and she delivered a detailed indictment of the running of the home, saying that inexperienced staff carried out 'regression therapy', that there was regular violence against children, and suggested that there might be sexual abuse of boys in care.

Almost ten years later, at the trial which ended Beck's career of abuse, Akram gave a vivid description of the atmosphere in The Beeches: 'I noticed the staff and children appeared to he intimidated by Beck. He would get personal details on them and use it against them and ridicule them in front of other children. I was the butt of his jokes – 'Paki, black bitch, middle class wog'. I was ridiculed for having a degree, in front of children and staff. He would ridicule anyone who had authority, police or teachers, everyone in authority was to be laughed at. He was the one to be listened to, it seemed to be him and the children against the rest of the world.'

One of the incidents she recounted to Noblett involved a 15 year old girl who was left bruised after a beating. Another concerned a 10 year old boy who was accused of stealing some money from a newsagent, but wouldn't admit it. One day, as she started work, she heard screams coming from the lounge and walked in to find Beck pressing his fingers into the boy's temples as he sat on his lap. The boy was screaming in pain and Beck was demanding 'Where is it?' Other children were laughing in a frightened and hysterical way. Beck explained that he had learnt the technique in the Marines, and told Akram it was 'brilliant' because the child could be in so much pain, but it left no marks.

Akram told Noblett she was disturbed by the sexual atmosphere at The Beeches. A younger member of staff and one of the boys spent a lot of time at Beck's house and even went on holiday with him, and there was constant innuendo about homosexuality. At the trial she explained that boys were encouraged to masturbate and told that homosexual relationships were part of growing up, but relationships with girls were discouraged. Akram described how Beck would encourage the boys at the home to fantasise about one of the women social workers who was particularly attractive – she was called 'the sex symbol of The Beeches' – and would then take the boys into private counselling sessions.

As someone with a psychology degree, Akram was very sceptical about Beck's therapeutic methods, particularly his version of regression. 'Frank expounded it and used it on children when all else had failed. The children were taken back and became so vulnerable. I felt it was wrong to break down someone's structure without offering them anything else. Again they were left helpless.'

Akram hoped she could pass on her concerns without Beck, her boss, finding out. But as soon as she returned to The Beeches she was confronted. 'Frank rushed out, pale and shaking and said 'I hear you've been to County Hall. Why did you go? Why did you go?' I was really frightened and said: 'Just ring up and find out'.' She later said she was 'aghast and betrayed' at the lack of confidentiality around her visit. After that, Beck made himself Akram's personal supervisor and promised her promotion and good references when she left The Beeches, and he tried to persuade her to tell him exactly what she had said. He was later to write in a reference that she was 'somewhat headstrong, but we have found her to be very competent... her strong will has caused some difficulties with staff... I think she will be more acceptable at a more senior level than she holds at present.'

Noblett told Akram it would be difficult to take action without first-hand statements from the victims. But he did speak to two other witnesses. One, a woman who had been a teacher at the home, reported some violent incidents and backed up some of Akram's other complaints. The second, Russell Mallison, was a former staff member at The Beeches who confirmed the attack against the 15 year old girl. Records kept by the 15 year old girl's social worker at the time, show that she suffered several beatings and that Beck had threatened to stop her being fostered and have her locked up in Polebrook House if she ever told anyone. Noblett did not check the girl's records.

The investigation simply petered out. The issues Akram had raised were very serious and the few interviews Noblett conducted produced supporting evidence. Noblett himself had recently investigated another complaint about violence at The Beeches and Beck was awaiting trial for assaulting a child. But nothing happened. There was no attempt to obtain first hand evidence from the victims. Not only were individual complaints dismissed, the accumulation of similar and disturbing stories emerging from The Beeches was also ignored. Akram, meanwhile, left Leicestershire for a job elsewhere.

At about this time, Beck wrote to the Director highlighting the increasing pressure on The Beeches. He said the centre was still working well, but warned that things could deteriorate. His main concern was that The Beeches was now being asked to take very disturbed children, which meant they had to stay at the unit beyond the normal few months. A meeting was set up to discuss the problem, and it became clear that Beck was admitting children to The Beeches on his own initiative – without permission from County Hall. 'It seems ironic that when some of the homes are carrying many vacancies, some being less than half full, The Beeches should be over-numbers with a waiting list,' Noblett noted.

A foster father

Even after Beck had been charged in 1983 and was awaiting trial, and while the Shimeld and Akram complaints were being investigated, the social services department was preparing to give Beck another astonishing vote of confidence: approval as a foster parent. Until early 1982, the law did not allow single men to foster children unless they were close relatives. When that restriction was about to be lifted, Beck applied to foster two teenage boys, Mark Tovey and Tom Wood, who were resident at The Beeches. He was already in the habit of inviting boys from The Beeches to his home, where some stayed overnight, and he was given permission for one of the boys he wanted to foster to live at his home as a lodger. Both later went with him on holiday to Tenerife.

Beck's formal application to become a foster parent was vetted by a social worker from an outside authority, in this case Northamptonshire. Even if they considered he was qualified to be a foster parent, social services managers also had to decide whether it was appropriate for someone in Beck's position to take on that role. The available information should have led to his rejection on both grounds. In June, the father of one of Beck's intended foster-sons went to see the boy's case worker and told her that another boy at The Beeches had alleged that he had been stripped and fondled by Beck. The father was worried that his son might be abused.

The social worker spoke to Beck, who denied the claims. He agreed that he carried children up to bed, undressed them and gave sexual counselling and therapy to some of them. She discussed his feelings for the boy – 'a very deep paternal affection' – and his sexuality, and decided there were no sexual connotations to their relationship. She decided that the boy's father was trying to wreck his son's placement with Beck. But at the time, no homosexual would have been approved as a foster parent, and so she passed on the allegations to the Northamptonshire social worker who was vetting Beck's fostering application.

The issue emerged again in one of Beck's references, from Ivan Carter, then the visiting psychiatrist at the Beeches, who had also written him a character reference for his 1983 trial. 'I have heard field workers make comments which might suggest that Frank is a homosexual,' Carter wrote, 'an opinion probably derived from his single status at the age of 40, his nurturant attitude towards children, and his occasional mannerisms and phrasing of words, which are like music hall characterisations of homosexuality. I do not personally know of Frank's sexual orientation but... he is without doubt responsible sexually and would not under any circumstances take advantage of a minor in his care.'

At the same time, a complaint that Beck was having a relationship with a male social worker had been submitted to Terry Smith, the deputy director of social services. Smith says that the complaint was forwarded to Mick Wells, the assistant director of social services with responsibility for fostering. Wells says he cannot recall receiving the complaint. The information had been submitted to Smith by the head of another· home, Tony Stamper, explicitly because Stamper had heard of Beck's fostering application.

Northamptonshire social services compiled a long and detailed report on Beck as a potential foster parent and he was questioned about his sexuality. The report on Beck stated enigmatically: 'Mr Beck does not believe himself to be a homosexual and has never had a homosexual relationship with another male... the allegations have had a profound effect on him, causing him to examine his own feelings and motivation closely.'

Beck's vetting as a foster parent was handled by the domiciliary branch of social services, and eventually reached the desk of Mick Wells, then assistant director. His approval was confirmed shortly after he was found not guilty in his assault trial, in February 1983. It is probably a side issue compared to the wider management failures surrounding his career, and both the foster sons loyally supported Beck for years afterwards, dismissing suggestions that Beck had abused them. But Barrie

Newell, who was later called in to investigate the Beck case, is still amazed by the decision. 'It had to go to a senior level to decide whether he should be approved – it called for a managerial judgement. But at the same time, the same department in the same building, there was all the stuff about Beck and children. Thirteen incidents in five years.'

Newell believes that the references to Beck's homosexuality in the foster investigation, put together with reports from the residential home, should have been enough to ensure he was refused as a foster parent. 'There is however no evidence who personally approved Beck – the County Hall record system is pathetic. But there must have been such a discussion – if there wasn't that's even more horrifying,' he said. The man who took the decision, Mick Wells, agrees. He was completely unable to remember the case – one of hundreds of such matters that crossed his desk every month – or his reasoning. But he was later to write: 'It is not with hindsight but with conviction that I say that if the employment history of Frank Beck at that time had been conveyed to the foster parent assessors, we would have objected to his approval.'

Above suspicion

In June 1983, a 14 year old girl who had absconded from The Beeches turned up at the Westcotes children's home and told police that Beck was 'forever hitting her and the other kids'. She said Beck had hit her when she refused to go out with a boy at the home. The police report quoted Mike Nerini, a residential care worker, saying that half his home's intake came from The Beeches, and that there had been repeated stories of ill-treatment. The police decided the allegations were too vague to be properly investigated, but referred them to Care Branch, where no action was taken on the grounds that if there was too little evidence for the police to act, the same applied for the council.

In March 1984, four boys were expelled from The Beeches one evening and ended up seeking help from the social services emergency team to find a place to sleep. That alone was cause for complaint. Without warning, the emergency team was expected to clean up the mess left by an internal problem at The Beeches. Beck's staff were uncooperative, suggesting at one point that the boys should walk back to The Beeches from Hinckley, ten miles away. The incident prompted one of the youths to make a statement complaining about his treatment. He said Beck had punched him and slapped him around the head, and that in an earlier incident he had been pushed to the ground and hit around the head by Beck, in a fight on the roadside outside The Beeches. The statement also accused another care worker of pushing a boy over and banging his head on the floor and recounted several other tales of violence by Beck against other children.

This was one of the rare occasions where managers were presented with first hand complaints from a child in care. John Cobb recommended that Beck should be called into County Hall to answer the allegations, but he thought it was unlikely that the story could be confirmed convincingly by other children because they were glue sniffers, had learning difficulties or were of low intelligence. John Noblett passed the information up the line to Peter Naylor, with the plaintive comment, 'you should be aware of yet another allegation about Frank Beck,' adding 'we never seem to get very far with these inquiries'. Naylor shared Cobb's doubts that any reliable evidence could be gathered from the children and he questioned whether the treatment of the children could be called abuse. He was also mollified by the news that Beck did not support the way the boys had been expelled by his staff. Nothing more was done.

The complaints continued. In January 1985, a 16 year old boy complained to a field social worker that he had been beaten and sexually assaulted by Beck, who had squeezed his penis and testicles. He added that another boy had said Beck was buggering him, but did not object because he quite liked it. A third boy had been made to strip by Beck, but nothing had happened. The boy did not want to press a complaint himself, but said he would give supporting evidence if another child decided to complain.

The information was passed to Mick Wells, then deputy director, who ruled that there could not be any further action unless a formal complaint was made. The police were not informed and no questions were asked within the department. Wells, who years later became the acting Director of Social Services at Leicestershire, cannot remember the case at all. Social services insiders say that, as Brian Rice's deputy, he was virtually running the department at the time, and that the strain and overwork were taking their toll. The boy would later take his complaint to the police, where it would be a significant factor in Beck's fall from grace in Leicestershire.

In the summer of 1985, two boys at The Beeches had a fight with a social worker called Gibson. He was throttled by the youths and taken to hospital unconscious. The boys were sent to the Glen Parva Young Offenders Institution in South Leicester and later charged with assault. It emerged that the first boy was trying to force Gibson to let go of the second, who was being restrained. The boy told his own social worker that there was more violence in The Beeches than he had seen at other children's homes, or indeed at Glen Parva. The incident was considered so serious that John Cobb was sent to interview staff at The Beeches – although he did not speak to the boys involved. The main worry for managers seems to have been the danger that the boy might make allegations about the home or individual social workers in court. The allegations about the level of violence at The Beeches were simply ignored.

In August more allegations surfaced. A 15 year old boy, who had been on The Beeches books for at least two years, had another spell at the home to deal with what Beck diagnosed as a 'normal adolescent sexual identity crisis'. He came to see Beck in his role as a foster father, and wanted to reject both his own family and his foster parents in favour of Beck. There was discussion about Beck taking over as the boy's foster parent, but then the boy went back to his mother and her new boyfriend. After problems at the family home, the boy was told he would have to return to The Beeches. He told his social worker he didn't want to go, because Beck had beaten him up and put his hands down his trousers. The allegation was referred to senior managers, who passed it on to the police.

The boy was interviewed and the police decided that it was nothing more serious than a possibly accidental grabbing of the boy's genitals. But they did turn up an incident where Beck went into a bathroom with another boy, undressed him and sat him on his knee. Beck remarked that 'everything was where it should be', and nothing more had happened. The boy thought the incident was 'weird'. The police considered there was nothing to justify a prosecution and, in line with their normal approach, Care Branch managers and Brian Rice decided that this ended the matter. Years later, Beck's immediate boss, John Cobb, would claim that he had personally forwarded about a dozen allegations to the police for them to investigate. Police records, though, do not confirm this. Why Cobb and his more senior managers felt unable to investigate the allegations properly themselves remains perhaps the most important unanswered question of the Beck case.

Another serious complaint followed in November, when David Alexander, an experienced social worker on placement at The Beeches, as part of a Certificate of Qualification in Social Work course, wrote to the Director, Brian Rice, complaining that Beck was hitting children and that other staff followed his example. Alexander was one of the most credible witnesses possible who came forward, but again there was no investigation and Alexander was not interviewed. Beck was merely asked for his comments. He replied with a robust defence of his staff who had to deal with aggressive, often violent young people, and were sometimes injured in the process. Beck wrote that he, himself, had suffered a black eye, a split lip and a broken tooth in one recent incident, but the staff were regularly reminded that there were limits to the force they could use against children and Beck insisted that anyone who overstepped them was disciplined.

Terence Nelson, the senior assistant director, who was handling the issue for Rice, accepted Beck's assurances – but ordered that he should be sent a written report on any future incident where staff at The Beeches used physical restraint. Even without investigating the complaint further, Nelson took a more cautious approach and signalled that County Hall would now monitor the level of force used against children at The Beeches.

Barrie Newell, who was called in after Beck's arrest in 1990 to investigate Leicestershire's social services management, says Beck survived the succession of complaints because of 'people, not procedures'. He added: 'I think managers' handling of Beck was inept. I particular think Brian Rice as Director and Peter Naylor as assistant director both acted lamentably over a period of time.' Complaints mysteriously short-circuited when they reached the top. Individual social workers kept detailed files on clients and discussions, yet County Hall, where the real decisions were made, kept files on virtually nothing. It frustrated Newell's investigation when time and again he found well documented complaints in the files, but no recorded explanation for the council's bizarre decisions. It was a frustration that was shared by the police, who found that enormous quantities of important files had simply vanished out of County Hall.

'There was a sullen despair about it,' explained Newell. 'First local inquiries were made, reports were passed up the line of command, and nothing would ever happen. None of those reports were even annotated in any way.' Newell's trawl through the County Hall archive left him unable to prove or disprove that meetings took place. 'People would say: 'I suppose we must have discussed it,' and this was at a level where such things must be written down,' he added.

John Noblett, the second in command at Care Branch, insisted that meetings had been held to discuss the management of Beck, but was unable to prove it. Commenting on Newell's findings he wrote: 'I can assure you that after every investigation there was a discussion involving staff of varying seniority, depending on the severity of the complaint, and a decision taken. Because you cannot find any written record of these discussions, which is very unfortunate, nevertheless it does not automatically prove that they did not take place.' He said that advice had been taken from the council's senior personnel and legal officials, and that Beck was interviewed and written to as appropriate. 'To suggest that he should have been given a verbal warning when there was insufficient evidence to support it is most inappropriate,' Noblett wrote.

His defence provides a useful insight into senior managers' view of Beck and of the complaints against him: 'Nowhere in your report do you take account of Beck's need for support from County Hall and, despite the complaints about him, his entitlement to receive it whilst still in the council's service. In giving that support, consideration had always to be given not only to the anxieties about Beck, but also to the difficult task being performed and the type of young persons being cared for. In those circumstances, good management practice would demand that staff on occasions would take Beck's side, but I do not consider such judgements justify conclusions being made that he was unmanageable or that managers turned a blind eye to his wrong doings.'

Peter Naylor, the head of Care Branch, recalls matters being referred to the police at least twice, and was aware of four police investigations of Beck. He believed that, given the type of adolescents placed at The Beeches, a higher level of complaints and incidents was not surprising. Naylor accepted that there 'did appear to be a collective lack of awareness of the cumulative evidence [about Beck].' He believes this was partly because, when allegations were referred to the police, the matter would have been handled via the county clerk's department – and staff in social services would not necessarily have been told of the outcome. What happened if the police investigation came to nothing was 'a matter of judgement'.

One of Beck's most important defence mechanisms was to make excuses in advance. He predicted complaints and allegations from the children, with phrases like 'this will happen,' 'it's par for the course,' 'all the theory would suggest that...', 'they challenge us to abuse them' and 'to trust us they have to see that we are not the same as the people who've abused them in the past'.

So when complaints or disturbing reports of goings-on at Beck's homes reached senior managers, rational-sounding excuses were already implanted in their minds, buttressed by Beck's reputation as a child care guru. The fact that the predicted complaints were made may even have enhanced his reputation.

Brian Waller succeeded Rice as Director of Social Services long after Beck had left and was still in charge when the Beck case came to light. From the fragmentary evidence available in the files, he believes that the incompetent handling of the complaints was the critical problem. But like Newell, he thinks that senior managers should have been alarmed by the sheer accumulation of cases.

'Care Branch was the poor relation and the managers were not high calibre people. Time and time again Beck could have been taken to a disciplinary hearing and brought up short there. You just have to see the files and think 'Christ, how did he get away with that?' There were 13 different complaints by children and staff – you could have missed the significance of up to four complaints, but when you had that many, it was blindingly obvious that this man was not a good employee. There was an overwhelming case for an investigation into The Beeches. Maybe people thought he was above the department, that it would not be possible to bring him to book.'

Bizarrely, Brian Rice's defence for his inaction relied on the crisis and the climate of allegations that pervaded the whole of his children's home responsibility. 'During this period, every other home attempting to deal with young people, particularly those who were on remand, was the subject of a complaint or presented senior management with problems. As examples, one home suffered the tragedy of the officer-in-charge committing suicide following his suspension on alleged sexual offences. At another home, the officer-in-charge was finally imprisoned for sexual offences after a period of suspension. In two other homes, the officer-in-charge was demoted for misdemeanours. This only goes to emphasise that the period from 1982-86 was indeed traumatic for residential child care services of the department.'

Still worse trauma was yet to come and as we shall see, Frank Beck was also implicated in some of these other sex scandals. Yet no broader investigation was ever carried out by Rice to see what connections existed between the various child abusers he was employing in children's homes, nor why his department's procedures were so lax that men who were to be convicted as paedophiles had risen to senior positions of trust. Rice's inability to see the connection between the range of disasters over which he was presiding is perhaps the most fitting testament to his term as Leicestershire's Director of Social Services.

CHAPTER NINE
Living to fight
another day...

*'We had rid Leicestershire of a man
we were all glad to see the back of.'*
**– Terence Nelson, senior assistant
director of social services.**

A complaint of sexual abuse finally ended Beck's career at Leicestershire in March 1986. But the complaint was not about abuse against children. The victims were two male social workers at The Beeches. Beck had made advances to them during staff supervision sessions.

Their complaint was part of a growing rebellion among Beeches staff against Beck and his methods. A group of 18 junior staff were holding regular meetings with Dr Chris Lewis, the visiting psychiatrist who had recently taken over the post. The sessions were held after the normal staff meetings, and Beck would send them off with derisive comments about staff needing a psychiatrist.

'They're all off to see their shrink,' he would tell the children. Beck had set up the sessions to help staff deal with the children, but he did not attend the meetings himself. This turned out to be his crucial mistake. Staff at The Beeches were often isolated, not just from the outside world, but also from each other, as the shift pattern meant they seldom had a chance to get to know each other. Now they had a forum where they could gain strength from each other against Beck.

One of the social workers, Liz Clarke, remembers that for several weeks the meetings were tense and inconclusive, avoiding the real anxieties that plagued most of them. But a level of trust was building up, and when the staff did bring themselves to discuss Beck and his methods, the floodgates opened. 'For weeks no one said very much, there would he the odd discussion about certain children, but then it all turned round and all anyone talked about was Frank Beck,' she said. 'Chris Lewis told us there was obviously a big problem at The Beeches, and it was mostly to do with Frank Beck. We said no one would believe us, we were just ordinary social workers, and there had been complaints before and nothing had happened. He told us we had the power. There were only three team leaders, the deputy, and Frank Beck who weren't in the group, so we had the power to do something about it.'

But they were also aware that Beck had beaten off serious complaints from his staff before. It says a lot about their lack of confidence in social services managers that they thought it necessary to build a watertight case against Beck. They signed a joint letter of complaint and took it to Beck's newly appointed deputy, Cliff Savage, an experienced social worker who did not get on well with Beck. Two of the male staff had a more specific complaint: they had been sexually abused by Beck during staff supervision sessions. The two men shared a house, and had built up a level of trust which allowed them to discuss their experiences. One was a career social worker, the other had first come to The Beeches to do community work in preparation for release from prison. They wrote statements and gave them to Savage, who passed them on to Terence Nelson, the senior assistant director, rather than to the normal line management for Care Branch, through John Cobb, Beck's immediate superior, or John Noblett, who was Cobb's boss.

'The statements told how the junior male staff had only gradually realised that most of them were being sexually harassed in supervision sessions. One described the process: 'Mr Beck told me to sit on the bed and close my eyes, saying that he wanted to talk closely with me. I did this without questioning the reason behind it, although I thought it was a strange request. Mr Beck then sat beside me with his hand on my shoulder and told me to relax and let myself go. 'Trust me' he said over and over. He then asked me to look inside myself and tell him what I saw. I started to feel uncomfortable at this point as he had untucked my shirt and put his hand against my back... he brought up the subject of homosexuality... he explained that everybody should try a bit of both as it is only society that has made us attracted to the opposite sex only. I was worried because he was all the time feeling my back, but didn't want to say anything because he after all was my officer-in-charge.

'He then said that if I ever wanted to understand the problems that these children face, I would have to let myself go and feel the need to be close to a member of the same sex. I then expressed to Mr Beck that I didn't want to carry on this supervision along these lines. He changed his tactics and knelt in front of me, putting his hands on my knees with a firm grip. He now had his forehead pressed against mine. Then he said: 'You know I could always delve deeper by touching a more sensitive part.' He then moved his hands along my upper thighs. It was at this point I stopped him, I couldn't bring myself to put up with any more of this apparent groping and brought the supervision to an end. He ended by saying, 'I don't want to push you too quickly yet, just think about what I have taught you.' I feel that this conduct was a diabolical liberty and now I am over the initial shock of this experience, I am prepared to stand up and voice my complaint.'

At The Beeches, staff knew their confrontation with Beck was under way. Clarke recalls leaving for a long weekend 'very, very scared that I would come back and not have a job'. Savage took the letters alleging abuse to Terence Nelson on March 3, 1986, and added that several staff had verbally complained of abuse by Beck and of sexual molestation and violence against children. Morale was at rock bottom. Savage himself reported seeing children 'slapped and thrown around, their arms twisted behind their back, their heads held between their knees until they cried out in pain and submitted'.

Nelson took the allegations to Peter Naylor, the head of Care Branch, who was in overall charge of residential homes. They agreed that Nelson should follow up the complaints by interviewing the two abused social workers the next morning. Only one of them was available, but the man described how he had been molested during supervision sessions, and said he knew of two others who had had similar experiences with Beck. They had kept quiet because they did not think their word would be believed against Beck's. The man told how it had become obvious that several staff had been groped, kissed or undressed by Beck during supervision sessions. Many of the women staff had been gossiping about homosexual activity by Beck for some time. He related a series of stories about a cleaning lady walking in on Beck in bed with another male social worker; about a staff member ending up in a psychiatric hospital because of sexual doubts after an encounter with Beck; and about sexual assaults on children and attempts to encourage two boys into a gay relationship. And he told Nelson he had been threatened with the suspension after protesting when a girl was called a slag, a bitch and a whore to her face.

Nelson moved rapidly. He consulted the council's Director of Personnel and was given authority to suspend Beck. That day, March 4th, Beck was due on duty at the Beeches at 12.30 and Nelson drove there, to intercept him as he arrived. Beck took the news of his suspension quietly and without argument. According to Nelson's detailed note of their meeting, he denied the allegations about abuse of children and asked if there was a possibility of criminal charges. He said he was 'totally dismayed' at what he called a betrayal by staff. After a quiet and rather anti-climactic conversation, in which he was warned not to contact staff or children at The Beeches, Beck agreed it would be inappropriate for him to stay for lunch, and left.

By the following day, news of the suspension was beginning to filter out. Beck himself had phoned Shirley Willetts, one of the social workers at The Beeches, talking about the ruin of his life's work and telling her he might 'precipitate an accident'. He had also been contacted by the *Leicester Mercury*, which had heard rumours of his suspension.

Into this rather tense and confused atmosphere walked John Hartshorne, a young social worker who had just joined The Beeches. He was a puzzled spectator as the other staff were called into a meeting with Naylor and Nelson, while he was left to look after the children. 'Everyone looked somewhat disturbed and pale faced, and there was a lot of mumbling and discussion going on,' recalled Hartshorne. 'I knew there were a couple of gentlemen in suits and they had called everyone else into a meeting. It lasted for ages, and when it was over this whole entourage of people came out, some were in floods of tears and had other staff comforting them. There were small groups of people talking in whispers and little huddles discussing what was going on – I didn't find out what was happening until I went home and read in the local paper that Frank Beck had been suspended.' Inside the meeting, Nelson asked if any other staff wanted to make statements, and each member of staff then had a 'strictly confidential interview' with himself or Naylor in the side office reserved for private business.

This produced a barrage of new allegations about Beck. There were stories about two 16 year old boys from The Beeches being invited to stay at Beck's home for the weekend. They all slept in the same bed, although there was no apparent sexual activity. Both boys were frightened by the experience. Two boys complained that Beck was 'messing about with them', and how one social worker had been sent to a boy's home to inform his family that he was gay. Another woman social worker described how Beck had told children she was suffering from a brain tumour – she was not. Later that day, Nelson rang Beck to tell him that five of his staff had added their statements to the original complaints against him.

For the first time an investigation had been effective, and brought immediate results. Beck was suspended and disciplinary action which seemed likely to end his Leicestershire career was in prospect. 'There was not the slightest doubt in my mind that by his conduct with his own staff – quite apart from whatever proof there might be for the allegations in respect of children – he had forfeited any right he ever had to be regarded as a caring person to whom the well-being of either adults or children could be entrusted,' Nelson wrote later.

Getting Beck out

Nelson now faced a tactical problem. His interviews with staff convinced him Beck had to be got rid of, but he was not confident that Leicestershire's internal disciplinary procedure would back his action. The Director, Brian Rice, did not have the power simply to sack Beck. He would have to take a charge of gross misconduct to councillors, at a disciplinary sub-committee, and Nelson had several reasons to be anxious about that.

First, it was clear that Beck still had some devoted supporters among The Beeches staff. A hearing, with different staff giving evidence on opposing sides, would split the unit down the middle, and make it impossible for it to continue operating. If a hearing was held, The Beeches might have to close while it was under way, and that would pose major problems – the department would have nowhere to contain its most difficult children. Second, politics, in the shape of Beck's Liberal Party connections, might intervene. Nelson did not believe the politicians would try to gloss over any proven offences, but what if the evidence put before them was inconclusive? Many of the allegations he had noted down from staff were hearsay or second or third hand, and staff who had alleged abuse might back down in the face of questioning by a committee, a subsequent industrial tribunal, or the police.

In a recent, unconnected case, politicians had over-ruled managers when two staff had been accused of gross misconduct. A councillor privately said that politics had been a factor. Nelson feared that Liberal councillors might give Beck the benefit of whatever doubt was raised during a hearing, and that Beck would then emerge from the incident in a stronger position than ever.

As managers wrestled with this dilemma, Beck gave them a way out. The day after the meeting with Beeches staff, his letter of resignation arrived on Rice's desk. It included the phrase: 'I cannot say how sorry I am, even though the complaints against me are overstated, I am aware that it would be impossible for me to continue.' In an application for unemployment benefit, dated March 24, Beck gave his account of the reasons for his resignation: 'I lost the confidence of my staff *and myself.* Without the full support of the staff, the damaged children in our care would have suffered. This would have been unacceptable, particularly as I was and have been 'washed out' for some time which has clearly led me into some mistakes of judgements. You have to be there to fully understand the strain one works under, something I've done for 12 years, I suspect one just dries up!' (Authors' italics.)

There was some debate at County Hall, about whether the resignation should be accepted, but ultimately it was. Barrie Newell, who conducted the initial investigation into the Beck case, believes Beck's departure was a considerable relief to the department, as it solved the problems attached to a disciplinary hearing. 'Rice sighs with relief – he has lanced the boil – so why spend a lot of time and trouble finding out what Beck had been doing? They were glad to get rid of him and were hoping it was under the carpet – but it came out again,' said Newell.

Nelson did not believe resignation would let Beck off lightly. 'His career was in ruins, with no prospect at all of him getting back into social work. At his age, and with his high profile professionally, no one was going to employ him in any social work capacity without prior reference to the department, and it was inconceivable, in the circumstances of his suspension, that anyone would give him support for any job of that sort.'

In practice, the council had no way to stop Beck from leaving, but there was one significant loose end – the allegations of sexual abuse against children. A complication was that – quite separately – the police were investigating a complaint of indecent assault from a boy who had been in Beck's care: the same boy who had complained to social services in January 1985. Beck was arrested and questioned on March 5, the day after he had been suspended over the allegations from his staff, and the day he wrote his letter of resignation. He denied the boy's story and was released on police bail.

Police officers investigating the complaint read about Beck's departure in the local press and wanted to know what was going on. They spoke to Rice, who referred merely to some 'innuendoes' that Beck had indecently assaulted children. Rice added that he could not hand over statements from Beeches' staff without permission from the politicians, and he had passed the statements and other paperwork to the council chief executive's department, asking for advice on what to do.

The view of the county council's solicitors was that 'misbehaviour with staff' was probably not a police matter. But the advice from a council solicitor added: 'As to the allegations regarding the children, however, there did appear to be a *prima facie* case here.'

Police should be advised, paperwork handed over and the police offered the use of social workers to assist with the interviewing of children in care. Remarkably, though, this advice never reached Nelson. To this day, it is unclear where and how the memo disappeared on its route between the council's solicitors and Nelson, the officer charged with implementing it. What is clear is that it represented an astonishing let-off for Beck, and one that angered and amazed police officers years later when they learned of it.

In the absence of legal advice, Nelson had the mistaken belief that the council could not interview children or invite the police to investigate, without rejecting Beck's resignation and committing the authority to a disciplinary hearing. If the children then failed to support the allegations Nelson thought: 'We would run the risk of losing the chance his resignation offered, of getting him out of social work, and secondly, of his resuming his post in a more unassailable position than ever. The action we took brought his reign to an end. If we hadn't taken it, he could have gone on as head of The Beeches for months or even years afterwards.'

The bizarre upshot was that the police were told of Beck's legal relationships with colleagues, but kept in the dark about the suspected illegal abuse of children – precisely the reverse of the apparently uncommunicated view taken by the council's solicitors. Nelson, his boss Rice and his subordinate Peter Naylor, agreed that the police should only be given notes of complaints from Beeches staff if the police asked for them, enabling the confidentiality promised to staff to be honoured. Rice and his officers believed that, because this approach had been discussed with the chief executive's department, and they had apparently received no further instructions, the chief executive had endorsed the plan.

On March 10, two police officers, Detective Inspector Pearce and Detective Sergeant de Haven, met Nelson and Naylor at County Hall. The police were told that the allegations against Beck included sexual harassment of male staff, violence against children, inappropriate professional conduct, and some indirect evidence of sexual abuse of children. Nelson and Naylor said that they had studied the allegations about children closely and decided that 'they did not in themselves represent direct evidence of sexual abuse'. They stressed that the children Beck dealt with were often disturbed. Pearce and de Haven accepted that physical contact was a major part of treatment at The Beeches, that there was a thin line between proper and improper contact, and that previous complaints had been investigated unsuccessfully.

A note of the meeting by Nelson recorded: '[The police] were not anxious to press charges against Mr Beck unless they were satisfied that he had behaved improperly in a criminal, as distinct from a professional or disciplinary sense. They were satisfied that the department had dealt with these aspects adequately and they were not wishing to press charges particularly if there were likely to be evidential problems in terms of proof in a court hearing. But they were concerned that the local press were taking a continuing interest, and if they were to drop the matter, they wanted to be in a position to indicate to the local press that they would not be justified in taking the matter further.' Nelson wrote later that: 'The general tenor of the discussion with the police was that, in getting Beck out of The Beeches we had rid Leicestershire of a man we were all glad to see the back of.'

Nelson denied vigorously that he had made any deal with Beck. He stressed that he had no personal motive – he had minimal involvement in Beck's career or in investigating complaints against him, and he did not know Beck socially. He accepts that he may have encouraged Beck to submit his resignation, but thought that would only have strengthened the council's position in a disciplinary hearing, because it would have been seen as an admission of guilt. He did not believe the department would have covered up information just because it was embarrassing. Indeed, he said, he expected a disciplinary hearing.

The police, at Nelson's suggestion, interviewed Cliff Savage, the deputy officer-in-charge at The Beeches, and concluded that there was insufficient evidence to justify charging Beck. No one apparently noticed that the legal advice to social services to hand over documents to the police had not been carried out. Nelson himself only became aware, four years later, that the advice had been issued, when he was preparing for Newell's investigation into the case. All the intellectual gymnastics to avoid passing on child abuse allegations to the police had been unnecessary all along.

Nor was Beck's name entered, as it should have been, on the Department of Health and Social Security (DHSS) Consultancy list – a list of people who had been dismissed from jobs involving work with children for criminal offences, or who had resigned in circumstances which might suggest they were a danger to children. Beck had been told, when he was suspended, that he would never work in social services again, but nothing was done to ensure that this would be the case. Adding Beck's name would not have totally destroyed his employment prospects, because it was not a straightforward blacklist, it was designed to encourage potential employers to make further checks about anyone who figured on it, but it would have been a clear warning signal. Much would still have depended on the reference given by Leicestershire County Council.

'You only get on the DHSS blacklist if you're convicted of an offence or sacked for a range of causes,' Newell explained. 'Local authorities are supposed to tell the DHSS if a person has resigned in circumstances where children might be at risk if they were put in charge of children again; many local authorities dodge this noose.' Rice did discuss whether he should enter Beck's name on the list with the regional head of the DHSS's Social Services Inspectorate, but decided against it because Beck had not been convicted of any offence. Beck was allowed to walk away from credible allegations of child abuse. It was the culmination of 13 years of misjudgements and managerial incompetence by Leicestershire County Council. The failures of previous years were now capped by a tangle of misunderstandings, miscommunication and cowardice at the end of Beck's employment.

But a further astonishing lapse was yet to come. Having been told his social work career was over, Beck was later given a reference by the council giving him the green light to continue in child care and carry on abusing children in new employment. Newell says that it indicates that references are handed out too easily by social services departments. One serving Director of Social Services backed him up, criticising a culture across many councils that continues to this day, of refusing to give bad references to social workers. The belief held by some social services bosses is that people should be given a clean sheet when they start a new job. There is no indication that such a conscious decision was taken in Leicestershire regarding Beck, but the effect was the same. Newell says it was very convenient for Leicestershire simply to draw a line under Beck, and try to forget he had ever worked for them.

Meanwhile, The Beeches erupted into anarchy, creating a crisis for social services managers. Without Beck – the ultimate deterrent – and with the remaining staff upset and divided, it became increasingly difficult to control the children. John Hartshorne, who had started at The Beeches the day after Beck's suspension, said that even after Beck was removed, there was no change in strategy or staffing at the home. But Frank Beck's methods of control needed Frank Beck to operate them; the children were simply not scared of the rest of the staff.

What followed, Hartshorne said, was a 'tremendous upsurge' of misbehaviour by the children, and suspicions about the cause soon began to crystallise. 'The team became aware that it was being orchestrated,' Hartshorne said. 'Some young people were saying that they were seeing Frank Beck and that he was supplying them with alcohol and money, which they were using to buy glue for sniffing. And he was advising them on how to protest without getting into trouble – passive resistance, almost. It meant a lot of overtime because the young people were almost running riot.'

On March 13, within a week of Beck's suspension, a letter from the county solicitor, Tim Harrison, was hand-delivered to Beck's home. It said he was making 'unwelcome' contact with Beeches staff and had suggested to some children that they should protest against his removal. The letter warned of further action against him, if the complaints continued.

One of the most serious incidents took place on the night of April 9, when a girl at The Beeches alleged she had been raped by one of the boys. The boy concerned was a chronic glue sniffer, with a string of convictions for assault, burglary, theft and car theft. He was a known 'groper' according to later reports into the incident, and both female staff and girls at the home had complained about him touching them. Beck had been the only member of staff able to exercise any control over this boy, and even he had struggled. After Beck's departure, he was one of a group of youths who disrupted the home. Cliff Savage, who had taken over as officer-in-charge, thought that The Beeches was a completely inappropriate place for this particular youth. On April 9, the boy returned to The Beeches at about 11 p.m. with several other youths. They had all been sniffing glue. The girl claimed the youth came into her room and raped her. A subsequent investigation revealed concerns about the level of disruption at The Beeches and the effect it was having on the staff: several had resigned or were planning to leave.

In November 1986, two youths from the Beeches were arrested for criminal damage after an incident described by the *Leicester Mercury* as a riot. The paper quoted neighbours as saying there was 'bedlam' at the home and windows were smashed. By this time, the county council was already planning to close The Beeches and was looking for a buyer for the property.

Some months later, Nelson gave Beck a reference for a 'menial' job as a security guard with Armaguard Ltd, in line with normal practice at Leicestershire. It was not an action that was open to serious criticism, as Beck was not to work with children, and there was no justification for giving a critical reference in a job of that kind. But it did open the way, a year after Beck's resignation, for what is perhaps the most bizarre and culpable error of all the mistakes that Leicestershire County Council was guilty of. Brian Rice twice provided references which allowed Beck to return to child care.

A request came from Reliance Social Care, an agency supplying staff to social services departments in London, and run by Nick Adjinka, a former colleague of Beck's in Leicestershire. It was addressed to John Noblett, but he had by then retired, so it was passed to Rice. The reference he supplied ran through the basic details of Beck's Leicestershire career, and said his methods were still highly regarded. It added: 'Mr Beck developed a highly personal approach to the care of children and young persons, which was reflected in the regime of his home. However he was able to demonstrate the effectiveness of his methods and was successful in modifying the more acute behavioural problems demonstrated by many young people.' There was a glowing tribute to his 'reliability and trustworthiness', and a suggestion that his forceful ways 'evoked varying responses from colleagues'.

The only warning note was the final paragraph: 'Mr Beck may have explained to you the reasons for his resignation. However you may wish to discuss these with him, as he undoubtedly found the constrictions of the authority's policy difficult to accommodate himself to on occasions.' The overall impression left by Rice's reference was that Beck's departure from Leicestershire was something to do with his being an awkward member of staff. There was no hint that sexual misconduct had been involved.

The same reference was subsequently sent to the North London borough of Brent's social services department when Beck applied for a post at the Woodcock Hill Children's Home. The request came from Alexandra Seale-Waithe, who had trained with Beck at Stevenage, more than ten years before. A few months later she became Beck's second wife. The marriage was brief and unsuccessful. Beck later told his trial that he realised it was a mistake within 48 hours.

A later police investigation found there was no evidence that Beck abused any children at Brent, but his methods and manner led to problems with the staff, who found him autocratic. He moved on to Hertfordshire, where he was accused of sexual relationships with two clients, one an adolescent boy.

CHAPTER TEN
Investigation and arrest – 1989

'I may have strayed, but I have not offended.'
– Frank Beck.

The complaint which finally led to Beck's arrest came from Pat Holyland, a former Ratcliffe Road resident, who now lived in Loughborough, a town to the north of Leicester. She had been convicted of neglecting her children, and when she gave birth to a subsequent daughter she was told by her social worker that she would have to go to counselling sessions and parenting classes if she wanted to keep the baby. Early in 1989, she began to attend parent-craft meetings run by social worker Eve Ball, at the Regent Street Nursery in Loughborough.

'We were talking about how childhood experiences affected your parenting,' Holyland said. 'One way or another I started telling Eve some of what had been happening in the kids' home I went to. I told her about the physical attacks by Peter Jaynes. She shut me up, because it was a meeting for everybody, and we could have talked about it for hours. But after the meeting she asked me to see her, and she told me she had met a young man who had been in the homes when she did in-house training as a social worker, and he had told her virtually the same story as me. She said she would contact her boss, Tony Shaw, which she did. He called the police in because I was making pretty serious allegations.'

Holyland's initial complaint related to a serious beating from Peter Jaynes, rather than anything about Beck – her contact with Beck was very limited. Her first police statement was about the general situation in the home and the attack by Jaynes. 'I knew the attack must have been illegal,' she said. 'I was bruised from head to foot, and the bruises lasted for over two weeks. I made four statements. The first was about Jaynes and his attack on me, but it didn't include anything about the tantrum sessions, because they had just been a natural part of life at Ratcliffe Road. I didn't know whether they were done in other homes. Someone else made a statement about the tantrums, and the police were gobsmacked – both by what was happening and by the fact that we could think it was normal.'

The police investigation into Holyland's initial complaint made little progress at first. Papers on the allegation bounced backwards and forwards between Loughborough and Welford Road police stations, and sat on desks for two months. The case almost did not take off – the allegation looked pretty implausible – and serious consideration was given to 'binning' it. But it was decided to interview five people whose names were given by Holyland as witnesses. The first four said they had no knowledge of the incident. However, the fifth said he knew nothing of the attack on Holyland, but that he had been buggered by Beck as a child. A sixth witness was then interviewed, and he made a similar complaint of sexual abuse by Beck.

An investigation that was to last two and a half years then began in earnest. It led to the police taking statements from nearly 400 children, and was of a scale that would normally only be matched by a murder enquiry. At first there were only two officers on the case: within six months there were 30. Just tracking down former children in care was an enormous challenge – they were to be interviewed in four continents. Tracing and interviewing witnesses even in Britain was difficult, and many police forces were involved, operating under the direction of the Leicestershire Constabulary.

The police delved into the archives at Leicestershire's County Hall to try to trace possible witnesses and victims – a process hindered by the chaotic state of the council's records. Many had never been properly completed; others were absent. It was not even possible to tell from the county council's records which children had stayed in which children's home – making it look as if it would be impossible to corroborate witness statements. The investigating police officers' state of mind was not helped by the dawning realisation that they could and should have prosecuted Beck years earlier, at the time of his resignation, if only the statements produced by Nelson's investigation had been passed to them.

By now, Brian Waller had been appointed the new Director of Social Services in place of Brian Rice. At first, Waller and his staff did not realise the magnitude of the police investigation: detectives simply asked for co-operation in seeing the files. No one in the department realised that there had been consistent criminal abuse of children. The size of it didn't dawn upon us at once,' Waller said. 'It took a while – weeks – before we realised how big the police operation had become, and how many young people's files were being looked at by the police.'

Giving police access to client files raised an issue of confidentiality which officials had to ponder, but once it was made clear that this was a major investigation, Waller insists no barriers were put in the way. But the police were unhappy because the information and documents they wanted were hard to find, or simply were not there. 'We put a person in to liaise with the police because the files were held in various places and took some finding,' said Waller. 'Historic files were kept in the basement at County Hall, but they weren't kept in good order. Clearly not enough attention had been paid to keeping them in a proper order where you could find things easily – they took some excavating. It was never seriously suggested that anyone had been burning files or withholding them from the police, it was just due caution. I made it absolutely clear to the staff that full cooperation should be offered, and there was no suggestion whatever of us stalling on that. We said: 'tell us what files you want and an admin officer will find them for you'. Some practical questions came up about whether files should be copied, read at County Hall and so on. Eventually we had a system where they were logged out and we would know where they were.'

But Waller's comments contrast with allegations made to the official Kirkwood Inquiry into the Beck case. The inquiry was told that Colin Clarkson, the officer-in-charge of Ratcliffe Road when the unit was closed in 1989, conducted a bonfire of records – a story Clarkson denies. Clarkson did, though, say that he filled ten bin bags with old records, which were collected and taken for shredding.

Mike Lindsay, then Leicestershire County Council's children's rights officer and a key player in the investigation, says that all the records at the Poplars and at Ratcliffe Road were destroyed. Records at The Beeches would have disappeared, too, he believes, if the building had not been securely locked up. Records at the homes and at County Hall disappeared, he says, but only for Beck's period – not before or after him.

The police had to rely on The Beeches pocket money book, which had been found in the attic at the home, just to prove that children had been resident, and when. Lawyers in the later compensation case were to rely on that as well. To the anger of police investigators, many records they were told did not exist were found only after Beck's trial was completed, and were presented to the Kirkwood Inquiry. It is possible that more charges would have been brought against Beck if the other files had been given to the police. These records included details of every child for who Beck and other care workers were responsible, for how long, which they punished, when and how. They would have given the police a much clearer idea which former residents they should concentrate on finding.

Police officers were especially angry that they were not properly informed by the county council of events that led to Beck's dismissal, particularly when it emerged that a county council solicitor had instructed officials to hand over all documents to police on the case, which had not happened. 'The police were very suspicious of the social services,' Lindsay recalls. 'This was not just professional jealousy. They did not trust the social services, or believe they had given information or were passing on allegations of criminal activity.'

The Beck case was the first child abuse inquiry of its size conducted by any British force. One key decision, taken in conjunction with the Crown Prosecution Service, was that they would not prosecute for comparatively minor offences, such as slapping children. This is contrary to the conduct of later cases, like that in Clwyd, but the view in Leicestershire was that they should keep to the main focus of the investigation, the sex abuse.

Arrested at last

A team of police officers pounced on Beck's home at 7.35 am, on the morning of Saturday April 14, 1990. Beck was told he was being arrested after an investigation into sexual misconduct in children's homes in the 1970s and '80s. Beck replied: 'Oh Jesus,

No!' He was to spend the next 18 months on remand in prison, and, after his conviction, the rest of his life.

Police officers had not, at this stage, understood the character of Beck's abuse. They were thinking of it as being about paedophilia – that Beck found young boys attractive. It was only later that police recognised that Beck used sex as an instrument of power, rather than being driven solely by sexual desire. They expected Beck's large collection of home-taped videos would contain paedophile material, but they were found to contain old films and innocuous TV programmes. As well as arresting Beck, the police also took in one of Beck's foster sons, Mark Tovey, who was staying with Beck and who later sued for wrongful arrest.

When news of Beck's arrest reached Hertfordshire, he was automatically suspended from duty, and an investigation into his conduct there was ordered. It found evidence of 'inappropriate relationships' with a teenage boy and a 27 year old man. Beck was told he would be dismissed and began an appeal. He even asked Hertfordshire councillors to hold his disciplinary appeal hearing at Gartree Prison in Market Harborough, where he was on remand.

Building the barricades

As the extent of the investigation and the magnitude of the charges began to dawn on Leicestershire officials and politicians, they realised they were facing a serious problem. The Liberal Democrat party, nationally as well as locally, faced perhaps the most difficulty. The party had a reputation for courage in calling for equal rights for gays and memories of the Jeremy Thorpe affair still persisted. Given the confusion between gay sex and paedophilia in the minds of some of the public, the party could be badly, and unfairly, tarnished by the revelation that a leading party member was also the country's worst ever sex abuser of children.

Beck was a Liberal Democrat councillor; he was the child care advisor to their county council group; and they were in the process of nominating him as a magistrate when the investigation began. Many members simply could not believe the allegations made against this close colleague. It was the basis of a long and upsetting discussion at a meeting of the Liberal Democrat's East Midland's regional executive. Anne Crumbie, the Liberal Democrat social services spokesperson on the county council, went to see Beck in the cells of Leicester Town Hall after a remand hearing. Crumbie recalls his distress: 'He told me: 'I may have strayed, but I haven't offended'. He was sobbing his socks off in my arms.'

She started visiting Beck regularly in prison, but was warned off by the county council solicitor, who feared she might be accused of a conflict of interest. Other leading Leicester Liberal Democrats continued to visit Beck. Bernard Greaves, a former policy officer for the national Liberal Party, was asked by the Liberal Democrat's regional executive to visit Beck, and see if he could assist. Greaves was a gay activist who had assisted other men charged with sex offences. He became a regular visitor, a close friend and a pivotal figure in Beck's defence team who continues to believe in Beck's innocence.

Labour, too, had cause for concern. The trial seemed likely to feature allegations by Beck against Greville Janner, the Labour MP for Leicester West, and a well known backbencher. Beck had already caused a stir by shouting allegations at a remand hearing, where he knew they could he reported by journalists with some legal protection against a libel action.

Janner was unable to make any detailed comment while the Beck case was *sub judice*. His solicitor, Sir David Napley, issued a short statement, vigorously denying the claims, and adding that the MP had been interviewed by the police at his own request. Janner launched a pre-emptive strike in private briefings to the local media. At a lunch with senior staff at the *Leicester Mercury* he insisted he had never done anything wrong – that the allegations were utterly untrue and he was an innocent man in the appalling position of being unable to defend himself in public. He and his family had tried to help a boy – he was one of a number of people who tried to befriend troubled children at local homes, as unofficial uncles and aunties.

Journalists on the national as well as local press were left in a quandary: the allegations were sensational but unsupported. Leicester has a venomous political culture, and the city was abuzz with increasingly fanciful embellishments of Beck's allegation, along with others alleging that there had been a masonic sexual intrigue involving children in care. But journalists could find no evidence to substantiate either claim.

Beck, too, ran a PR operation. Local reporters including the *Leicester Mercury* crime correspondent Mark Dorman and BBC TV's Leicester reporter James Roberson interviewed Beck at Leicester prison. Roberson, a senior and experienced reporter, came away impressed. He told colleagues that Beck was either an innocent man or an Oscar-class actor. Dorman found Beck complaining of being spat on and beaten up, because of the media, the police and what he termed 'the conspiracy'. After two weeks in prison he consulted a psychiatrist because he thought he might have been deluding himself about his innocence. Beck said the prison officers had treated him 'like dirt' at first, but later asked him to keep an eye on other remand prisoners, to watch how they coped.

An internal investigation

Senior county councillors were given an initial, but insubstantial briefing on the Beck case in spring 1991. They did, though, authorise the council to initiate its own investigation. The motivation was as much about public relations as it was about getting to the truth. Jim Roberts, then Labour's social services spokesperson, accepts that what they wanted was a report that would avert a full public inquiry. Councillors and officers wanted something that could be shown to the trial judge and the press to demonstrate that the matter had been properly examined. They also wanted to know what other dirty washing would come out. The suspicion at the time was that it would reveal a Leicestershire version of pin-down: the sexual element to the abuse came as a shock.

Barrie Newell, a retired assistant director of social services from neighbouring Nottinghamshire County Council, was called in to conduct the inquiry. Initially he simply trawled through the files and wrote a report on what he found. His findings were so alarming that an expanded report, based on interviews with key figures in the social services department, was commissioned.

'We wanted to get a grasp on what had happened over the period of Frank Beck's employment,' said Brian Waller, the then Director of Social Services. 'It took about three weeks, and it was by no means a profound piece of work, but I was alarmed when I received the report. It catalogued serious concerns about the way Frank Beck had been managed over a long period of time. We wanted an external view of what had happened in order to report to members. When we commissioned Barrie Newell we didn't know how awful it would be – we didn't know how many witnesses were going to turn up, how many offences Beck was alleged to have committed.'

A flavour of the attitude towards Newell's investigation came from the former Director, Brian Rice. In his response to Newell's preliminary findings, he wrote: 'We share the same view, I am sure, Brian [Waller] and I, that the matter be appropriately resolved by the courts and that there be no further inquiries. In the event that one should be called for, let us hope that the efforts you have made on behalf of the council will suffice and that there will be no further need to find 'scapegoats'.'

In reality, Newell's report dispelled any hope of avoiding a major inquiry into Leicestershire social services' handling of Beck. The chain of failures – the ineffective investigations of complaints, the failure to inform the police about the allegations which surrounded Beck's resignation, the failure to add Beck's name to the DHSS consultancy list, and the reference which allowed him to return to social work – amounted to appalling mismanagement. Worse still – in an atmosphere of fevered anxiety – it left scope for suspicion of something more sinister than mere misjudgement.

Newell did not really touch on the abusive nature of Beck's therapy, or his lack of qualification to act as a therapist. But his central finding, that the sheer accumulation of incidents involving Beck should have been enough to trigger a thorough inquiry into Beck and the running of The Beeches, was damning enough. Newell pointed out that his report was not based on hindsight; he had reached his conclusions using the same files that had been available to Beck's managers at the time. Their failure to take action, even given Beck's vital role, difficult personality and political connections, amounted to weak management. 'What seems to me extraordinary about the evidence I have seen, is that no one actually did anything about Frank Beck until 1986,' he wrote.

Waller was glad that he and the department were at least forewarned: 'Newell looks a bit thin now, but it served the purpose of giving us a semi-objective view. We wanted an outsider so that we could show it wasn't an in-house gloss on what had happened. Members were worried, as we all were, about the police turning their attention onto the department.

Some were saying that it could not possibly have happened –
they could not have imagined that Frank Beck had done this.
Armed with the Newell report early on, we were able to prepare
them for the outcome of the police inquiry.'

There were also discussions about how to handle the
developing media circus. Lawrie Simpkin, a former Executive
Editor of the *Leicester Mercury*, was consulted about a damage
limitation strategy. Simpkin had been the second in command at
the *Mercury* for several years, and had cultivated close personal
contacts with politicians and officials. He was later to act as
press officer for the diocese of Leicester, and handled regional
press work for the Conservative Party before moving to the
Referendum Party.

Simpkin's advice was that the social services department
should build up a cushion of good news stories, to absorb the
impact of the bad news which was on the way. He also advised
them that a key objective should be to stop the case becoming
known by a shorthand term which permanently linked it to the
county, in the manner of the Orkney and Cleveland cases. If
they wanted to avoid talk of 'The Leicestershire Child Abuse
Case' or something similar, they should try and control the
terminology by always calling it 'The Beck Case'. This proved
a dazzlingly successful stratagem.

What *The Guardian* was to call 'unprecedented defensive
measures' were taken in advance of the trial. MPs and journalists
were briefed about the findings of the Newell report, but it was
carefully pointed out that few of the senior managers from the
Beck era still worked for Leicestershire, and that the system
had since changed almost out of recognition. The press were
also told that the area child protection committee had checked
the present state of Leicestershire children's homes and given
them a clean bill of health.

Councillors began to be concerned about the potential impact of the Beck affair. On August 30, Jim Roberts, the Labour social services spokesperson, wrote in his diary: 'Members need to be part of any strategy – what is their [the officials'] problem?' It was rumoured that junior staff loyal to Brian Rice were passing information to Alan Taylor, Central TV's crime correspondent, and there were complaints that the *Sunday Times* had been briefed without councillors being informed. Questions were being asked about the conduct of several managers who were still around. Ray Fenney, a senior personnel officer, had recommended that Beck should not he suspended during his court case in the early 1980s. Fenney had thought that was the right course at the time, but now recognised he had been wrong. He had been part of the team handling the Beck affair, and now withdrew from the process.

On Saturday, September 7, Roberts returned home to a message from Bernard Greaves, one of the people supporting Beck's defence, saying the story was about to break in the national press. Gail Gerrard, the county press officer, visited Roberts to brief him and Sue Middleton, another leading Labour councillor, went to see Waller. The next day, details of the Newell report were published in the *Mail on Sunday*. It had been in the hands of the politicians for some weeks and had been leaked to selected local journalists. No other paper has been prepared to publish, because publication might have prejudiced Beck's trial and risked a prosecution for contempt of court. The *Mail* report led to suggestions of moving the trial to avoid prejudice, and the county council and the *Mail on Sunday* were later hauled before the judge to explain themselves. The county's defence was that no one was authorised to release the report, and the editor of the *Mail* was severely reprimanded.

On Monday September 9, a crisis meeting was held at County Hall, with party leaders and the three social services spokespersons in attendance. Bob Angrave, the Conservative leader, refused to agree a statement that the county council had complete confidence in the present management of the department. He wanted a public inquiry. The other parties disagreed and a 'troika' approach was worked out, under which all parties should be in the room when legal advice was taken.

Roberts and Middleton also made their own efforts to brief Labour Party officials about the Janner allegations. They tried to arrange a meeting with Joan Lestor MP, a shadow minister and member of Labour's national executive, who was due to visit the area, to warn that allegations would surface during the trial. They were told that they could have a word while riding in a taxi with her, but rejected this idea. They next approached Peter Coleman, then Labour's regional agent and later a senior figure at party headquarters. He said he had been briefed by Willy Bach, a barrister, former city councillor and close confidant of Janner, and was convinced there was nothing in the allegations.

Politicians then met Municipal Mutual Insurance, the county's insurers, together with the council's lawyers, for a briefing on the case. The councillors were relieved to be told that MMI had been shown the prosecution barrister's draft opening statement, which said that the issue of blame for the county council was not a matter for the court. The legal advice was that there were three tranches of charges stacked up against Beck and his co-accused, and that the whole matter could be sub judice for years – statements made after this trial would have to be very cautious, to avoid the risk of prejudicing future trials.

Councillors felt that if they put a foot wrong, MMI would pull out and they could he left liable for millions of pounds in damages – money that would then have to be found from their general budget, at the expense of services. It was even possible, in the most extreme circumstances, that councillors and officials could be held personally liable for any losses suffered by the council, if it could be shown that these were incurred because legal advice was ignored.

Robert Pritchard, then the Liberal leader at County Hall, remembers 'It was clear from the start that this was very serious – there were signs of panic. There was tremendous pressure from Municipal Mutual that it was most important that no one should prejudice any possible proceedings by speaking off the cuff. So it was all handled through press releases at appropriate intervals.'

Brian Waller thought the politicians showed steadiness under fire: 'We had no difficulty with members, except right at the end when people were getting a bit panicky about TV and media attention. There was no objection about the way we had gone about this – a number were mortified to think that this had been going on while they had been responsible for developing the childcare strategy – they had taken an interest in children's work in Leicestershire and turned it round. It was a highly commendable strategy – but almost because their attention had been turned to alternatives to residential work, Beck had been able to become more influential and carry out abuses.'

Another possible interference with the trial came from an unexpected direction – the National Society for the Prevention of Cruelty to Children. The case was already generating headlines and distressed victims were asking for help and the NSPCC wanted to set up a helpline. Mike Lindsay, a former child protection officer at Leicestershire social services, thought the proposal was 'the biggest *faux pas* of any specialist organisation I have ever known'. The publicity for the helpline and the effect it might have on potential witnesses could have caused the case to collapse, so the NSPCC was instructed by Mr Justice Jowitt not to set up the service while the case was being heard. After Beck was convicted however, and when it became clear that there were going to be no further trials, the NSPCC did set up a helpline (*see Chapter 15*).

CHAPTER ELEVEN
The Trial

'You are guilty of the grossest
breaches of trust imaginable.'
– **Mr Justice Jowitt.**

By the time Beck entered the dock at Leicester Crown Court, on
Tuesday September 17, 1991, the excitement around the case had
reached fever pitch. For the media, local and national, there was a
horrifying story to he told in salacious detail. For the politicians
and professionals at Leicestershire County Hall, there was the
prospect of career-shattering revelations. And for the people of
Leicestershire, there was the expectation that the major scandal their newspapers and TV programmes had been hinting at,
would now come to light.

But at first all this was frustrated by a media blackout, ordered
by the trial judge, His Honour Judge Edwin Jowitt. He imposed
a reporting ban, because there were two further indictments
against Beck which were expected to come to court after this
trial. But the ban was lifted ten days later, after three national
newspapers and the Press Association challenged the ruling in

the Court of Appeal. The coverage which followed was a parade of horrifying stories of rape and violence, of weeping witnesses and scathing cross-examinations.

Beck faced 29 charges at the start of the case, including various counts of buggery, rape, assault occasioning actual bodily harm and indecent assault. Five charges were dismissed during the trial, but more were also added – when the jury was sent out he faced a total of 32 charges dating from the mid-1970s to the mid-'80s. In the dock with him were Peter Jaynes, his former deputy at The Poplars, and George Lincoln, his former deputy at Rosehill and later a team leader at The Beeches. Jaynes was charged with two counts of assaulting a boy and indecently assaulting a boy and a girl. Lincoln was charged jointly with Beck with buggering a boy at Rosehill, and with assaulting a boy.

The choice of Jowitt as the trial judge was controversial, and worried Beck and his defence team. Jowitt had presided over Beck's assault trial years before, when he was considered sympathetic to Beck. Now, Beck feared, Jowitt would he hostile, feeling that he might previously have assisted a guilty man to go free.

The trial was held at Leicester Crown Court – a modern red brick building in an isolated corner of the city centre, which housed a series of antiseptic, atmosphere-free courtrooms. Space in the courtroom – Leicester's largest – was at a premium. There was intense competition for seats in the public gallery – including a number of characters who matched the 'dirty mac' paedophile stereotype. Relatives and friends of the victims and onlookers were clearly unable to cope with some of the more chilling evidence, and many left the court in a state of distress. Even hardened court reporters found the evidence hard to bear. Burly adult men, who had been victims, sobbed like children as they recounted humiliating encounters from years before. Some were hesitant and deeply embarrassed, others couldn't wait to have their moment in court after years of denial. The fact that the abuse victims included adult social workers, as well as children, was one of the biggest surprises. There were long pauses between the revelations – with just the sound of a pen or a page turning, as the legal teams noted verbatim accounts of the evidence. It was during those pauses that witnesses cast venomous looks at Beck in the dock. The man who sat there seemed thin and prematurely aged. To some of the victims, he was barely recognisable as the confident, strapping figure who had presided over The Beeches.

Robert Pritchard attended much of the trial, because as then leader of the county council Liberal Democrats, he was worried about the political fallout – the Conservatives were already attempting to make capital out of the case. He heard most of the prosecution case, but after he was asked not to take notes by an usher, he wrote to the judge, saying he was attending as a county councillor. This caused the judge to say in open court that he was representing the county council, which later prompted questions from the county's insurer and Tim Harrison, the county secretary, warned Pritchard off.

At the trial, the nature of the evidence ensured regular drama. The prosecution painted Beck as the central figure in a 'reign of terror' – the co-defendants were his satellites, victims of his overwhelmingly powerful personality. The first few witnesses gave harrowing accounts of the sexual and physical abuse they had suffered from Beck and the other defendants.

One witness, Mary Bell, gave a forceful description of the abuse she suffered, as if she had been waiting for years for her day in court. She was a sad figure, who described absconding from the home, and going to hide in the bushes in the garden of her parents' home, to watch her mother wash up. It was the only family contact she had. Like many of the prosecution witnesses she was accused by the defence of lying in order to win lucrative criminal injuries compensation payouts. She pointed at Beck saying she might have a criminal record, but she wasn't a liar and Beck knew what he had done. Beck, simply sat with his head lowered making notes on a clipboard as the prosecution witnesses gave their evidence.

The name of Greville Janner cropped up early on in the testimony of Jenny L, one of the most seriously abused victims (*see Chapter 3*). Cross-examined by Beck's defence barrister, John Black, she described overhearing an argument about whether a particular boy – who boasted of being a rent boy – should be allowed to see a man named Greville Janner. But she rejected suggestions from Black that Beck 'utterly disapproved of any form of homosexual conduct between men and boys'.

At the time, the purpose of this exchange was probably lost on the jury. But the allegation that Janner had conducted a relationship with a teenage boy, [referred to in this book as Boy A], and that Beck had tried to stop it, later emerged as a major plank of the defence case, when Beck and Boy A entered the witness box. These allegations did not, however, impress the jury.

Some of the most telling evidence came when Peter Jaynes entered the witness box. The former deputy at The Poplars admitted his complicity in the violent regime at The Poplars, and admitted being 'thoroughly ashamed' of his conduct. He said he had colluded with therapies he now realised were abusive because he was 'an idiot'. He described his own seduction by Beck and said he had gone along with it because he was frightened of him. But it had never crossed his mind that he might be abusing children, even though he knew Beck was having sex with other members of staff – an attitude he now realised was naive. Jaynes admitted sitting a young boy he was accused of indecently assaulting on his knee, but denied the actual assault. It had been a very foolish thing for a care worker to do, but he had not intentionally touched the boy's genitals, he said.

In her evidence, the former Director of Social Services, Dorothy Edwards (who held the post from 1974-1980), agreed there were question marks over Beck's regression therapy. She had seen adolescents run up and embrace Beck and other social workers, during her visits to his homes. 'It seemed an odd thing for adolescents to do,' she said, 'but nevertheless it seemed to us, during his time there, some of the children were helped by this therapy. They had disturbed backgrounds and this was helping them to put their personalities right.' She believed Beck had been anxious to help children, but insisted that all complaints were investigated and that she or one of her staff would have contacted the police if criminal allegations had been made.

The witnesses highlighted the dependency Beck created in his victims. Men and boys who had been abused visited him at home for years afterwards, sought his advice or invited him to their weddings. One described how he had gone to see Beck after he had an argument with his girlfriend, and punched him when he made sexual advances. 'I can't understand why, but I still looked up to the man,' he said. Years before, he had been abused by Beck during 'counselling sessions' and threatened with borstal if he complained. At the time he thought the sex was a small price to pay for getting away from his family.

A former Beeches resident described how he got a job as a cook at the home, years later. He had planned to stab Beck with a chef's knife, to take his revenge. But he was recognised and left after six days. Another man, a prisoner serving a sentence for burglary, described how he became a rent boy after leaving care. He said he had hoped he would he brought into the courtroom to give his evidence via the dock, which had a direct entrance from the cells. He wanted a chance to hit Beck as he passed him in the dock, but in the event he was brought into court another way. He had been buggered five or six times by Beck when he was 13 or 14. But he had kept in touch, and had even written to

Beck after giving a statement against him, saying he hoped his court appearance would go well.

One witness whose evidence was later rejected by the jury, claimed to have been raped by Beck and Lincoln at the Rosehill home. The man didn't recognise Beck in the dock, and admitted he had been smoking marijuana when the police arrived unexpectedly to take a statement from him. He also admitted being confused about the incident, since a road accident in which he had crashed head-first through a windscreen. And he agreed that Beck's successor, after his brief spell in charge of Rosehill, had been Ken Scott, who had been convicted of buggering two teenage boys at the home.

Beck's arrival in the witness box, at the end of October, some six weeks into the trial, represented the defence's last throw of the dice. Some charges had been dropped, some witnesses had been discredited, but most had survived cross-examination. The defence had produced witnesses who said they had benefited from the regime at The Beeches and Ratcliffe Road, who had seen no abuse and who insisted Beck had been like a father to them, and had put their lives in order. Social workers including Richard Loweth had given evidence about Beck's 'selfless and exemplary' conduct. But these alone would not he enough to offset the prosecution's accounts of abuse and violence. For Beck to be acquitted he had to convince the jury, as he had convinced so many of his friends, that he was simply incapable of the offences he was charged with.

The 'Janner defence' quickly emerged. Beck broke down and sobbed three times, as he claimed to have protected Boy A, while a teenager, from an alleged abusive relationship with the MP. Beck said Boy A was 15 when he arrived at the Ratcliffe Road Unit. 'He had major sexual problems,' he told the court. 'He thought he was a girl and behaved in a homosexual manner – he would basically offer his body to anyone who wanted it and actually rubbed his body up against any male person and children.' Beck said the boy was used to mixing in 'top class company' and boasted he had a powerful friend who would put Beck in his place. He claimed the boy had received presents from Janner, and that eventually he reported the relationship to the then Director, Dorothy Edwards. The police say no relationship was ever reported. In fact Beck had merely requested managers to ask Janner to stop giving the boy presents, because it was causing problems in the home, as other children were getting jealous.

Beck also said he had written to Janner at the House of Commons, in 1977 or 1978, asking him to leave the boy alone. He began weeping as he told the court: 'That boy had been abused something chronic and I wasn't going to have it.' But people close by were able to see that the weeping produced no actual tears and this was seized on by Peter Joyce QC, the prosecution barrister, in his closing speech, when he reminded the jury of 'the tearless tears of Frank Beck'. Beck claimed the police had known about the alleged relationship and took no action. All Janner could do was issue a statement through his solicitors, saying he was prevented from commenting.

Beck's cross-examination began late on a Friday, and within ten minutes a bravura piece of advocacy by the prosecution barrister, Peter Joyce, revealed Beck as a liar. Beck categorically denied ever having any homosexual encounters or experiences, especially during his time in the Marines. At the push of a button, Joyce played an extract of his police interview to the court.

The jury heard Beck recalling a masturbation game with other marines in Borneo – called the five knuckle shuffle. Joyce sat down, his point proved. Beck was visibly flummoxed and the court rose, leaving him to sweat for the weekend. It was a moment of high drama, which demolished the respectable facade he had built up during his earlier evidence. Whatever credibility he had established with the jury was badly cracked.

The demolition continued when Joyce began to ask Beck about his approach to therapy. Within minutes it was clear that Beck had not read many of the books he had so often cited as the basis of his theories. Joyce was later heard to complain he had spent weeks studying complex psychological texts, only to discover that the target of his cross-examination had barely looked at them. The incident further dented Beck's credibility.

It was revealed that Beck had twice written to Janner after his arrest, asking for a character reference. Joyce accused him of maliciously dragging the MP into the case, after his requests for support were spurned. Beck also claimed that the charges against him were fabricated to justify a vast and expensive police investigation, which had failed to come up with real evidence.

Tension and media anticipation were at their height when Boy A gave evidence. Smartly dressed and articulate, he was a confident witness. He supported Beck's story, claiming that he had had a two year 'affair' with Janner, which started when he was 13. His story included tales of sexual encounters in a hotel in Scotland and at the swimming pool at the Leicester Holiday Inn, the hotel where Janner normally stayed during his constituency visits. The star exhibit was a letter signed with the words 'love Greville'. H said their friendship cooled when Janner discovered that he was stealing money from the MP's wallet.

But under cross-examination, he admitted changing his story. His statement to the police said intercourse did not take place; he later claimed it did. He said he had not admitted this in his police interview because 'it didn't feel right' to do so. Boy A also denied prosecution claims that he was negotiating to sell his story to the *News of the World* or *The Sun* for £5,000 or more. He said he had talked to the papers because he wanted protection after receiving threats, and he did not reply when asked why he hadn't talked to *The Times* or *The Independent*. He also denied he was being 'minded' by a journalist who had been seen leaving court with him.

The defence said this story illustrated Beck protecting children from abuse, rather than abusing them himself. If the jury believed it, it showed a man quite unlike the abuser portrayed by the prosecution. They also asked how Leicestershire social services could have failed to spot violence and abuse on such a scale – quoting evidence from Dorothy Edwards that County Hall officials were proud of the achievements of Ratcliffe Road and The Beeches.

The prosecution dismissed the whole Janner tale as a 'red herring', a distraction to suggest Beck was the victim of some vague but powerful conspiracy. The story had been badly damaged under cross-examination and did nothing to contradict the vast mass of evidence from other witnesses, which described a pattern of abuse lasting more than a decade. The only doubts the defence had raised surrounded the fact that many abuse victims maintained contact with Beck and The Beeches. In his closing speech Joyce dismissed this as irrelevant. The reason some of them had kept in touch was that he had given them the only kindness they had ever known from an adult – even while abusing them. Joyce compared their conduct to a puppy that crawls back to a master after being kicked.

The other two defendants, Jaynes and Lincoln, had sometimes seemed bystanders at their own trial. Jaynes' barrister, Graham Buchanan, told the jury that they had to decide whether he was an abuser or a 'stupid fool', a victim or a villain. His client's evidence had been one of the most dramatic moments of a dramatic case – it was the evidence of a man who recognised his errors and was genuinely trying to tell the truth, who had been influenced by Beck, but did not seek to make excuses.

Lincoln's barrister, Stuart Rafferty, said his client should not be found guilty by association. The former boy in care who had claimed he had been buggered by Beck and Lincoln at the Rosehill home, was a liar, Rafferty added. There was reasonable doubt about the evidence against Lincoln, and the jury had no choice but to acquit him, he said.

Mr Justice Jowitt's summing up focused on the discrepancies in Beck's story – he noted that the defence never asked Dorothy Edwards to confirm that Beck had written to her about Janner and asked if Janner's alleged behaviour was really plausible – would he not have run too great a risk of exposure if the stories were true? He too recalled the 'tearless tears' in Beck's evidence, telling the jury they would have to decide whether Beck's tears, as he gave evidence about Boy A, were real or crocodile tears.

Jowitt said the jury would also have to consider Beck's sexuality and its implications for the case. Was Beck a homosexual? If they decided he was, that did not mean he must be a child abuser, and most homosexuals would abhor the thought of abusing children. But if he was homosexual, that raised the question of why he lied about his sexuality. Was it because he thought a candid admission would condemn him, or because he was deliberately seeking to mask his guilt. The jury would have to decide whether they believed Jaynes' evidence, which had been dismissed by Beck's defence as 'a pathetic story'.

The jury was asked to consider Beck's therapeutic methods; was his regression therapy a sound method of helping damaged children, or was it a mechanism for domination? And was the evidence of some of the witnesses coloured by their resentment of it? Finally, the jurors were reminded that many of the key witnesses had criminal records and that memory was not like a tape recorder which always replayed the same message. It could mislead.

On Monday November 25, over two months after the case had begun, the jury retired to consider its verdicts. Over the next two days, they began to deliver their decisions a few verdicts at a time, convicting Beck on some charges, and rejecting others. After 34 hours of deliberation, stretched over several days, they had convicted Beck of three counts of buggery against boys in care, one count of buggery and one count of rape against a girl in care, two attempted buggeries, six indecent assaults (including two on male social workers) and three counts of assault occasioning actual bodily harm. Jaynes was convicted of indecent assault on a boy in care and ABH against a girl, but cleared of indecently assaulting a girl. Both Beck and Lincoln were acquitted of the joint charge of buggering a boy at Rosehill together. Lincoln was convicted of one count of common assault.

Jowitt then delivered one of the most severe sentences seen in this country since the abolition of the death penalty. Beck was sentenced to life imprisonment on each of the four counts of buggery, and for the rape. And he was sentenced to 24 years for the remaining charges. Jowitt told him: 'You are a man whose character combines considerable talent and very great evil, sadly, you chose to use your talent in pursuit of your evil and lustful desires ... what many of the children suffered at your hands was harshness and perversion where there should have been wholesomeness. It is tempting to think your arrogance led you to think you could excuse yourself because of the good I accept you otherwise did. No one can say the extent of the harm you have done by committing these offences. Much of it has been considerable and long-lasting – that is only too apparent from what I have been able to see from some of the witnesses who gave evidence. You are guilty of the grossest breaches of trust imaginable by someone in your position.'

Jowitt agreed with a comment by Jaynes that Beck wanted too much from those around him, he cared for them and then abused them. As long as Beck retained any sexual potency, he would be a substantial danger to young people, and that demanded a sentence which would ensure their protection. Beck remained impassive, occasionally muttering 'not true, not true,' as the judge catalogued his offences.

Jaynes, now a pathetic, shrunken figure in the dock, was sentenced to three years. He stood with his head bowed as Jowitt said he was now clearly 'a broken man'. The judge had taken into account that he was following Beck's instructions and his example when he carried out regression therapy and choked children with towels. Lincoln was given a 12-month conditional discharge for the single offence of common assault of which he had been convicted. The judge said that the offence of dragging a girl out of bed and slapping her would probably have resulted in no more than a severe reprimand, if it had been reported at the time. He hugged his family as he walked free from the court.

Outside a scrum developed as photographers crowded round the exit where prisoners were driven from the courts. Beck was among a group of prisoners driven out in a minibus. TV pictures show a gaunt face with a fixed, grim smile, illuminated in flashes from cameras. A former boy in care shouted: 'I hope you rot in hell Becky', and he slowly extended two fingers in reply. Then he held up a piece of paper with 'This is not the end!' scrawled on it. The van accelerated away, pursued by photographers.

That night, East Midlands Today, the BBC regional television news, broadcast a recording of Beck's reaction to the verdict, made by his solicitor, Oliver D'Sa. It was an emotional interview. Beck was sobbing as he protested his innocence. He told D'Sa: 'I can only hang on for so long, they keep saying the same thing, you can't keep it up, someone has got to listen, I have got feelings.' To many children from The Beeches and his other homes, the sobbing, at times almost hysterical voice was unrecognisable. It was a minor journalistic coup for the BBC, but one which prompted furious criticism from several MPs.

With the success of the prosecution, the police and the Crown Prosecution Service decided not to proceed with further charges against Beck. With Beck clearly inside for decades, there was no public interest justification to put against the enormous cost of a further trial.

On December 2, almost immediately after Beck's trial was completed, the then Health Secretary, William Waldegrave, announced in the House of Commons that there would be an inquiry into the case, and a wider report into the selection of staff for children's homes. The latter was to be chaired by Norman Warner, a former Director of Kent social services. 'This trial shows the dangers that work with vulnerable children, particularly in residential homes, may attract the very people who should be kept at the greatest possible distance from it,' Waldegrave said.

The announcement gave Greville Janner his first chance to hit back at the allegations against him. He was cheered by MPs as he rose to his feet. He told them: 'There was, of course, not a shred of truth in any of the allegations of criminal conduct made against me during the trial, by Beck and his accomplice, Boy A. As my wife, my family and I have had a taste of the suffering that Beck can impose on innocent people, will you join me in sending to the real sufferers, the individuals who endured Beck's homes and whose lives have been wrecked at his hands, the profound sympathies of us all.'

That night, Janner made a second and more extensive statement in an adjournment debate, organised by a fellow Leicestershire MP, the Conservative David Ashby. Surrounded by his Leicestershire parliamentary colleagues, and by a number of other sympathetic MP's, Janner produced a letter from a man who had shared a cell with Beck, which he said made the motive behind the allegations against him 'blazingly clear. He writes that Beck told him that he, Beck, was going to frame me. According to Beck, that would take the light off him'. The letter quoted Beck as saying he planned to enlist the help of Boy A.

Janner said that the law of contempt of court should be changed. His good name had been 'unjustifiably savaged' in the court, and the media had been able to report the allegations made against him with impunity, because court reports carried absolute privilege. At the same time, the law of contempt meant he was forced to remain silent. 'Anyone involved in a trial can make any allegations they wish about anyone else, providing that the judge cannot disallow them as irrelevant – however harmful, horrendous and vile the lie may be,' Janner said. 'I effectively had no legal right in the matter and I was not even allowed to nail the lie. No wonder many people were mystified by my uncharacteristic silence.' His call for some change in the law was rejected by the Attorney General, Sir Nicholas Lyell, who warned that changes to the constitutional safeguards for justice could he dangerous. 'We interfere with this at our peril and at peril to our liberties and system of open justice,' he said.

The media spotlight swung from Beck, and on to the organisation rapidly being built up as the second major villain of the piece, Leicestershire County Council. For the then Director of Social Services, Brian Waller, who had inherited the crisis from his predecessors, it was an uncomfortable experience: 'During the trial we had a person in court and were getting daily transcripts – it dominated our lives and my life, the whole thing dominated my professional life for many months, to the point that when Frank Beck was convicted, the world's press was there – a frightening experience for any chief officer. But on the whole the press and even the tabloids were very fair. We gave a confidential briefing and that was very well received. I even had a letter of thanks from one reporter.'

In fact Waller proved a difficult target for the press. His department had clearly failed the children in its care over a period of more than a decade, with appalling consequences. But he had not been the man in charge at the time, and most of the senior managers from the Beck era were now drawing their pensions. Waller's mild manner and open acceptance of failure helped defuse the criticisms now levelled against Leicestershire. It was Waller who plunged into a whirlwind of media interviews, to explain the county's position. In a post-trial press conference, he said he was 'sick to the pit of one's stomach, that in a department ostensibly there to help people – and in many ways providing a very good service – for a significant period of years these quite awful events were taking place'. But he also highlighted the changes since the Beck era. Then children's voices had not been heard. Now the county council had appointed a children's rights officer to give them an effective voice. And he emphasised that Beck's regression therapy 'had no place in child care today'.

'We were spurred on to an enormous effort to clear the department,' Waller recalled. 'Not to draw a veil over what happened, but to show that it wasn't happening any more. A prodigious amount of effort was put into making sure that our children's homes were safe places and I think our reputation now is a good one. Although people still put Leicestershire alongside Clywd and pin-down, I don't think it is felt that our homes are anything other than safe. I said I would resign if systematic abuse – not one-off incidents, but systematic abuse – came to light in Leicestershire homes while I was in charge. We had six to eight systems in place, and while any one of them would not guarantee nothing could happen, taken together they were a solid safeguard that it couldn't happen now.' (In 1997, Waller was again before a press conference explaining the past failings of a social services department, this time as acting Director in Cambridgeshire, when a damning report on the department's handling of the case of the murdered five year old, Rikki Neave, was published. Again he had taken charge after a tragedy and dealt with the aftermath.)

The police in Leicestershire also had some explaining to do. If Beck could be convicted in 1991 of offences in the 1970s and '80s, it must have been possible for them to have caught him earlier. Deputy Chief Constable Tony Butler was very unhappy at what the investigation threw up in terms of earlier police failings, including the failure of police to respond seriously to allegations from children who had run away from the homes. Butler had convened a press conference after the trial to say 'mea culpa', and to apologise publicly to the victims. Half an hour before the conference, the county solicitor advised him not to say anything which might compromise the police's defence to any potential claims from victims, or cause their insurers to withdraw cover.

The subsequent press conference was very embarrassing, and Butler was slammed by the press for refusing to say anything worthwhile about the case. But he did commission a Police Complaints Authority investigation, which was led by officers from the West Mercia Constabulary. Ironically, when Butler later became Chief Constable of Gloucestershire he found himself in the same position as Brian Waller, explaining past failings for which he was not personally responsible, when the murderous career of Fred West came to light.

CHAPTER TWELVE
Official Inquiry
– 1992

'Work with vulnerable children may attract the very people who should be kept at the greatest possible distance from it.'
– **William Waldegrave, Secretary of State for Health**

The inquiry announcements by Waldegrave and the Police Complaints Authority put an end to the bleatings of official explanations and justifications. Neither the county council nor the police wanted to compromise their positions before they gave evidence.

Andrew Kirkwood QC – an expert in child care law, a barrister for 25 years, who was soon after to become a judge – was put in charge of the inquiry ordered by the Department of Health. Kirkwood was assisted by two assessors, Maurice Le Fleming, former chief executive of Hertfordshire County Council, and Hilary Simon, senior assistant director of social services at Berkshire County Council. The terms of reference were to report on Leicestershire County Council management's response to allegations and other evidence of abuse in children's homes between 1973 and 1986, and any other relevant management and personnel management matters during that period, or subsequently. In practice, though, the inquiry team focused on the activities of Frank Beck, and looked only in a very cursory fashion at his co-abusers.

One key decision, resented by the media, was to hear almost all the evidence in private. Kirkwood announced the decision and gave his reasons in a statement on the opening day of the inquiry, January 22, 1992.

'I am extremely conscious of the continued public interest in and concern about this whole affair,' the statement said. 'It is plainly right that the public should have the fullest possible information about it. At the same time, I bear in mind that at the core of all the evidence lies detail of young people at times of particular difficulty in their present or past lives – detail, moreover, which has been recorded in circumstances of confidentiality. I intend to respect the right of all those people to confidentiality and I shall do nothing to add to the burdens upon any of them. I am certain that the fullness of my final report, by which the public will be informed, depends upon witnesses feeling able to talk freely and frankly to me, and that some may feel inhibited in that respect if their every word is in public audience.'

The inquiry was held in a newly built primary school building in the middle of a new and largely unoccupied housing estate, at Thurmaston, just north of Leicester. Kirkwood did allow the photographers to take a few shots of the inquiry team, sitting and chatting amiably around tables in the school hall. And he allowed some witnesses to give evidence in public session, where they said they would find it helpful to do so. But for the most part, the media had to be content with shooting pictures of key witnesses such as Brian Rice, Terence Nelson and John Noblett as they arrived at the school. Cameramen and reporters quickly became adept at playing cat and mouse with witnesses who had been warned about their presence and tried to avoid them.

There was a well-orchestrated attempt by politicians, lawyers representing the victims and the press to open-up the proceedings. Michael Latham, then MP for Rutland and Melton, and the late Sir John Farr, MP for Harborough, both criticised the exclusion of press and public. 'It never crossed my mind that the whole inquiry wouldn't be in public,' Latham said. 'Although it might occasionally be necessary to have private sessions to protect the reputation of third parties, in general the public have a right to expect it to be held in the open. I can't understand why it should be held in private when the Orkney and Cleveland cases were not... The Health Secretary was asked to 'look into' the issue, but in the end did not intervene.

One senior Leicestershire politician, Martin Ryan, then Labour leader at County Hall, asked to give his evidence in public. Ryan was egged on by several local journalists, keen to get their teeth into some public testimony. But after a meeting with Kirkwood, he said he had been 'dissuaded'. A motion calling for the proceedings to be opened was proposed at a Leicestershire County Council meeting by the then Conservative leader Robert Angrave – but it was ruled out of order by the chairman, Alec Strachan, who said it would be quite improper for the council to try and influence the conduct of an independent inquiry.

A *Leicester Mercury* leader focused on the central reason for taking at least some of the evidence in public session; the need to scrutinise the performance of officials. 'This man Beck ruined many lives and the reputation of Leicestershire. He could have been stopped. We want to know why he was not,' the leading article said. 'The answers lie in Mr Kirkwood's investigation. We must hear them as they are given, not at a later date.' By then it was clear that the inquiry was likely to last for many months and cost the county at least a million pounds – equivalent to

£1.80 on Leicestershire poll tax bills. Several of the key players, notably Peter Naylor, Mick Wells and Brian Rice, were unable to recall some of the most important events. Occasional snippets of evidence were leaked. In January 1993, BBC TV's East Midlands Today broadcast details of the county council's failure to pass information to the police when Beck resigned, and other revelations from the key officer witnesses. But it was Kirkwood's conclusions that aroused the greatest interest.

The conclusions were finally published on February 8, 1993. But the long awaited event proved something of an anti-climax. Kirkwood refused to take reporters' questions. Instead he simply delivered a short statement to a press conference. Although his inquiry dealt with events at least seven years in the past, it was not safe to treat it all as 'merely past history,' he said. 'I hope that minds can be focused beyond my adverse critical remarks, so that lessons can be learned – not just in Leicestershire – from the very worrying events I have described,' he added. Then, pursued by shouted questions he beat an undignified retreat, leaving embarrassed council officials to take questions on a report they had not seen until 48 hours before.

If Kirkwood wanted the lessons of the Beck case to be understood, his behaviour hardly helped – at least as far as the public and the media were concerned. One of the purposes of such reports is to provide the definitive explanation. Kirkwood not only prevented public scrutiny of the key evidence about what had gone wrong within Leicestershire social services, he also ducked out of giving a public explanation of his conclusions.

Those conclusions included, nonetheless, some damning criticism of social services officials. Brian Rice, the former Director, was 'grossly negligent' in writing a reference for Beck after his resignation. Dorothy Edwards, his predecessor, had 'an unwarranted faith in Beck and his methods,' and should have recognised the warning signs emerging from his homes.

Terence Nelson, the senior assistant director, was right to accept Beck's resignation and was not responsible for the fact that it did not, as intended, exclude him from future employment as a social worker. He added, though, that 'Mr Nelson may also have been inappropriately influenced by recent publicity arising from the trial of another officer-in-charge'. This was a reference to the fact that another children's home officer-in-charge, Kenneth Scott, had just previously been convicted of sexually abusing children in his care.

Mick Wells, the deputy director, was criticised for failing to respond to a complaint in 1985, and for overlooking an allegation of homosexual behaviour by Beck, which came to light during Beck's application to become a foster parent. Wells was the only senior officer criticised in the report who was then still employed by Leicestershire social services, and a further, internal, investigation was held into his conduct. It concluded that he was a valuable officer who had made a major contribution to the work of his department, and he was not disciplined. A further demonstration of continuing confidence in Wells came when he was appointed acting Director of Social Services at Leicestershire County Council, succeeding Brian Waller on his retirement in 1997.

Kirkwood was especially withering about the managers in Care Branch. John Noblett was 'dangerously influenced by the supposed indispensability of Mr Beck'. Kirkwood said Noblett was 'a poor, unenthusiastic and unimaginative' investigator of complaints, and 'bore a heavy burden of responsibility for his own inadequate handling of complaints'. In particular Kirkwood believed his failure to act on Nasreen Akram's very detailed allegations constituted 'serious managerial negligence'. Peter Naylor, the head of Care Branch, was criticised for poor leadership and for failing to investigate a complaint of sexual assault in 1977. John Cobb, Beck's immediate line manager was 'conscientious, willing and cheerful, but he was out of his depth'. Cobb always passed on complaints, but his failure to inspect the daily log at The Beeches – which would have revealed the level of violence to children and other problems – was heavily criticised. There were also general conclusions about the weakness of management, the unwillingness to confront Beck and the failure to supervise him properly. None of those who received the most serious criticism were willing to comment.

At long last, the county council was able to contemplate disciplinary proceedings against staff. This had been an awkward area for the council, with some internal debate over whether staff could be disciplined on the basis of the evidence they gave to the inquiry. Jim Roberts, the Labour social services spokesperson, at one point contemplated going public with his objections to any immunity being granted. Brian Waller wanted a thorough house-cleaning exercise.

'We never felt we had to protect our staff, that people who had sinned should somehow be protected,' he said. 'I was very keen to clean out the stables. I did not have any historic baggage attached to me. We just cracked on with the investigation into people who'd been named in the trial. We had evidence from the files, original complaints about members of staff and new allegations made in the trial, and we processed these one by one. Some people had left or retired, and some were still with us. We didn't know where some of the people concerned had gone, and we were very meticulous about that. We wrote to every authority in the country giving the names of people we had concerns about, asking them to contact us for information about any of their staff who appeared on the list. There were some concerns raised about possible libel, but I said, don't worry about libel. If they want to take us to court, let them.'

It remains unclear, though, how many of Beck's former staff – many of whom were entirely innocent of any wrong doing –

are still employed as social workers, and children's residential homes' staff. Many people who had worked at The Beeches moved to other local authorities after Beck was charged. Staff who were still employed by Leicestershire County Council were dealt with through the normal disciplinary machine – the principal offenders were the ones who came to court. 'There wasn't anyone in that league left in the department or elsewhere, no one who manifestly needed to be turfed out and never allowed near children again,' Waller said.

This left two groups to deal with: managers who were taken to task for mismanagement, and people who had committed lesser offences against children – hitting them or taking part in cruel regimes or abusive therapy. No one was dismissed, but Waller remains confident that the process was handled properly. 'In a way it would have been nice to have found someone to dismiss, to have been able to say that we had dismissed them,' he said. 'The hearings were left in the hands of the people chairing them, and several final written warnings were given out. One person who'd retired might have been on the receiving end of dismissal – but the main offenders had already been brought to court. I don't know what happened about the people I wrote to the other authorities about, but if there had been any really serious, I mean criminal, allegations about them, I would have followed them up personally with the Director of the authority concerned. I think we were pretty energetic, we did all we could possibly do to tell other authorities.'

The main county council trade union, NALGO, was privately critical of the disciplinary exercise. It suspected some staff were being scapegoated and that the disciplinary agenda was being dictated by the council's insurers, with an eye to the Beck victims' impending court case. Waller rejects this: 'The insurers weren't interested in the disciplinary proceedings at all,' he said. 'Where they came on strong was at the time of the public pronouncements we made when Beck was convicted. I never found them as difficult to handle as other authorities on other cases did. I never felt their behaviour was unreasonable. It was a pity that we had to follow the whole legal process; I wanted to say the county council had got this terribly wrong, that we owed an enormous apology for ruining these young people's lives, and were dreadfully, dreadfully sorry for that. They would not let us do that. But they never stopped us doing anything about the disciplinaries – that would have been highly improper.'

CHAPTER THIRTEEN
The case for the defence

'I am personally convinced of his total innocence.'
– Lord Longford

It is easy to overlook the charm and friendship Frank Beck could deploy. It is, though, instructive – child abusers can appear to be nice people. That charm goes a long way to explain why so many people refused to accept that Beck could be guilty as charged and convicted. The judicial atmosphere of the early 1990s should also be recalled. Various miscarriages of justice were unravelling, and it was perhaps more plausible to believe that Beck had been wrongfully convicted than to admit that his bosses had been duped for 17 years.

Lord Longford, the prison reformer, was the most famous and public advocate of Frank Beck's innocence, but by no means the only one. Beck had a close network of friends and they and his foster sons steadfastly argued his total innocence long after his death. On a day-to-day basis, the co-ordination of Beck's defence was handled by two men, working through the law firm

Greene, D'Sa. One of these was Ian Henning, an investigator employed by their firm who became absolutely convinced of Beck's innocence. Ian Henning, who has since died in a road accident, was himself an intriguing person.

A former Metropolitan Police officer, Henning retired on grounds of ill health after being in dispute with his bosses because of their corruption, according to his friends. A source within the police argued the opposite – that Henning was himself sacked for corruption. Either way, this former police officer readily and energetically went into conflict with the Leicestershire police.

'Ian was determined to do whatever he could to get any client found not guilty, even if he knew they were guilty,' explained a former colleague. 'He used the police's tactics against the police. It was Ian Henning that enabled Greene, D'Sa to be so successful on criminal cases.' Henning was equally successful in annoying the police – to such an extent that he was banned from all police stations in Leicestershire, after officers accused him of attempting to pervert the course of justice in a rape inquiry at the same time as the Beck investigations.

Beck's other leading campaigner was Bernard Greaves, a person at least as interesting as Henning. Greaves was a leading member of the Liberal Party, later the Liberal Democrats, being a member of its national executive for a while. It was Greaves who warned Cyril Smith, then Liberal chief whip in the House of Commons, about leader Jeremy Thorpe's private life and the enormous risk it posed to the Liberal Party. As an active gay rights campaigner, and frequently involved in assisting the defence of men accused of sex offences, Greaves was an obvious person to ask to help Frank Beck's defence. Anne Crumbie, a Leicestershire county councillor for the Liberals and a close friend of Beck's, raised the arrest and charging of Beck at a meeting of the party's East Midlands regional executive committee, where Greaves was also a committee member.

The committee agreed that Greaves should assist Beck in his defence, and do all he could to keep the Liberal Party's name out of the newspapers.

When Bernard Greaves met Beck in jail he was pleasantly surprised. Frank Beck did not conform to the usual stereotype of men accused of molesting children. He was a physically strong man, with enormous presence. Nor did he give the usual signals of being gay – though Greaves himself made no secret of being gay (he was a founder member of the Leicester Lesbian and Gay Helpline). Greaves quickly became absolutely convinced of Beck's innocence – a conviction that he holds to this day. It was a classic case of wrongful charge, believed Bernard Greaves. In his view, Frank Beck's attempts at giving harmless encouragement and support to children who had been starved of love, had been misinterpreted. 'Frank showed the children physical affection, including caressing them,' Bernard Greaves explained. 'He spoke a lot about sexual feeling.' As well as this, believed Greaves, a lot of the people who had been in Beck's care had been traumatised by earlier events in their childhood, and made unreliable witnesses. 'There was a consistent pattern in the prosecution evidence that some of the former children in care were recounting real events by displacing them onto Frank,' said Greaves. 'But I did not think that was confusion, the easiest way to lie is to state something that is basically true, but adapt it. There were people with horrendous experiences. Some of the things that Frank was accused of had to be at the hands of other child care workers.'

One of the charges against Beck was dropped when it emerged that Beck was not the officer-in-charge at the time of the alleged offence (though he was still a frequent visitor), and, more relevantly, because the witness making the allegations could not identify Frank Beck in court. Given the number of other child abusers employed in Leicestershire children's homes at around this time, it would not be surprising if there was some confusion as to exactly which of them had abused which children. However, the witness was later paid compensation by Leicestershire County Council in an out of court settlement – so the weight of evidence alleging abuse by a child care worker did persuade the insurer to concede liability.

Greaves argues that the Leicestershire Constabulary was convinced from the outset of Beck's guilt, and was looking for evidence against him, rather than searching out the truth. He says that the likelihood that victims would receive compensation if Beck was convicted made their evidence unreliable. Equally, he suggests, the fact that many were approached while in the hands of the criminal justice system, in prison, on remand, or on bail and sometimes seeking home leave, made their statements unreliable. He continues to believe that Frank Beck was falsely convicted, one of the great miscarriages of justice of recent times.

To achieve a result, some plea bargaining was entered into, alleged Greaves. 'George Lincoln was incidental, he was convicted of a minor charge. Peter Jaynes tried to save himself by co-operating with the prosecution, and he was not charged with any major offences.' He says that Beck's co-worker, Colin Fiddaman, was actually the person who committed vast amounts of abuse, and that Beck was 'stitched up' because Fiddaman had died – arguably because of a police error – and Beck had to be convicted of very serious charges to save police face.

'Colin Fiddaman was a major player,' suggested Greaves. 'The defence never saw the evidence against Fiddaman. There was very likely a case against him. Fiddaman took over the Ratcliffe Road home when Beck took over the Beeches.' The problem with this argument, though, is that most of the abuse allegations against Beck relate to his period in charge of The Beeches. Fiddaman never worked at The Beeches.

Some of Bernard Greaves' other complaints have the ring of authenticity. One solicitor who has read the 500 or so statements from the former children in Beck's care – and who believes that Beck was guilty – says that the repetition of phrases and consistency of style is striking. Children appear to have been led on to make the statements the police wanted them to make, rather than the ones they might themselves have made.

But, as this solicitor points out, the police writing statements for victims is common practice. In effect they put the witness' experiences into police language. This does not make the statement false, it merely suggests that police officers helped victims write them out, which is normal practice. As most people who have made written statements to the police will know, it is common for the police to write out their own version of what witnesses have said for them to sign.

Another element of Greaves' complaint, which can be verified, is the nature of the contact between police and victims. A social worker told the authors that many victims were first approached via prison warders at Leicester jail, when the police made an informal request for allegations against Beck. Victims in prison, including some on remand, were encouraged by the police to make statements, and were aware of the possibility of compensation and the prospect of mitigation when charges came to court. Whether this is enough to discount their statements as false is a different argument. Statements from victims who settled across the world were so mutually corroborative that a miscarriage of justice is only possible if more than 30 police officers conspired in a massive attempt to pervert the course of justice.

Another person who was convinced of Beck's innocence was one of his occasional visitors, prison reform campaigner Lord Longford. 'Personally I am convinced that not only did Frank Beck act throughout as an idealist, but that he did not exceed the bounds of propriety and certainly did not commit any criminal act,' wrote Longford in his autobiography Avowed Intent. 'Those who spoke against him were usually, it would seem, likely to gain financially if he were convicted.' But in an interview with the authors, Longford admitted that his support for Beck was not the result of having seen any evidence. It was merely that Longford liked Beck so much that he could not believe that Beck could be guilty.

Lord Longford has, in any case, changed his position from one of belief in Beck's innocence, to one of agnosticism about it. 'I liked him very much', said Longford. 'He was like those school masters who liked boys. You can care for people too much. He was a friendly person. I visit prisoners as human beings – it is not about whether they are guilty or not. It is not for me to say whether he did it, or not. He was a devoted man: devoted to young people. 75 years ago I started visiting boys' clubs. I have been in touch with youth work, so I do realise you want to love young people, but have to do so in the right way. I always had the greatest regard for what he did for young people, but he may have gone too far, given too much love. It can be dangerous.'

Longford stressed to the authors that prison visiting was not about making judgements about people, and that he does not believe Myra Hindley is innocent, merely that she is 'a wonderful person'.

But not all of Beck's supporters have remained loyal to him. Oliver D'Sa, Beck's solicitor, took a very strong liking to Beck as a person. 'He was very kind to me, and I could not help but really like him'. D'Sa was not merely a paid lawyer doing his job. He was absolutely committed to Frank Beck's case, and believed him totally innocent. Beck's conviction was a clear miscarriage of justice, argued D'Sa when the case was over. After Beck's conviction, D'Sa continued to argue Beck's innocence, organising the basis for an appeal application and writing to the local evening paper, the *Leicester Mercury*, complaining of the way it had covered the trial, and pleading for a more enlightened attitude, one that recognised that Beck might, after all, be not guilty.

'The catalogue of miscarriages of justice evident in the cases of 'the Guildford Four', 'the Birmingham Six', 'the Maguire Seven', and 'the Tottenham Three' have shown the fallibility of the system of criminal justice,' wrote D'Sa. 'I have received during the course of the case many testimonials and references from children who have been in the care of Mr Beck and fellow social workers, who testify to the help, kindness and devotion to his work,' continued D'Sa. 'This should be borne in mind in any assessment of his overall character.'

But although D'Sa was convinced of Beck's innocence at the time he represented him, he has since changed his mind. 'I don't know where the truth lies. It is one of the cases that has been a conundrum to me. I think Frank Beck was a mesmeric character and very intelligent. Since then I have represented a number of his victims in the local magistrates courts. The victims have given their accounts with such clarity that I think it is unlikely that all those complainants could have lied. The spread of victims, in terms of timescale and geography, makes it impossible to have collaboration on that scale. I think Frank Beck believed in his own lies – he believed that he was innocent.'

D'Sa's explanation is that Beck was mentally ill, and able to convince himself that he was not guilty. Beck could not have been so convincing with his friends and legal representatives unless he had also convinced himself that he was innocent – that he had within his own mind re-written his own history – D'Sa believes. It is a view that could help explain why so many other friends of Beck, people who are honourable and just, were persuaded by him. It is also a possibility that Beck himself suggested when he asked to see a psychiatrist while he was on remand.

What should also be recognised, says D'Sa, is that Beck genuinely did good for many of the children in care, and that the majority did not allege he committed abuse against them. 'Some of the children said Frank Beck was the next best thing to God, and are now computer programmers, carpenters, and in these open children's homes had not seen any kind of abuse. You can do a lot of good, but if you do one bit of bad it is cancelled.'

While in Whitemoor, Beck was vigorously planning his appeal, which eminent barristers Anthony Scrivener and Michael Mansfield had shown an interest in taking. 'My own feeling was that the chances of appeal were very remote,' said D'Sa. 'He was convicted by a jury hearing, and by the evidence and facts. There were no errors in law. Only if new evidence came to light did he have a chance of success. There were questions of misdirection of the jury and whether screens should have been used for some of the victims, but this was in the discretion of the trial judge. Frank Beck, right up to the end, was determined to appeal. He was not going to let the matter rest. I think he regarded the sexual allegations as lies. But if you accept they did happen, the only way to explain his ability to behave in such a persuasive way is to believe that he had a form of madness, that he did believe nothing happened. A victim explained to me the brutality of the regime, and as a result of it he went to London Piccadilly and became a male prostitute. I just don't think he could have been lying.'

In any case, some of the things that Beck's friends report him as saying amount to an admission of some guilt. Bernard Greaves says that Beck admitted to having hit many of the children in his care – even though Beck pleaded not guilty when the initial prosecution for assault came up against him in 1983. Beck also admitted to having seduced other residential social workers. 'The 'personal development sessions' [where Beck met with individual members of staff] did involve sexual contact with other child care workers,' Bernard Greaves told the authors. 'This was to help workers deal with difficult children. I was told this by Frank.' Beck claimed that care workers became better at their jobs after they had sexual contact with other workers. This, he told Greaves, allowed them to see relationships in a less restricted manner. And where care workers began to have gay relations, it enabled them to identify more easily with children, who were themselves struggling with their emerging sexual orientations, which may be gay or straight, or a mixture of the two. Beck's resignation letter, sent two days after his suspension, did not directly deny the allegations against him; he said they were 'overstated'. This again suggests that Beck did not persistently maintain his absolute innocence.

Some of Beck's friends make a further point in his defence, which needs to be examined. They argue that in the same way that he made his colleague social workers better at their jobs, by introducing them to new sexual experiences, so, too, he helped to mature children in his care by encouraging them to have new sexual experiences. The argument is that it is discriminatory against children to prevent them from having sex until the age of 21 (as the age of consent for gays was at the time of Beck's offences) or at 18 (as the age of consent for gays currently is) or even at 16 (the age of consent for heterosexual relations). Beck was therefore doing the boys and girls a favour by allowing them to have sex at an earlier age, and adopting a libertarian approach which society should copy. This same argument holds, say its advocates, whether that sex is with other children in care, or if it is with care workers, and whether the sex is straight or gay.

There is one fundamental problem with this argument, which is the nature of 'consent'. Consenting relations between children under the age of 16 cause problems of their own – the risks and damage of pregnancy, possible damage to young bodies not yet developed enough for some forms of penetrative sex, and the lack of knowledge for a child to protect himself or herself. But these problems are nothing compared with relations between a child and an adult. A child may supposedly 'consent' to sexual relations with an adult, but how is it possible to judge whether this consent is real? Of the 200 or so allegations of abuse against Beck, none suggested that a child attempted to seduce Beck. It was only ever the other way around.

Pressures on a child are such that it seems absurd to argue that the child has free will to consent to a sexual relationship with an adult – especially one who, like Beck, had effective control of their liberty. The man who is attempting to seduce the child has taken the place of parents (who in many cases also abused the child), and has a position of enormous authority over the child. There is, too, a great age difference. Beck was in his 30s when most of the offences were committed – other social workers were in their 20s and some were even older than Beck. These were not relationships of equals. They were initiated by manipulative men who forced themselves onto unwilling children either by physical strength, or by force of personality. The supposed 'consent' of the children was used to make the children feel complicit, to ensure their silence. In the process, it had the effect of forcing the victims to live through a perpetual inner torment of guilt for the rest of their lives.

It is the paedophile's habitual defence. And it no more justifies Beck's behaviour than it does any other adult who abuses children.

CHAPTER FOURTEEN
Scant compensation

---

*'Whilst these defendants did not rape the plaintiff,
their negligence permitted Beck to do so.'*
– Mr Justice Potts

By the time it reached the High Court, on January 23, 1996, the Beck victims' battle for compensation had been raging for six years. Eight former children in care were suing Leicestershire County Council for damages. Many more had already accepted settlements and still more were waiting on the results of the case.

For the claimants, the legal process had already forced them through several gruelling re-examinations of events they would much rather have forgotten. They had to give some details of the abuse they suffered to claim legal aid. They had to make a detailed statement as the basis for their claim. They had to be medically examined – usually by a psychiatrist, to determine the emotional damage they had suffered and they had to be examined by experts representing Leicestershire County Council. Further detailed statements were needed by their solicitors and they had to comment on documents disclosed by the council. Now they faced their turn in the witness box. This constant replaying of trauma had taken its toll. The strain and humiliation on the faces of the victims was painfully clear.

'It takes a lot of psychological strength to bring these claims – to face the fear and shame and every single emotion that you or I would run from,' said Bilhar Singh Uppal of the Leicester law firm, Marron, Dodds, which represented most of the claimants. 'It's like standing on the edge of an abyss for them, and hearing someone telling them to jump. It's additional abuse, really.' For some, according to Uppal, bringing the action had meant a painful reassessment of their lives: 'It was very difficult; to realise that the individual they had hated, loved, worshipped, even revered as a father, was the real cause of their problems. They had trusted Frank Beck as their saviour and moral guide, and for some, it was a revelation that they didn't want to face, about the only person they had ever really respected.'

In some cases, this had been exacerbated by the police. When the police began to contact children from Beck's homes for the original criminal investigation, they had simply turned up on doorsteps or left messages on answering machines. Many of the victims were already nervous and upset because they had seen news of Beck's arrest in the media; some had bad experiences with the police in their past, and a number who might have sought damages were simply frightened off by the insensitivity with which they were approached.

About 400 children went through Frank Beck's hands and a quarter of them brought claims. For the majority, it was not that they were not abused or that they suffered less – The Beeches' log book records maltreatment and regression and severe physical abuse against people who didn't claim – they just did not come forward. Uppal believes some victims simply could not face re-living their time in care. 'There were a whole host of people who trembled on the brink,' he said. 'There was also the category who simply could not get beyond the insidious nature of Beck's harm, and believe that he did them a service.' Some people were less affected by their experiences because they had a stronger personality to start with, or were able to turn to their families, who helped them over the damage.

There was plenty of time for the lengthy legal preparations. Between 1991 and 1993, the whole process was frozen, awaiting the report of the Kirkwood Inquiry. Its findings were certain to have a considerable bearing on claims that the county council had been negligent. When Beck was convicted, the council already knew that about 30 former children in care were planning to bring claims against them – a number which eventually rose to 102. At the time, they had promised to treat the claims sympathetically, although there was no admission of liability. But suddenly, a few months after the publication of the Kirkwood report, the council's position hardened.

Claimants were told that the county's lawyers were contesting the issue of limitation – of whether they had left it too late to pursue a claim. This opened up the complex legal issue of whether victims were allowed to seek compensation for abuse that had been inflicted as long as 20 years ago. They responded by issuing proceedings and the county council – whose defence was now being conducted by their insurers, Zurich Municipal – sent back a 'waterfall defence' which effectively denied everything.

Their defence was first, that Beck and other council staff did not abuse the children; second, that if he did, it wasn't at the behest of the council so they weren't responsible; third, that even if they were the responsible authority, they were not negligent because his actions were unauthorised; fourth, that even if they were negligent, his actions were not the cause of the claimants' later problems; and, fifth, that even if they were the cause, they were not the whole cause of their problems. And above all, they argued that it was now too late to claim because of the rules of limitation.

Leaving aside the fact that the defence was denying the findings of a criminal trial and an official inquiry (and the county council had publicly accepted its findings just a few months earlier), it was now advancing the extraordinary argument that it had no duty of care towards children looked after in council homes and that it was not responsible for the actions of council employees in council homes. To the layman, at least, it was an astonishing defence, and one which made managers and politicians at County Hall squirm. 'The duty of care argument placed us in a very difficult position,' recalls Brian Waller, who was Director of Social Services at the time. 'We had to answer to the press for that kind of statement – and we clearly did feel that we had a duty of care and it was unfortunate that they adopted that argument for a period of time.'

The council may have been the defendant, and it might be thought it could have rejected a line of argument it found unacceptable. But officials and politicians at County Hall did not believe they were in control, and their perception was that any public protest or interference would result in Zurich Municipal claiming a breach in the terms of their insurance and walking away from the case. If that happened, the council would be left to pay the costs and settlements from money earmarked for services. The longer the negotiations and then the court case dragged on, the more uncomfortable politicians and officials became.

'I was unhappy that the system didn't allow us to recompense people for what had happened to them, quickly and generously,' Waller said. 'The accountants and lawyers called that naïve – they said all claims had to be tested and justified through an adversarial court system, because that was the way these things work. But as the person who was managing the department at the time I thought that was a terrible position. I could see that the young people were being damaged even more as a result of the protracted nature of the proceedings. I remember seeing one man in his 30s, married, who'd been abused by Frank Beck. He came to my office and asked me to do anything I could to finish it quickly. He said the amount he got wasn't an issue. The process was just killing him, the time taken and the suspense were damaging him and damaging his marriage. It spoke volumes for what it was doing to these poor people.'

One claimant settled for £8,000 compensation before his case came to court, because he could not stand the pressure. This was the man whose evidence about being abused by Beck at Ratcliffe Road had been rejected at the criminal trial, because he said that Beck was the officer-in-charge, and Beck had already left Ratcliffe Road by that time. It later emerged that Beck returned to Ratcliffe Road regularly and spent extended periods there, parading around as if he were still the head of the home. In fact the head of the home was Jaynes, who was totally dependent on Beck – so the confusion was understandable.

The county council had promised to deal sympathetically with all the claims, but now the defendants seemed to think there was a long-term interest in discouraging more claims. Perhaps they feared opening the floodgates, not only to more claimants in Leicestershire, but also to more claimants from the growing list of abuse cases in children's homes across the country. The county's original insurers had been Municipal Mutual, which had specialised in insuring local authorities. But the firm had collapsed and been taken over by Zurich Municipal. ZM denies that the level of the potential payout in the Leicestershire child abuse case helped destroy confidence in MMI's ability to meet its liabilities. Municipal Mutual had been forced to cease trading, and was bailed-out by Zurich Municipal, in 1992, because its reserves were insufficient to meet likely liabilities. This was before the value of compensation payments to Leicestershire victims became known, but the recognition of likely settlements in Leicestershire – and those in similar cases emerging elsewhere in the country – were a major factor in Municipal Mutual being forced to cease trading as an independent business.

There was a limited pool of money available to meet the claims and it appears that Zurich Municipal wanted to test the legal issues in the case and discourage a bandwagon effect from pulling in more claims. It had the reverse effect – many of the claimants wanted an apology more than anything else; the majority were not all that interested in the money. They wanted help in rebuilding their lives and dealing with the trauma. Uppal believes the sudden resistance may have increased their resolve. 'The insurers efforts to guard what they called the floodgates ensured they were opened,' he said. 'What they didn't understand was that they were dealing with people who had suffered as children because they were disempowered, but who were now in a position to fight back against an authority which they saw as treating them abusively. All the promises that their claims would be handled sympathetically had evaporated, so it became a painful reciprocal fight – the harder they were pushed, the harder they pushed back.'

The first step was to deal with the issue of limitation – the cut-off date by which claims normally have to be made. Here there was good reason for hope. With limitation in damages for negligence, claims normally have to be made within three years of the date of the negligence, or if the claimant was a minor at the time, they would have to claim within three years of their 18th birthday. But there is the proviso that the limitation period starts from the point when the claimant knows, or should have known that they had suffered significant harm from the actions of which they were complaining.

So, for example, a claimant could argue that the limitation period should start from the point where they knew Frank Beck's therapies were the cause of their psychological problems. This would not necessarily have been obvious to them before Beck was prosecuted. After all, Beck was able to convince experienced managers that his therapies were valid; scared children in a home were in no position to realise that they were not. And there were people who, even when the police were taking statements, didn't immediately realise that their difficulties were attributable to Frank Beck.

Different rules apply to limitation for damages caused by criminal acts – 'assault and trespass' in legal jargon. Claimants have six years to lodge a complaint from the date of the act complained of, or six years from their 18th birthday, if they were minors at the time. Limitation was an issue for most of the compensation claims – Beck had left Leicestershire County Council in March 1986, and had not been arrested until 1990, or convicted until 1991. Some of the claims were for abuse in the mid-1970s. The victims had to demonstrate that they had not understood that their treatment by Beck was the root of the later problems, until he was prosecuted.

At the time this was still uncharted legal territory. Apart from the Staffordshire pin-down case, which had been settled out of court, there were no real precedents for a large scale action for damages against a council for child abuse which had taken place in council homes. The defence even raised the issue of public interest immunity on council documents. They said some documents were confidential personal records, and they did not want to release other documents on policy issues because it would injure the public interest; if such papers could be released, the council would be unable to record policy discussions candidly, for fear that the records might later be published. But they also wanted to avoid disclosing council and committee minutes that were normally automatically available to the public. The claimants' lawyers retorted that the confidential records were those of the very people who were making the claim. They wanted access to their own records. And if councils were to be given a blanket immunity from disclosing documents about internal policy discussions, they would have the power to set policies and carry them out with no public accountability at all. The court ordered that the majority of the documents should be handed over – but it was clear that the defence intended to fight each issue in the case every inch of the way.

A particularly important battle was fought over the admissibility of Barrie Newell's original internal report into the management of Beck – a document which highlighted the level of negligence involved in the case, and left the county council extremely vulnerable. It had already been extensively leaked and its contents had probably encouraged many victims to claim. The insurers learned their lesson and a few years later the same solicitors, representing the same insurers, were issuing stern warnings to Clwyd County Council in Wales about the handling of their internal inquiry into child abuse allegations at their children's homes. Their solicitors demanded stringent precautions to avoid a leak, warning that if the document was made public, 'the newspapers will publish the usual lurid and alarmist articles… any deviation from this mode of proceeding could well prejudice the insurance position'.

The preliminary skirmishing over, the High Court hearing began in Nottingham on January 23, 1996. The atmosphere was low key, in comparison to the criminal case. There were few theatrics because there was no jury to plead to, and such tactics would not impress an experienced judge like Mr Justice Potts. Inside the nondescript modern courtroom, great piles of documents, some contained in stacks of two or three cardboard bookcases, surrounded the judge and the two legal teams. Weeks of complex legal argument and detailed evidence, with just a few moments of drama, began.

Sue Morton, a care worker at Ratcliffe Road and The Beeches gave telling evidence about how her position had been undermined by Beck. He had once thrown her into a river in front of the children. 'I did not realise he was bullying children, I thought he was just bullying me,' she said. 'He hit me quite often, when things were not going well for him. He was particularly derogatory towards women, saying we were just there to do a bit of caring. He would say to me 'What do you know? You've got no intelligence'. When I went there I was not a very mature 20 year-old, he was a very intimidating man.'

The judge believed she was 'totally subjugated' by Beck. Morton described seeing Beck lying on top of a boy, moving up and down. He told her to get out, and later explained that he was trying a new form of therapy. He said the boy thought he was a woman and Beck was treating him like a woman, but if she said anything about the incident and the boy heard about it, he would be damaged. She also confirmed that various forms of provocation were used against children, to make them break down and cry. Her evidence helped confirm the nature of Beck's regime, and the domination he exercised over staff and children.

The contents of the Beeches' log, with its entries about regression, physical punishment and temper tantrums was also helpful to the plaintiffs. They had hoped that the Ratcliffe Road log would be equally helpful – it was known that it existed at the start of the Beck affair, but it subsequently disappeared. It also came out that Fiddaman had a relationship with a 16 year old boy in The Beeches as late as 1985-86. The boy was going down to see Fiddaman in Devon where he then lived. He also stayed with him in the Grand Hotel when Fiddaman visited Leicester.

In the first week of the trial the council dropped part of its defence and admitted that it did have a duty of care toward the plaintiffs, and that their managers had failed to monitor the homes properly. But the defence did not concede limitation and the plaintiffs still had to prove they had been abused and had suffered damage from it. The total legal costs of the case were about £2 million, half spent by the defendants and paid for by their insurers, half spent by the claimants and mostly paid for through legal aid. If the money spent on legal fees – and most came by one route or another from the taxpayer – had been put in a fund and claims had been dealt with purely on the issue of how much should be paid to each claimant, Beck's victims would have been spared the repeated re-living of their abuse and the process could have been finished much more quickly and cheaply.

But the defendants wanted certainty about whether each claimant had been abused and whether they had a claim in law. So each plaintiff had to establish that they had been abused and had to demonstrate the extent to which they had been harmed – the issues of liability and quantum, in legal jargon. This meant they had to lay their life story before the court, including their psychological, sexual and criminal histories, so that the judge could decide the extent to which their subsequent problems resulted from their experiences in care. The results could be harrowing.

Expert witnesses described the problems of particular victims. One woman had been subjected to regression therapy, temper tantrums, verbal abuse, including taunts that she had been abandoned by her parents, and beatings. She had been denied privacy, even in the lavatory, and was often bathed by male staff. She had been dragged upstairs by the hair, on one occasion she was stripped by male staff, 'to check for love bites' after she had absconded with a boy from the home, and she had been beaten for failing to carry a cuddly toy when she was supposed to be undergoing regression. These experiences meant that she would sometimes behave childishly and use babyish talk. She continued to use cuddly toys and furry hot water bottles. She was left with a great deal of bottled-up emotion and would deal with her distress by slashing her left forearm with a razor – a habit which she began within days of entering Ratcliffe Road.

Her self-mutilation continued at intervals through the subsequent years and had left her arm seriously scarred. She suffered flashbacks and bad dreams, and abused tranquillisers and alcohol to control anxiety attacks. She believed she was mad and had difficulty controlling her anger. She had been left with 'an enormous amount of anger and aggression and fears she might hurt someone seriously,' according to one witness. She also found it hard to show affection to anyone other than her daughter.

The judge had to untangle the roots of these problems. Were they exclusively the result of her experiences in care at Ratcliffe Road? Or were they also the result of her earlier family life, with a mentally ill alcoholic mother and a sometimes violent father? The woman admitted being terrified of her mother, who she described as 'mad, unpredictable and frightening'. Some of the most crucial evidence showed she had managed to recover from some of her earlier problems as a result of care she had received before going into Ratcliffe Road. But there, according to one expert witness, Dr Andrew Clarke, a consultant adolescent psychiatrist, 'she encountered an atmosphere of denigration, humiliation, physical and emotional abuse, where she should have been encouraged to greater autonomy, self awareness and independence. She should have been consolidating the gains she was making. Instead she was deprived of the opportunity for normal growth and development by the regime'.

Another expert, Dr Trevor Friedman, a consulting psychiatrist, said she had suffered some problems due to her mother's mental illness, but her condition had worsened dramatically after she was subjected to the regime at Ratcliffe Road. It was, he said, 'tormenting, overwhelming and akin to torture'. He added: 'She may have had one or two problems prior to being in their care, but one would expect, with a reasonable standard of care, that these would have improved. In fact they increased in severity devastatingly. In particular her self-mutilation appears directly attributable to occurrences in the children's home and her efforts to escape.'

This woman was one of two plaintiffs who refused out of court settlements. The others gradually accepted offers which would end the ordeal quickly. The other plaintiff who was determined to take the case to judgement was Jenny L., whose experiences at Ratcliffe Road were described in *Chapter 2*. Her evidence was particularly painful. Her mother had threatened to cut out Jenny's tongue if she referred to her boyfriend as 'dad'. She was frequently beaten, and had become seriously disturbed. She was admitted to a children's psychiatric unit at the age of eight, and after a spell in another children's home, she was placed in The Towers, an adult psychiatric hospital, because of violent behaviour and self-mutilation. The Towers was clearly not an appropriate institution for a 15 year old girl. After an attempt to abscond, Jenny L was put in a locked ward. She said later there were only 'a load of old women, I had no one to talk to, they were giving me drugs'.

After six months at The Towers, she was visited by Beck. He told Jenny L about the new children's home he was opening at Ratcliffe Road. It had no locked doors, no rules and the children were given plenty of attention and freedom. It seemed a much more attractive place to live than The Towers, and Jenny L Agreed to move there. She arrived at Ratcliffe Road on March 31, 1975, and it was not long before she was subjected to physical and sexual abuse and the abusive therapy regime practised by Beck and his co-abusers.

Jenny's evidence was attacked as unreliable by the defence. They said that at various times during her childhood, she had claimed to be pregnant, to have been raped by her brother and to have feigned symptoms that led to an operation to remove her

appendix. Mr Justice Potts, however, took into account that she
had been severely disturbed at the time, and thought her evidence
to the trial was honest – and that she did not deliberately lie. He
accepted that she suffered numerous rapes and sexual assaults as
well as being throttled with a towel, beaten, kicked and dragged
around by the hair. She suffered 'regression therapy', and was
threatened with a return to The Towers if she complained.

The judge did not accept two specific claims: that she had
been gang raped by Beck, Jaynes and Fiddaman and that
long term damage was caused to her right ankle by sustained
attacks on it by Jaynes and Fiddaman – her ankle problems had
developed recently, and during the compensation trial she was
on crutches. The judge decided that the evidence about the gang
rape incident was unreliable because Jenny had not mentioned it
in her original statements to the police. After hearing detailed
medical evidence he was not convinced that her ankle injury
could be attributed to abuse at Ratcliffe Road. The evidence
about her later life demonstrated the damage she had suffered.

Jenny had remained at Ratcliffe Road for almost a year after
her care order expired, because Beck refused to let her leave and
threatened her with a return to The Towers if she disobeyed.
She left only after overdosing on paracetamol and whisky. She
explained to the court that, by then, she was convinced that she
would only leave the home in a coffin or an ambulance.

After treatment at the hospital, Jenny was told she could
not return to Ratcliffe Road. She drifted between jobs and
hostels and psychiatrists, suffering episodes of depression while
bingeing on drugs and alcohol and mutilating herself. Her
life began to stabilise when she formed a lesbian relationship
and moved in with her partner. Then, cruelly, news of Beck's
arrest and the revelation that she had been sexually abused
undermined their relationship.

Again, the judge had to try and distinguish between the psychological damage which pre-dated her arrival at Ratcliffe Road and the damage which was caused by her period in Beck's care. Arbitrary figures were bandied about by expert witnesses. The defence argued that she was already severely disturbed by the time she arrived at Ratcliffe Road and that only 25 per cent of her problems could be attributed to her experiences there. Her own expert witnesses said that, with proper therapy, she would have coped fairly well with her pre-Ratcliffe Road problems. They said the majority of her problems were the result of her experiences at Ratcliffe Road. She was a survivor, who had coped to some extent with horrific abuse. They pointed to the fact that she had been doing quite well until the police contacted her as part of their investigation into Beck. Then her life fell apart. By the time of the compensation case, Jenny was suffering from depression and had no sense of self-esteem of self-worth. She was abusing drugs and alcohol, mutilating herself and suffering flashbacks in which she saw Beck's face in front of her. She was not alone; the other claimants also showed visible signs of intense stress.

Having accepted that both the remaining plaintiffs had suffered abuse, and that this had left them with lasting psychological damage, the judge turned to the complex issue of quantum: that is, the amount of compensation to which they were entitled. The damages came under three headings: pain, suffering and loss of amenity, past and future; lost earning capacity or handicap on the labour market between leaving care and the time of the court case, and the cost of therapy.

The first woman was awarded £50,000 for pain and suffering, £10,000 for handicap in the labour market and £20,000 to pay for future therapy. Jenny was awarded £80,000 for pain and suffering, £40,000 for lost earning capacity and £25,000 for therapy. It was a bitter result for Jenny, who, just days earlier, had turned down an offer for an out of court settlement which was substantially greater than the £145,000 she was now awarded.

Potts was conscious that his awards might seem small compensation for the horrific treatment both women had suffered. 'A layman who has heard the evidence in this case might be tempted to think that the awards made for personal injuries are too low when compared to the ordeal suffered by the plaintiffs,' he said in his judgement. 'I wish to emphasise that these awards must be in scale with awards for personal injuries generally. If the scale of the awards is too low, that is a matter for a higher court or Parliament. In any event suffering on the scale endured by the Plaintiffs and monetary compensation may be thought to be incompatible. Money can never adequately compensate the plaintiffs for what they have suffered in consequence of the defendant's negligence.'

In the chaotic impromptu press conference on the High Court steps, Jenny was visibly distressed. The other claimant was simply relieved that the case was finally over. She praised her lawyer, Uppal, for his support. Uppal took the opportunity to condemn the defendant's promise to fight all future claims just as hard. Already, he was looking toward the next battle.

For claimants like Pat Holyland, the process was financially disappointing and emotionally unsatisfying: 'I got £40,000 and I think I was pretty well cheated,' she said. 'I never got anything for the physical injuries, although I lost most of my teeth because of drinking sugary drinks from those bottles. I was never called to testify at the first trial, since my assault was in the second batch of offences that never came to court. And because I was in the second batch, I wasn't allowed to go to the main trial, either. I never had my day in court – I gave evidence to the inquiry, but it was never challenged or disputed.'

Holyland felt cheated of a confrontation she had been anticipating for years – she would have liked a chance to do battle with Leicestershire County Council, but they avoided a clash. She was never allowed to confront her abusers: 'My over-riding wish is to see Peter Jaynes and ask him why? And why me?' She believes the compensation process could have been made much easier. 'In the beginning we all thought it had been admitted and compensation would simply be paid over,' she said – 'then it was all going to court. I had been given £5,000 by the Criminal Injuries Compensation Board, but the legal process to get the rest lasted for about six years. The lawyers got millions, but the compensation paid out was a few hundred thousand at most.

'Leicestershire County Council had no case, they didn't dispute any of my facts, all they tried to do was make me tell the judge I was OK now. My reply was that I might be OK today, but tomorrow I might not be. We sat there for weeks bringing out our stories, then they said that we were too late in bringing the case. There was this wind-up, let-down process. They tried to get us to settle out of court – their first offer to me was £6,000, and each time it was Christmas they sent offers round, knowing that some people had kids and they were on the social and didn't have anything. I told my solicitors to tell them I already had extra presents, so I didn't need the money...'

At the time of writing it appears that almost all the remainingclaims will be settled out of court. One exception is Peter Bastin – a convicted murderer who took Leicestershire County Council to court in a separate action in 1998. An out of court settlement was agreed on terms which remain secret. Some reports say he was awarded £50,000. All Bastin's solicitors would say was that their client – who was due to be considered for parole two years after the case – was 'delighted' with the outcome.

CHAPTER FIFTEEN
Beck's network of abusers

'It is too much of a coincidence.'
— **Mike Lindsay, former children's rights officer.**

There was no network of child abusers around Frank Beck, concluded both the police investigation and the Kirkwood Inquiry into abuse in Leicestershire. The police even drew up a matrix of the worst child abusers in Leicestershire, Clwyd, Merseyside and Calderdale to see who worked with whom. They reached the conclusion that there was no obvious link between abusers in Leicestershire and those around the rest of the country.

The finding that there was no Leicestershire network was, to say the least, bizarre. There may not have been overt connections between abusers inside Leicestershire and those who operated in children's homes elsewhere in the country, but the evidence is plentiful that there was contact between abusers operating inside Leicestershire. Kirkwood simply ignored the evidence. The police, on the other hand, took a cynical view – they became so jaundiced by the Beck enquiry that they began to expect child care workers to be abusers. If lots of care workers are abusers anyway, why be surprised that so many of them worked with each other?

Care workers are rightly affronted by this. Inquiries by the police and by Kirkwood wrongly glossed over the connections between Beck and other child abusers employed at the same time by Leicestershire County Council. They should have examined, in particular, the role of Beck in recruiting staff who turned out to be abusers, and investigated more thoroughly why so much evidence inside Leicestershire County Council was apparently destroyed after Beck was taken into custody.

Whether there was a network of child abusers in Leicestershire in the end comes down to a matter of semantics. The police could not prove there was an organisation that brought together the abusers, or supplied them with victims, and therefore concluded there was no network. An alternative view is that it is clear that the abusers did not simply work together. Many of them had socialised together before they began to work together and continued to do so when they moved on to other jobs. If this does not constitute a network of abusers it is a pretty strange definition of the word 'network'.

'Some of these people had paedophile connections before they came into the care system,' said Mike Lindsay, Leicestershire's first children's rights officer. 'They may have been members of the same organisation. All of them seemed to descend on Market Harborough. Why there? Eight, or something, known abusers from this area, and all seemed to have worked in Market Harborough. It is too much of a coincidence.'

There is some slight indication that there might be wider connections, going outside Leicestershire. Rod Ryall, the Director of Social Services at Calderdale council in Yorkshire, was convicted in 1989 of sexual abuse of young boys. Among the papers taken from Beck's home when he was arrested were copies of letters from Beck to Ryall, including one commiserating with Ryall's plight, and with the supposed severity of his six year jail term.

Psychologists have argued that child abusers can form an unspoken bond, allowing one abuser to identify quickly that another man shares his predilection. Non-verbal signals may be used between established abusers. Beck, like other strong, manipulative characters, may have been on the look-out for weak characters who he believed he could seduce or bully into co-operation by drawing into a ring of abuse. Peter Jaynes, Beck's co-accused, can be categorised as a weak man who strayed under the influence of a charismatic leader. But this description does not apply to all of Leicestershire's other child abusers.

One of Beck's co-abusers, more than any other, emerges as distinctly unpleasant. 'By comparison with Beck, all the others seem bit players. But Colin Fiddaman was more important than that,' said Mike Lindsay.

Colin Fiddaman

Colin Fiddaman is – except to his victims – the forgotten figure of the Leicestershire child abuse scandal, because he never faced trial. He was a much more serious abuser than the two men who did share the dock with Beck in 1991. Fiddaman's abuse of children in care in Leicestershire was second only to that of Beck, who personally recruited him to the Ratcliffe Road home in 1973 as a 22 year old. He was already a friend of Beck's – the two met in Northampton, after Fiddaman replaced Beck as a care worker at Northamptonshire County Council's Highfields Children's Centre. Friends say Fiddaman trained as a teacher, but never taught.

Soon after Fiddaman began work in Leicestershire, he instituted a system of physical punishment of children in care that was simply sadistic. He was Beck's deputy officer-in-charge at Ratcliffe Road (he continued for a while as acting officer-in-charge at Ratcliffe Road when Beck took over at The Beeches) and the two had a close relationship, emotionally and physically.

Fiddaman had a long standing gay relationship with Beck as well as a series of sexual relations with boys in care. But he also had a wife, Debra, and two children, though people who knew them say it was not a happy or close marriage. Had Fiddaman stood trial, he would have been the leading co-accused alongside Beck, and would in the view of lawyers and police have been given a very long sentence, probably at least one life term.

'Colin Fiddaman was a bit more sophisticated than Jaynes and Lincoln,' explained Mike Lindsay. 'I think Colin Fiddaman was the architect of some of the punishment regimes.' In one of the compensation hearings, one victim told of the punishment regime at Ratcliffe Road overseen by Fiddaman. She was humiliated over a six week period for absconding – itself a reaction to earlier humiliations – by being forced to wear pyjamas during daytime hours, and was frequently stripped by Fiddaman and other male staff. The judge, Mr Justice Potts, in summarising her evidence said: 'On occasions the staff would pull her hair and tell her to 'get her feelings out'. Colin Fiddaman, the deputy, frequently bent her wrists back. Members of staff would sit on her from time to time and cover her face with a pillow or cushion.'

Mr Justice Potts continued: 'On one occasion she absconded with [another resident] and was away for some days. When she returned she was taken to the bathroom and forcibly stripped by [care worker Tim] Ankers, Fiddaman, Lavender [another care worker] and [Peter] Jaynes, all members of the staff. They told her that they had to check her body for lovebites. They examined and touched her body. In evidence, Ankers denied that such an incident occurred. I did not believe him. I believed the plaintiff.'

Another victim of Fiddaman says she remains upset, over 20 years later, by the way Fiddaman treated her. 'He gave me a good hiding' She says he gave her a black eye and severe bruising for disobeying his instructions, but he never sexually interfered with her. 'He was not that way inclined. Although he was married with children, he only seemed interested in boys and men.'

Some of the children have recovered psychologically from sexual abuse by Beck better than from the gratuitous physical abuse handed out by Fiddaman. Mike Lindsay, himself brought up in a children's home, explains that it is almost possible to legitimise some types of abuse – or at least forgive that which is not the symptom of hatred and contempt. 'I was physically and sexually abused myself, which I can rationalise, but not the cruelty,' says Lindsay. 'You cannot rationalise what Fiddaman did in terms of the way he dispensed punishment. Forcing young persons to sit on a stool in the middle of a room, and not move. It is cruelty. There can be no justification for that however you look at it. So I can understand why a lot of young people had a lot of complaints against Fiddaman. The problem with social workers is that they assume that sex abuse by Beck was worse than the physical abuse. Fiddaman's punishment regime was a lot more harmful for a lot of people.'

So who was Colin Fiddaman? He stood out from social worker colleagues by being distant, socially apart from them, by being smarter, and by wearing sunglasses indoors. This had an unsettling effect on co-workers, who felt they could not trust a man whose eyes they could not meet. 'He wore dark glasses throughout the meeting,' recalls one social worker who met him once, 'which is very odd for a social worker. It's against the ethos. I thought it strange and commented so. You could not make eye contact with him.'

'He seemed a bit over-confident in some ways,' recalled Barry Graham, area manager for the National Society for the Prevention of Cruelty to Children in the East Midlands, which employed Fiddaman as a child protection officer for Rugby and Wellingborough after he left Leicestershire. 'It is unusual for the profession. It is not an area you can feel wholly confident in, all the time. It was nothing more than that – a certain brashness. He started wearing dark glasses after he began working for us. He was about 5' 10', or 5' 11' tall, he dressed well, not a suit, but a jacket and tie, and quite formal in social worker terms. I doubt if he made any friends. He was not grossly different. You can see certain aspects of the way he behaved or dressed that were different. We are all individuals. But he was not so different that people felt very uncomfortable, or suggested that something else might he happening.'

A former NSPCC colleague of Fiddaman was less sanguine. 'Colin Fiddaman is someone who I wish never came into my life. It has taken me a very long time to recover from it, if I ever will. There are things which if they came out are really quite awful – very difficult. Fiddaman was an extremely destructive member of the team. He was a member of that whole Beck gang.' He suggested that Fiddaman was guilty of continued wrong-doing after he left Leicestershire.

While working for Leicestershire County Council, Fiddaman remained a close friend of Beck's and was recruited by Beck into the Liberal Party. In May 1983, Fiddaman was one of three workers from Ratcliffe Road and the Beeches who stood for election to Blaby District Council as Liberal/Alliance candidates. Beck was elected, Richard Loweth, another Beeches care worker stood with Beck for the Winstanley ward but lost, while Fiddaman stood for the nearby Narborough ward, coming fifth with 567 votes.

The month after, Fiddaman became a parish councillor for the small town of Narborough, on the edge of Leicester, but lasted just 18 months before he gave it up. The clerk to the parish council, Douglas Maas – who was himself a Liberal councillor before he defected to the Conservative Party – remembers Fiddaman as an 'unremarkable, ordinary' person, who suddenly appeared, and then equally suddenly disappeared again. Following the convention of most parish councils Fiddaman stood for election as an independent, though he was an active member of the Liberal Party.

David Pollard, a long standing Liberal Democrat county councillor in the Blaby area, says it is not significant that Beck, Fiddaman and Loweth had all been selected as candidates for the party. He says that the party operated an autonomous branch structure, with no vetting of local candidates by the county party, let alone the national party. 'Anyone who volunteered was put up as a candidate,' recalls Pollard. But activists in other parties in Blaby recall Fiddaman as an active Liberal party member, and certainly more than just a 'paper candidate'.

Colin Fiddaman would have been charged with between 20 and 30 offences against children in care, had his case proceeded. There is little doubt that he would have been convicted of both physical and sexual abuse against children. With hindsight, it looks as though the police made their one really serious mistake in interviewing Fiddaman before they had taken statements from the many children who had been at Ratcliffe Road. At this time, the police were only looking for evidence of crimes at The Beeches, and it had not seriously occurred to them that Beck, let alone others, had been guilty of serial child abuse in children's homes in Leicestershire, pre-dating The Beeches.

In his police interview, Fiddaman said that he might have gone too far, but did nothing seriously wrong. He claimed that he, too, was a victim, seduced by Beck into sexual relations. The police believed Fiddaman's story, and indeed had no reason not to. They warned him, though, that they would be 'questioning every child he had ever had care of', and if they had evidence that he had been guilty of any kind of abuse against them they would 'throw the book at him'. Fiddaman was given bail in May 1990.

As the evidence started rolling in, Fiddaman became more anxious, and in September he returned to his digs in Nottingham and persuaded the teenage son of the unsuspecting couple he was lodging with to go with him – and he skipped bail. For four months, police across Europe chased Fiddaman on behalf of the Leicestershire force, who by now had credible statements alleging physical and sexual abuse from former children in care, as well as the implication of the disappearance. Eventually Fiddaman gave up the chase. On January 6 1991, in a flat in Nieuwe Achtergracht in Amsterdam, at the age of 39, Fiddaman took an overdose of pills, killed himself, and denied the police and victims their judicial revenge. A friend says he had attempted suicide several times before. He left behind a note for his divorced wife, Debra, saying that as a younger man he had 'done things that were unwise'. Fiddaman's teenage friend returned home to his parents.

This was not the first time that Fiddaman escaped justice. There are no records to suggest that Fiddaman might have been successfully prosecuted for child abuse while employed by Leicestershire – though he was cautioned by Leicestershire police for cottaging with a youth in a public toilet in Leicester – because they ignored warning signs from this period pointed at Beck or at the Ratcliffe Road home generally, rather than specifically at Fiddaman. But things were very different at one of Fiddaman's later jobs.

After leaving Leicestershire, Fiddaman took a series of posts as a child protection officer, one of them for the NSPCC, the major children's charity. Why Fiddaman wanted to work in this field is open to interpretation – there is no evidence that he abused children in any of these jobs. He may simply have felt that it was a good career path. His subsequent employers all state categorically that the jobs were office based and gave Fiddaman no access to children in care. Employers also state that although one of Fiddaman's roles was to chair case conferences, it did not give him the opportunity to cover up abuse, protect abusers or allocate children to other abusers, because he was always working in teams with trusted and experienced colleagues. It is difficult to believe though, that this role did not at least give Fiddaman the opportunity to influence these decisions, and his influence may, on occasion, have been decisive.

A former NSPCC colleague alleges that doubts were expressed at the time of Fiddaman's appointment about the quality of his references and criticises the charity for employing him. The NSPCC dismisses the complaint, saying that Fiddaman was properly vetted, with references taken up and a check made on the DHSS consultancy index. 'The NSPCC was and still is confident that the vetting procedure available to it at that time was always carefully implemented,' said an NSPCC lawyer.

Fiddaman's co-workers found him obstructive and negative and he was despised by some in his office. His boss, Barry Graham, however, showed great loyalty even when suspicions began to arise. The police found Fiddaman in a compromising situation with a teenager, below the age of consent, in a lay-by in a NSPCC-owned car. The boy had been in Fiddaman's care in Leicestershire, and Fiddaman explained to the police that he was merely maintaining contact with him. The police officers involved did not believe Fiddaman's explanation. However, the police had no evidence of anything illegal taking place, and were told by the NSPCC that it had no concerns about Fiddaman's behaviour.

'We had an unofficial call from a police officer from Nottinghamshire,' explains Graham. 'He was [ostensibly] checking that the NSPCC was happy that Fiddaman was using a car outside his area. He expressed some discomfort with finding him with what I understood to be a young man of 17 or

18, expressing concern in some vague and unspecific way, not suggesting any offence.'

The NSPCC regarded this, not as an issue of child protection, but as a matter of a discriminatory and unjust age of consent for consensual relations between two adults. It appears to have ignored the underlying question of whether it was appropriate for a care worker to have a sexual relationship with someone he used to have care responsibilities for, and the related question of when that relationship began.

'It was pursued with him [Fiddaman], and an explanation was given which, in the light of the unofficial nature of the police contact, had to be accepted,' said Graham. 'A lot of this [issue] is around the definition of a young man. It raised with me a question about his sexuality, but not about child abuse. We did not have any knowledge or any reason to believe he was sexually interested in children while in our employment. The only issue was that he may be gay, but being gay and being interested in young children and young people is another distinction which one has to be careful of. We were concerned enough to take it further, but we did not have enough information or concern to take it [even] further because the police officer was not making any formal allegation.'

However, Fiddaman's responsibilities at the NSPCC were in regard to children from the age of six up to 16, and Fiddaman's evident willingness to have sexual relations with a youth might have rung more warning bells at the NSPCC than it actually did, even on the basis of the comments of Fiddaman's own boss, Barry Graham. Nor was this the only question mark over Fiddaman's behaviour while with the charity. Colleagues believe he was not managed effectively. For example, he was not properly disciplined on one occasion when he failed to turn up to a meeting.

Barry Graham is satisfied that Fiddaman was not in a position either to abuse children or to provide other abusers with access to children, as a result of his work at the NSPCC. 'We did an examination of all his work, and there is no evidence or cause for concern that we had. But you can never be certain. Most of his time was spent chairing case conferences. A lot of people very aware of key issues in the child protection area would be present, so it would be very difficult to conspire with other paedophiles. Paedophiles are often very clever and we know they are. There was no evidence and no concern from other professionals that wrong decisions had been made.'

Fiddaman worked as a generic social worker for Warwickshire between leaving Leicestershire and joining the NSPCC, and was employed by Northamptonshire afterwards, again as a generic social worker. Northamptonshire council has refused to discuss its employment of Fiddaman, or whether there is any evidence to suggest that he abused children while there. The Northamptonshire police have destroyed their records for this period, so cannot say whether they investigated Fiddaman, or had allegations made against him.

Fiddaman left Northamptonshire to work as a child protection officer for Lincolnshire County Council. Lincolnshire says it did conduct a subsequent inquiry, which found no evidence of wrongdoing by Fiddaman while in its employment. It pointed out that the recruitment of Fiddaman was conducted on a multi-agency basis, involving the council and independent child protection agencies. The police may also have been involved in the appointment, though as full records no longer exist from this time it is impossible to be certain. Fiddaman was sacked in November 1990, after he failed to turn up for work – because he had absconded while on the bail he had been placed into the previous May.

'I am told that it had been noticed by colleagues that he was to be involved in proceedings,' says Mat Bukowski, the subsequent Director of Social Services at Lincolnshire County Council. 'It is just conceivable that someone worked for us while on police bail, but it is very unlikely.' However, Fiddaman was questioned and bailed in May, continued to go into work for Lincolnshire until September, was only sacked in November, and there are no records at the council to suggest that he was transferred onto other duties or was given leave. The clear implication is that Fiddaman continued his child protection work between May and September, while on police bail as a suspected child abuser.

'His job gave him the responsibility of chairing case conferences on children at risk of abuse,' adds Mr Bukowzki. He says that as far as he can now ascertain, this did not give Fiddaman personal access to any children in care. Fiddaman's career as a child protection officer after leaving Leicestershire must raise questions, though, about why the poacher wanted to turn game-keeper. Was it just to pursue his career, did it give him access to children, or did it enable him to protect other abusers? These are questions that it is just not possible to answer now.

The local police force in Lincolnshire has destroyed its records from this time, so it has no way of knowing whether they were suspicious of Fiddaman's behaviour. Northamptonshire council, too, refused to discuss the activities of the Highfields Children's Centre, where Beck was employed after he finished his social work training, and which also employed Fiddaman. It can hardly be a coincidence that the same centre employed both Beck and Fiddaman, and Susan Morton, another of Beck's initial appointments at Ratcliffe Road. Morton has not been accused of abuse, but was victimised by Beck and has testified that she was often hit by him. The centre is of great importance because it is where Beck came across ideas that evolved into his version of regression therapy.

Colin Fiddaman's story is, in its own way, as cautionary as Beck's. Warning signals were ignored and someone who should have been prosecuted for child abuse at an earlier stage in his career was, instead, given promotion to the job of protecting children from abuse. It was as appropriate as putting the mafia in charge of a police drugs squad.

Ken Scott

Another appointment in which Beck was involved was that of Ken Scott, who was interviewed in 1978 by a recruitment panel consisting of Beck, Peter Naylor and John Noblett of the county council's Care Branch. Scott was employed as the permanent officer-in-charge at the Rosehill home in Market Harborough. He took over from Beck who had been in charge on a temporary basis in 1978. This was presumably why the comparatively recently appointed Beck was invited to take part in the employment of the new manager of the home. Given Beck's character, it seems likely that he would have had an influential voice in the selection process.

Scott's career as a paedophile came to light in a very different way from Beck's, and had a touch of farce. A 17 year old, who lived in the Holt children's home near Leicester, burgled Scott's home in Market Harborough in 1986. His motive was to recover photographs Scott had taken of him as a boy from the age of 12 onwards, and to steal obscene videos of various boys who had lived at Rosehill. After he stole the photos and videos, he attempted to blackmail Scott, asking for £100 for the return of the items. But police located the stolen pictures after they detained the boy for a variety of offences, including other burglaries and criminal damage, following a spate of vandalism in a churchyard.

It soon became obvious that for seven years Scott had been indecently assaulting boys in his care and offering them money for being video recorded. Mr Justice Rose, when sentencing Scott to eight years in jail, said: 'You repeatedly incited [the boys] to commit sexual acts by showing them pornographic videos and books. You repeatedly paid them money or bought them clothes to encourage their submission and you recorded on film activities which you induced them to perform.' One boy said he had performed sexual activities for Scott 60 times, and another said that he was just eight years old when Scott first had sex with him.

Leicestershire County Council responded to the Scott case by closing the Rosehill home, and within days of Scott's conviction initiated an inquiry to find out why the child abuser Scott had been employed and why his activities were not discovered. But the council decided that the inquiry would be conducted in secret. The results were reported, again in secret, to the county council's social services committee a year later, and have never been revealed. Even the Kirkwood Inquiry into Beck did not refer to the results of the earlier inquiry. Whatever lessons were supposedly learnt in the Scott case, they were badly applied – abuse in other homes was still then taking place, and continued to take place after Scott was convicted. The obvious conclusion would have been that children in care should have been interviewed independently, on a regular basis, but no such steps were undertaken.

The whole rationale for the inquiry into Scott seems to have been no more than public relations, to stop the press and public taking any interest in the case. In this it succeeded. The local press made little effort to find out the results of the inquiry, and completely failed to link a growing number of care workers who were prosecuted for abusing children in care. If the local media had been more effective in investigating behind the headlines, rather than simply reporting the outcome of apparently isolated court cases, then many children would have been saved from abuse.

The Kirkwood Inquiry found that, as in the Beck case, Scott could and should have been detected earlier. Brian Rice, the then Director of Social Services, had not passed legitimate concerns onto the government's Social Services Inspectorate.

Ron Bloxham

In April 1981 Ron Bloxham, the deputy officer-in-charge of the Camden Road children's home in Leicester's Braunstone area, near to The Beeches, committed suicide. He was on police bail at the time, and his death prevented a case coming to trial that would have seen him prosecuted for a number of sexual offences against girls in care. After Bloxham's death, it emerged that his officer-in-charge, Colin Hawley, had harboured suspicions for some time. 'We had no positive proof at that particular time at all, and it was always mentioned that unless one had proof that one couldn't do very much about it,' Hawley told the Kirkwood Inquiry.

His colleague, a Miss Tyrell, told the inquiry that one girl had told her that Bloxham had instructed the girl to pull her knickers down. Miss Tyrell said that Hawley had said that a complaint on the incident had been forwarded to the county council. Hawley also said that his gut instincts and what he had heard 'along the grapevine' had made him uneasy about Bloxham. 'Mr Bloxham was a strange man,' said Miss Tyrell. 'He was not a man who put himself forward to offer you anything. You always had to talk to him and make the first approach.' Eventually the concerns of Tyrell and Hawley became more concrete, were referred to the local police, and statements against Bloxham obtained – which is when he killed himself.

Before working at Camden Road, Bloxham worked for the Woodlands Observation and Assessment Centre, a remand home in Leicester.

Brian Davis

Brian Davis had been a colleague of Bloxham's at the Woodlands and had worked there for five years. In July 1980 Davis was convicted of four charges of gross indecency and indecent assault of boys between the ages of 13 and 15. The boys were of very low intelligence – one had an I.Q. of just 47. Some of the offences occurred at the Woodlands, others while on a camping holiday. Davis was jailed for a year. His defence barrister said that Davis had 'a relationship of affection' with the boys, and had been unable to resist the temptations he came across while working with them.

Peter Blastock

Peter Blastock was another residential child care worker employed by Leicestershire County Council who turned out to be a paedophile. In August 1982, Blastock was convicted of an act of gross indecency with a boy of 13. He had approached boys in Abbey Park in Leicester and asked them to spank him after he had shown them pornographic pictures. He stripped to his underpants before the boy hit him with a cane.

There was no allegation that children in Blastock's care were abused, and he was placed on probation for two years, and ordered to go for psychiatric treatment. As well as being a child care worker, Blastock had also been a scout leader. He left the council's employment upon conviction.

More cases

Other children's homes staff were disciplined during the 1980s for sexual offences and offences involving violence over this period, but the allegations were not as severe as against Beck, Fiddaman, Jaynes and Lincoln. Several other staff were prosecuted for alleged sexual offences against children in care, but were acquitted. Another man, Robert Dent, was convicted in

1981 of repeatedly sexually abusing boys in care after breaking into a county council children's home.

Upon Beck's arrest, government inspectors conducted an inquiry within all Leicestershire's children's homes to establish the extent of further abuse by care workers. This led to another two workers being accused of alleged sexual abuse of children and another of physical 'rough-handling'. One of the alleged sex abusers was sacked by the authority in 1989, the other left when accused, while the worker alleged to have used excessive force on two children was given tighter supervision. The inquiry found that the sacked worker's references had not been in order, and that allegations of sexual impropriety had circulated at his previous place of work.

In addition, a number of teachers employed by the county council were convicted, during this period, of sexual abuse of children. These included several music teachers. One of these had boasted of his connections and close friendship with Beck. Some local teachers have alleged that abusers made a conscious effort to be trained and employed as music teachers, because of the opportunities it gave them for after-hours contact with children. In 1988 a survey of children in Leicestershire County Council schools found that sexual abuse of girls was prevalent in the schools, with teenage girls frequently subjected to pressure to have sex with male teachers.

No apparent attempt was ever made by Leicestershire County Council, either before the Beck case came to court, or afterwards, to link the cases involving care workers, and ask whether it was merely a coincidence that so many people, often with social links, had turned up in Leicestershire, committing so many similar offences, over such a short period of time. Even during the Kirkwood Inquiry, only a superficial investigation was conducted into a few of the cases. That inquiry was hindered by the widespread disappearance of relevant files at

County Hall and the destruction of potentially vital records at various children's homes.

The suspicion that some people had more than a passing connection is unavoidable. Concern would have been ever greater if more than a few people had known of the information passed to NSPCC workers on the helpline set up to counsel victims of Beck's abuse. Helpline workers were given allegations that never came to court, and have never previously come into the public domain. Some former children in care at The Beeches told the helpline workers that they had been taken to Beck's home, and had there been introduced to other abusers who took them away for evenings, and even to Leicester hotels for overnight stays.

One victim, who has sought continued counselling, has alleged that he is still in contact with one of the abusers he was introduced to by Beck, despite repeated attempts to break away from him. He says that on one occasion, while still at The Beeches, he attacked a man who had taken him away for the night and stole money off him. Although these stories were given to the NSPCC helpline workers, they were never passed to either the police or to Leicestershire County Council. The police say that no similar allegations were made in the 500 or so statements they took from former children in care.

The NSPCC undertook that this helpline would be absolutely confidential. Although it took to the county council a report on its operation, this gave information on the number of calls received, and how successful its counselling had been. The NSPCC felt it could not pass to the council or the police any information regarding new allegations made to its counsellors. As a consequence, the police were not aware of the suggestion that children in Beck's care had been introduced by Beck to other child abusers.

It is far easier to take a view on the recruitment policies of Beck himself, who carefully selected the children he was taking into care on the basis of those who seemed the most vulnerable. It is likely that he did the same thing when appointing his own staff – without interference, for the most part, from the county council. As one of the social workers who counselled Beck's victims commented: 'I have no doubt that Beck was selecting his workers.'

CHAPTER SIXTEEN
Those who did not survive

It would be pleasant to write a heroic tale of Beck's survivors, about how they overcame adversity to put their past behind them, to lead successful, well-adjusted lives. And, for some of the victims of Leicestershire's abuse, this is a true picture. Unfortunately, for many of the victims, it is not.

The truth is not politically correct. Some social workers have condemned the suggestion that victims of abuse are more likely to go on to commit abuse themselves. This is not because of some statistical analysis which has examined what happened to those children after they left care. It is because it is what they want to believe, because the alternative makes it more difficult to work with abuse survivors, who are often tormented by the fear that they might go on to do to others what has been done to them. If the victims believe that they might themselves become abusers, they may be too scared to come forward to say that they had ever been abused. Social workers want to be able to tell these victims that their fears are unfounded, that they are no more likely to commit abuse than anyone else out there in the wider community.

'That is a convenient view to hold,' said Dr Chris Lewis. He was the psychiatrist who helped to put an end to Beck's reign of abuse, and tried to support some of the victims afterwards.

'Abused children have more of a tendency to become abusers themselves in the future,' he explained. 'This is reflected in the acknowledgement that children do abuse other children. It is a statement of the effect on them. We know it occurs, especially with adolescent abuse. Because someone is abused it does not mean they are going to abuse others. We are just talking statistics.' The inference that Dr Lewis is drawing is that it seems unlikely that a child would sexually abuse other children, unless they had themselves been abused.

It has to be recognised, however unpleasant the truth is, that sexual abuse on children can make victims more likely to abuse other children, to commit suicide, to be unable to control their temper, even, at the extreme, more likely to commit murder. But the effect on victims must not be overstated, and it is difficult to disentangle cause and effect. Most victims of abuse are female – most perpetrators are male. If there were a simple relationship between being a victim of abuse, and going on to become an abuser, then by now most perpetrators could be expected to be women.

Even experts on the effects of child deviancy are unsure what impact sexual abuse in childhood has on later life, and on adult criminality. Professor Donald West of Cambridge University, perhaps the world's leading expert in this field, says he is unaware of any research that had been conducted. One problem is that convicted criminals cannot be believed when they put forward abuse in mitigation. In one survey, he pointed out, half of rapists in the United States had claimed to be childhood victims of sexual abuse by females. This was very unlikely to be true, Professor West suggests.

Research conducted by Professor West and by Lee Robins and others in the United States, has shown a strong relationship between childhood offending and repeated criminality in adulthood. It has also indicated that children taken into care are much more likely to go on to become serious criminals – a child abused at home is likely to develop more slowly, and becomes even more likely to turn to crime if taken into care. But physical and sexual abuse as a factor in this has been impossible to quantify because of the difficulty of obtaining verifiably accurate information.

No research has been undertaken among Beck's survivors to examine the long-term damage they suffered. But analysis of victims of comparable abuse elsewhere shows severe problems, directly related to their experience. In Clwyd, where a similar level of abuse was committed by care workers on children in care, it was found that victims were 19 times more likely to commit suicide than was the general population. It also found that they were seven times more likely to die violent deaths.

It is impossible to untangle cause and effect. Many of the children put into Leicestershire's care and abused had already been sexually abused in their own homes. Many of them were already hardened criminals by the time they were teenagers. Even without the abuse, they may have gone on to commit crimes. But in all probability, fewer of them would have gone on to commit crime, or commit so many crimes. Nor would they, as in some extreme cases, have so precisely copied the abuse that was inflicted on them in the way they abused others. 'The individual case needs to he looked at, and the type of abuse committed,' says Dr Lewis. 'Look at the pattern of behaviour, and ask was it too much of a coincidence?'

Of the 200 or so children who were sexually abused by Beck and Fiddaman, four went on to commit murders. One of these is now a long-stay resident in Ashworth special hospital in

Merseyside. Another of these murderers was to copy exactly
the abuse inflicted on him by Beck and Fiddaman on the young
child he raped and murdered. Others went on to become rapists
and serial arsonists, one inflicted a razor attack on a nurse in
a Birmingham hospital. One ran away from The Beeches to
become a child prostitute, and when last heard of was still a
rent boy in London's West End.

Another, Mary Bell, was raped by Beck, became a drug
addict, repeated shop lifter and fraudster, and has spent much
of her adult life in prison. In one of her many criminal trials,
her defence counsel told the court: 'It is difficult to think of
someone more damaged by their past.' A judge said he found a
psychiatrist's report on her 'heart-rending'. And there was Lee
Taylor, who at the age of just 20, raped a 60-year-old woman
while wearing a mask and then carried out a telephone campaign
of harassment on the same woman.

Some victims died young, like Dale Elkington, who died of
an AIDS-related disease. Then there was Darren Bradshaw,
who ran away from The Beeches, stole a car, and died when
it crashed. Another was Andy Biggins, who died sniffing
glue while absconding from The Beeches a few miles away on
Braunstone Park.

These were not the only lives ruined by the abusive regimes
practised in Leicestershire's children's homes in the 1970s and
'80s – they are merely some of the most extreme examples. What
they illustrate is that abuse is like throwing a pebble into a pond
– the ripples spread on out, with effects so distant that they may
still be felt even when they are no longer seen. Frank Beck's
abuse is continuing to have its impact, not just in the distress
of its victims, but also in the hurt, injury, crime and even death
that some of the victims inflict on those around them. Those
who were the worst treated by Beck and his co-workers were
among those who went on to commit the worst crimes. This is

just a small but poignant sample of the personal tragedies that Frank Beck and Colin Fiddaman left behind them.

Simon O'Donnell

Simon O'Donnell's body was found hanging from a light fitting in toilets at the GEC sports club in the Leicester suburb of Whetstone in the early morning of the 4th October, 1977. He was a disturbed and sad 13 year old, who had been admitted to Ratcliffe Road mainly because a place could not be found for him in a specialised psychiatric unit.

Pat Holyland was in care at Ratcliffe Road at the time: 'Simon was a friend of mine, he was a tiny, weeny little boy, with a lot of black curls, a cheerful little lad with an elfin face, happy-go-lucky; he was in the home because he had smashed up a milk float depot. One night he just disappeared. The next day they fetched us back from school (it was not long after we had got there), and told us that Simon had been found dead. That night they threw a party, a kind of dinner party with presents for everybody, to cheer us up.'

At Simon's inquest, the Leicester coroner, Michael Charman, heard evidence from Mark Salisbury, then one of the Ratcliffe Road staff, about the regression treatment the boy had received. Salisbury described how Simon was given relaxation and regression treatment in which responsibilities were removed from the child. 'We allowed the child to regress and re-live the experience he may have missed in childhood, so that he would live a more normal life,' Salisbury said. 'On occasions, when he needed comfort, he had a bottle at bedtime, and as he regressed and relaxed, he allowed people to carry him around. He was becoming happier with the regression.' Beck also gave evidence, telling the court he believed Simon's treatment was beneficial and he had become very relaxed, after two months.

Charman was not impressed, commenting that he was 'extremely unhappy' about the circumstances surrounding Simon's death, and about the fact that he was being given therapy by social workers at Ratcliffe Road who had no psychiatric qualifications and did not have adequate professional supervision. He added: 'I do not think they understood what was wrong, maybe nobody understands what was wrong. I have no doubt he was given a great deal of care and concern, particularly at The Poplars, but I have the impression the treatment he was given was fumbling in the dark by those responsible for looking after him. I am not at all happy with the idea of making someone so regressed. Although Simon was clearly immature, he was of average intelligence.' The comments were splashed in the local press, yet no thorough investigation into O'Donnell's death ever took place.

A 5,000 word council report was presented to councillors by Dorothy Edwards just three weeks after his death, but it was more concerned with whitewashing the incident than investigating it. Simon's death was accepted by councillors as no more than a very sad story. It included a defence of the Ratcliffe Road unit and of regression therapy by Edwards: 'I recognise that many members of the public and indeed many members of this committee, will be shocked at the thought of a 13 year old boy wanting to be cuddled or wanting to have a baby's bottle, but I can only say that the experience we have had at the unit leads me to believe that with many children who have experienced early deprivation, this form of treatment works.'

She quoted figures to demonstrate the success of Ratcliffe Road. In four years, 37 children were admitted, 30 of them were considered uncontrollable, 27 were extremely aggressive, 24 had sexual difficulties, 17 were thought dangerous to others, 11 had attempted suicide and 19 had been expelled from school. Eight of these children were considered untreatable and seven had previously been in closed psychiatric wards. Edwards said 14 of these children had since been discharged, and seven had committed no offences. Four had committed minor offences but were living happily in the community, and only three had been placed in other institutions. 'The unit is being far more successful with disturbed children than any similar establishment I know,' she added. The source of these figures was not given, so it is impossible to assess their validity, but they do provide further explanation of management's confidence in Beck.

Edwards revealed – presumably on the basis of comments made to her by Beck – that just before he died, Simon had talked about a dream in which he stabbed and strangled his parents. He had talked about his feelings of confusion and worthlessness, he had cried, but seemed more relaxed afterwards. Beck told his bosses that Simon's shoes and trousers were taken away every night and his room checked, but on this occasion at 7.15 in the morning, he was found to be missing. His body was found a few hours later, with another boy's shoes and clothing. A clear case of suicide caused by depression, the circumstances suggested.

To some former Ratcliffe Road inmates, the story sounded quite different. The method of apparent suicide – a towel round the neck – sounded more like one of Beck's restraining and provocation 'paddy attacks' that went wrong. Holyland remains highly suspicious of the circumstances around Simon's death. 'I don't believe personally that he did kill himself, and there should have been an open verdict and not one of suicide,' she said. 'It's not true that he was talking about killing himself or running away, of anything like that. They said he was saying all sorts of things about his parents, but they were the kind of things they tried to get you to say in the temper tantrums – they told me I wanted to sleep with my father. If Simon did say those things it was because they forced him to. You would say anything to get out of it. I think what happened was he was in a temper tantrum that went wrong. He was found hanging from a towel rail – if you were going to kill yourself you would jump off a bridge or something, not something like that.'

Dramatic new evidence to support this theory emerged in 1998, when another Ratcliffe Road resident, Peter Bastin (see below), took Leicestershire County Council to the High Court to win damages for his treatment by Beck and Fiddaman. He told how there had been a 'strange atmosphere' at Ratcliffe Road on the night Simon disappeared. Bastin had been unable to sleep. 'My bedroom was at the front, and when I looked out of a window, I saw Colin Fiddaman and Beck,' Bastin told the court. 'They had something wrapped in a blanket, which I now believe was Simon O'Donnell.'

Bastin said he had considered going to the police, after he read reports of Simon's death in the local papers. But instead he went to see Beck, who told him Simon was an epileptic and that Beck had decided to stop his medication. It is not clear quite how this was supposed to explain what Bastin had seen, but at any rate the boy never went to the police. With hindsight he told the court he wished he had 'had the guts' to speak to them.

The official account of Simon's death sounded all wrong to Bastin. 'In the paper it said Simon was supposed to have run off in the middle of the night and hung himself in the toilet,' Bastin told the court. 'But if you knew Simon you knew he couldn't have done that because he was scared of the dark. Yet he was supposed to have broken into a dark building to hang himself. He was petrified of the dark and couldn't go to sleep without the light being on.'

Mike Lindsay, who was appointed as Leicestershire's children's rights officer, some years after the Beck era, also believes the O'Donnell case should be re-examined and was critical of the inquest. 'There should have been a public inquiry. It was an unusual way of doing it [committing suicide], and some doubt whether it was possible,' said Lindsay. 'I would have thought he would have blacked out doing that. It links with the punishment regime in the home.'

The official verdict on Simon's death may be correct, though in retrospect either deliberate murder, or death from too tight a ligature under provocation by Beck and Fiddaman, is more likely. All hindsight can achieve with certainty, at this distance, is to raise unanswerable doubts. Simon clearly needed psychiatric help, but was instead treated by a quack.

Ironically, the tragedy produced a vote of confidence for Beck and, at least ostensibly, for regression therapy. In private, though, Beck was told to exercise more caution in the use of regression therapy – something that was never revealed to councillors, the press, the public or parents of children in care. Management's priority can be clearly seen as ensuring a clean bill of health, even where legitimate concerns were expressed privately.

Leicestershire social services were determined to apply the coat of white wash very liberally. Beck received a fulsome tribute from one social services committee member, Mrs Jane Simpson: 'He seems to have a love for his children, they trust him and he can do extraordinary things with the majority of them. We are extremely lucky to have people like Mr Beck.' Even O'Donnell's father stressed, at the time, that Beck and the other staff at the Ratcliffe Road home were not to be criticised. 'The treatment was first class, and I have nothing but admiration for the staff,' said James O'Donnell.

If Leicestershire County Council's members and officers had listened more seriously to the coroner's comments in October 1977, the tragedy caused by Beck would have been much less severe. Instead, some councillors immediately expressed their full confidence in Beck and in regression therapy, and the superficial response of the social services committee helped reinforce Beck's aura of untouchability.

After Beck's arrest in 1990, the police and the Crown Prosecution Service – without the benefit of any co-operation from Peter Bastin – briefly considered charging Beck with either manslaughter or murder in respect of O'Donnell's death. This was rejected, not because Beck was cleared of responsibility, but because the other serious charges were expected to produce a clear guilty verdict. Re-opening the O'Donnell case from that distance, they concluded, would unhelpfully muddy the water, as well as sensationalising the trial for no good purpose.

Peter Bastin

Simon O'Donnell was not the only person at about this time to have died with a towel around his neck. So, too, did Mohammid Aslam Ibrahim, a 10 year old boy living in the Highfields area of Leicester. It was one of Leicester's most publicised and most notorious murder cases, but it was only in 1998, 20 years after the boy's death, that it was publicly recognised that Ibrahim's death was connected with Frank Beck's career of abuse.

Aslam was murdered on 29th May, 1978 by Peter Bastin, who was himself just 18 years old at the time. Bastin had, until shortly before, been a resident at Ratcliffe Road. As with O'Donnell, Ibrahim's death had a disturbing connection with the punishment and control methods used by Beck and Fiddaman. Bastin abducted young Aslam when the boy asked him the time after a game of football. Bastin took him to his nearby house where he fastened a towel round his neck while he raped the boy. Thinking that Ibrahim was already dead, Bastin packed him into a suitcase where the boy slowly died from suffocation.

Dr Peter Andrews, a Home Office pathologist, told the inquest: 'The ligature was tightly fixed and the restricted space of the suitcase further aggravated the asphyxia.' A police hunt was launched when Ibrahim was reported missing, and his naked body found in a suitcase in Bastin's room in a shared house.

Bastin was missing, having stolen £200 from two barmaids who also lived in the house. Ibrahim's clothes, including the football kit he was wearing when abducted, were lying around Bastin's bedroom.

Detective Sergeant Alan Wilson, one of the investigating officers, told the inquest: 'The suitcase was closed, fastened with clips, and tied with a piece of plastic cord. Inside we found the body of the deceased boy, lying on his side completely naked, with a leather strap like a large dog collar fastened around the neck.' Police officers who many years later investigated Beck's methods of control and restraint, were to he horribly struck by the similarities.

A nationwide hunt was launched for Bastin, and his description released – a pigeon-toed, stockily-built, youth, 5' 10' tall, with dark brown hair, grey-green eyes, a mole on his chin, and a pale spotty complexion. In March 1979, Bastin was convicted of the murder, and sentenced to life imprisonment, after a trial at Nottingham Crown Court. Bastin declined to put forward an explanation for the crime or a plea of mitigation, even after the judge urged him to do so. Throughout the trial Bastin was counselled by just one person – Frank Beck. Beck and Bastin had formed a close friendship while Bastin was at Ratcliffe Road, which was maintained through the trial and afterwards. Bastin refused to brief his solicitor properly, and the only person who he would talk to for any length of time was Beck. In later years he came to believe he should have pleaded guilty to manslaughter on the grounds of diminished responsibility. He told his compensation hearings it was Beck who persuaded him to plead guilty to murder.

For the next 12 years, Beck was the only visitor that Bastin was willing to see. Until Beck's death, Bastin also refused all offers of counselling offered him in prison. However, when Bastin was interviewed by the police during the Beck inquiry,

Bastin told them that he had been sexually abused by Beck. Prosecution counsel and the police decided against referring to the Bastin case during Beck's trial, on the grounds that it would unnecessarily further sensationalise the trial, without assisting the conviction of Beck. Bastin spent much of his sentence in the Leyhill open prison at Wotton-under-Edge in Gloucestershire, where he sought parole and continued to receive psychological treatment with a view to his eventual release and resettlement. However in 1993 he absconded from the prison, leading to a further national hunt for him, and delayed his possible release.

Bastin's background was typically tragic. His mother was a prostitute, and – according to his evidence during his High Court compensation claim – both he and his sister were sexually abused by their stepfather Fred Quin and made to sleep in his bed. He was eight, his sister was nine. He didn't tell his mother, and from that point their relationship deteriorated. Bastin became a regular runaway. He was eventually picked up by the police in Hull, and placed in council care in the Westcotes children's home in Leicester. He continued to abscond and drifted to London where he became a rent boy. He told the court he was 'passed around from one paedophile to the next'.

'I didn't like any of it to start with, but over time I grew used to it,' Bastin added. 'They were giving me money and buying me clothes. I had lots of free time going to pubs and clubs. I regret what I did now, but at the time I felt needed and wanted. It seemed better than the children's home.' In 1974, after being returned to the Westcotes home, he absconded and indecently assaulted a ten year old boy. It was this incident which led to his being referred to Beck at The Poplars home in Market Harborough.

His case was almost forgotten until early 1998, when an application for compensation from Leicestershire County

Council for the abuse he suffered in care at the hands of Beck and Fiddaman reached the High Court. Bastin spoke in public for the first time about his abuse by the care workers – particularly by Fiddaman, who was his key worker at The Poplars before Bastin was moved to Ratcliffe Road, and who undressed him each night. Bastin also spoke of being a witness to the removal of Simon O'Donnell's body from Ratcliffe Road and of seeing Beck sexually assaulting a young girl. He still suffers nightmares about the home. But perhaps most significantly, Bastin also disclosed how the regular use of belts and towels around his neck, as implements of control during sexual abuse, developed into something he found exciting.

'If I struggled he [Beck] would tighten it a bit more,' Bastin told the court. 'In the end I found I liked it. I found it sexually stimulating.' Soon after Bastin left Beck's care, he was to use the same restraint on young Ibrahim while raping him. The cause and effect in this instance is obvious.

Peter Bastin accepts a share of responsibility for the murder – but believes much of the blame lies with Beck and Fiddaman, because of their abuse against him. His compensation claim was settled out of court. Reportedly, he received £50,000.

Barry Samuels

Barry Samuels was Simon O'Donnell's room mate at Ratcliffe Road and the shock of O'Donnell's death was something he never got over. Samuels was not in any case one of the children happy to be in Beck's care. He had been removed against his will from the Catholic Carmel children's home in Kirby Muxloe, near Leicester, where other children and adults describe him having been 'a lovely child'. At the Carmel he had lived with his two sisters, who were seldom allowed by Beck to visit him at Ratcliffe Road, which precipitated a rapid worsening in his behaviour.

It was some years after he left Leicestershire's care that the real tragedy hit Samuels' life. In 1987 he married his girl friend Serena, and in the middle of the next year they had a son, Isaiah, who was immediately placed on the 'at risk' register by the social services department, because of what had already become regular physical abuse, including severe beatings, by Barry on Serena. As soon as Isaiah was horn, Barry began to hit him, too. Eventually, in December 1991, Barry Samuels lost his self-control so badly that he inflicted a hard blow on Isaiah's stomach, and, after an agonising 12 hours, during which he received no medical help, the child died. Barry Samuels was charged with the murder of his son.

In jail on remand, Barry Samuels was wracked with guilt and was placed on Leicester prison's own 'at risk' register, because of the fear that he might commit suicide. His depression appeared to lift, and he was taken off the register and put in a cell by himself where he hanged himself shortly before he was due to face trial. Serena was subsequently herself sentenced to two years probation for failing to obtain medical help for Isaiah, instead going out in a taxi to look for Barry.

Samuels was questioned by the police about his treatment while in care, and he disclosed that he had been sexually abused by Beck. But Samuels had become a 'big man' in the criminal world of Highfields, Leicester's hardest inner city area, and admitting to being a victim of sex abuse as a child would have humiliated him. He refused to make a formal statement to the police about his time in care.

Beck even had an impact on another generation. His managers suffered what might be termed traumatic stress when they realised the full extent of the consequences of Beck's guilt and of the regime with which they had colluded. Several developed forms of mental illness. Police officers, too, found the Beck investigation extremely upsetting. One was to take a year's leave on completion of the case, because of a nervous breakdown, while another was driven to early retirement resulting from the stress.

CHAPTER SEVENTEEN
A better future?

What went wrong?

The Beck case was not simply another instance of a sexual predator operating undetected within an otherwise healthy, competent institution. Leicestershire's child care services were subverted to such an extent that Beck and his followers were able to sexually abuse young children at will. This was possible, partly because of Beck's remarkable personal qualities, but also because of the weakness of the managers – and, to a lesser extent, the politicians – who were supposed to be in charge of him and his co-abusers.

There can be no question that Beck was a charismatic, bullying, manipulator. Weaker spirits wilted before the force of his personality, accepting unwanted sexual advances and dubious professional practices, whatever their qualms. He cultivated political contacts and exploited the political environment of Leicestershire with ruthless opportunism, to bluff and bluster his way into a position of power. On the rare occasions that he was challenged, he defended his domain ferociously. At the core was the compulsion to dominate children and adults, physically, emotionally and sexually. But had he operated within a stronger, better managed organisation, or in an environment where children's complaints were taken more seriously, he would have been stopped much earlier.

Beck was arguably the worst child abuser in British criminal history. His suspected toll of 200 children is probably the highest number any one abuser has victimised. But Beck's behaviour is not without parallel. The 'charismatic' aspect of Beck's personality fits the mould of several of the central figures in abusive regimes in children's homes. Jocelyn Jones, head of social services policy at Leicester University, highlights the nature of the power exercised by Beck and by Tony Latham, the key figure in the Staffordshire pin-down scandal. Both men were well-connected, politically. Both were able to control the relationship between their institutions and the outside world to protect their own power. But they had something more, a power which derived from their charismatic personalities and their unique attributes and abilities. In Beck's case this was the ability to 'get results' with the most difficult children in a way which became vital to the smooth running of the county's social services, but using a therapeutic approach which was not properly understood. This was the key to Beck's success and his survival as an abuser. Beck's rule was exercised by cutting children off from the outside world and from their families as much as possible and by encouraging them to see him as their father – and mother – figure.

Beck's regression therapy made children even more vulnerable. He employed a potent combination of affection, shame, humiliation and domination which mentally paralysed many of the children in his care, and even some of the vulnerable young men who worked at the homes. It was the show of love from Beck that was in a sense the most crippling element – it was the first positive emotion many of the damaged children had ever been offered. This made it all the more difficult for them to reject Beck's physical advances. The cuddling, nurturing, bottle feeding treatment gave Beck the traditional 'maternal' role, and he could play the stern, controlling patriarch as well. It is easy to understand how children were unable to resist him, psychologically as well as physically.

Residential care for children remains a low paid, low status backwater within the world of social services – whether it is administered by local authorities, charities or the private sector. Reforms such as those implemented by Leicestershire as part of their own child care strategy (*see Chapter 3*) concentrating – for sound reasons – on avoiding the use of children's homes, may well have marginalised residential care still further. Yet the retention of some children's homes is probably unavoidable. Their work is vital and the consequences when they go wrong can haunt society for decades. Without proper treatment, children who are alienated from their families and society are likely to go on to become the hard core offenders of the future – as did many of Beck's victims. The worst part of Beck's so-called 'regression therapy' was not that it tried to 'treat' or 'reform' children – but the converse, that it did not try to do so, and merely acted as a facade for sexual abuse. Damaged children do need treatment, provided it is legitimate, effective, monitored and administered by genuine experts.

Society produces a significant number of difficult children – they may be violent or emotional, abusive, disturbed, substance abusing, criminal, or all of these. Their problems go beyond mere delinquency and they may need to be contained for their own safety and that of others. But containment tends to become the priority. Once these children are out of sight, they are usually out of mind as well. Some may be fortunate enough to receive genuinely helpful care, even treatment. Others, as we have seen, became the victims of sexual predators, sadistic guardians, or quack therapists. Frank Beck was all of these.

The children's status was such that their complaints were not believed. It is hardly surprising that, when they emerged from their containment, many simply took a deeper plunge into the adult penal system.

Research in a recent book, *Whistleblowing in the Social Services*, by Dr Geoffrey Hunt, suggests that physical and sexual abuse of children and adults in care by social workers is much more extensive than has previously been believed, and continues despite attempts at improving the care system. One in three of 400 social workers surveyed by Hunt said that, during the two years prior to the survey, they had complained of clients being verbally abused by care workers. One in four had alleged physical abuse. One in 12 social workers involved in the care of children, the elderly and people with disabilities had made allegations of sexual abuse of clients.

A series of other problems emerged from Hunt's survey. It found that many residential homes operated a system of racial segregation, with white only homes refusing to admit ethnic minorities. Physical neglect, theft, fraud and breaches of confidentiality were widespread. Falsification of reports on patients was commonplace and sickness and absenteeism were serious problems. The survey also found that the numbers of unqualified staff made the difficulties worse.

Child abuse experts, such as academic Jocelyn Jones and Allan Levy, the leading child care QC who chaired the inquiry into the pin-down case in Staffordshire, said that the Frank Beck case had great significance because it brought together all the main elements of the other child abuse cases. It contained sex abuse, excessive physical restraint, a punishment regime that contained elements of torture, denial of civil liberties for children in care, and epic managerial incompetence.

Levy believes that the poor quality of management in many social services organisations is an essential component of institutional child abuse. 'It is consistently reported that managers in social services are ill-informed about the quality of care in the homes; that, at worst, they are remote, ill-informed and incompetent,' Levy told the authors. 'That is not true everywhere, but it is true in a very significant number of places, and I think that is extremely dangerous. In some respects it has not got better, it has got worse.'

Bob Lewis, a past president of the Association of Directors of Social Services (ADSS) says that bad managers are traitors to the children in their care. 'One of the things that concerned me [about the Leicestershire case] was some of the management issues. Did management, when they became aware of some of the issues, deal with them? Of course, the answer is that they didn't. You can put all your whistle-blowing systems into place, you can put all your professional guidance to the workforce. If something does go wrong, if somebody does slip through the net, you have to have the management quality to be able to deal with it. Some of the issues that have emerged more recently in South Wales, post-Beck, indicate that there are still significant areas of concern about the quality of middle and senior management when faced with the sorts of problems that Beck posed for the management of Leicestershire.'

Out of control

Failure to deal with complaints properly nourished an environment where sex abuse flourished. But other managerial weaknesses were just as important. Many abuse scandals have been possible only because managers' weakness allowed rogue empires to operate within social services departments. These empires flourished because they were seen as delivering results that the parent organisation needed. They were fortified by neglect – the reluctance of senior managers to supervise those in charge or to scrutinise the methods by which the 'results' are delivered. Once a semi-independent body has emerged, there are border clashes with other parts of the department and any challenge to the authority of the empire's ruler is vigorously resisted. Within the empire itself, the normal rules do not apply, events are shrouded in secrecy and abusers can thrive. The subjects – junior staff and children – suffer an arbitrary and oppressive rule against which they see no possibility of appeal.

Beck's personal empire fits this description, and similar conditions are a common theme in other scandals, not only involving children, but also the mentally ill and the elderly. Beck was seen as an expert therapist, and none of his managers had the expertise to challenge him, even if they had wished to. He pacified previously uncontrollable children, which made him a vital resource for the department. His political contacts gave him far more independence than an official at his level could normally expect. And officialdom was disinclined to believe the complaints of children who were regarded as completely untrustworthy. A striking aspect of the case was Leicestershire County Council's blasé acceptance of Beck's therapeutic methods and of his credentials as a child care expert. An important factor here was that most of the hierarchy above him were generic managers who, typically, had no specialist knowledge of fields like child care, even while they administered them. Allan Levy shares the view that placing generic managers in charge of social services departments has been to blame for much of the care tragedy of recent years.

'Such management as there is, is by people who have not had experience of services in the front line,' he says. 'They are people who have been brought in to manage money and resources and organisations. It is an inherent weakness, and it is happening all over the place. It is happening in the universities and elsewhere. We are being ruled by accountants and administrators. Even at directors' level, they seem to accept that many supervisors have no experience of the work being done on the ground.'

An additional problem with this kind of management is that many policy makers have been too ready to suspend their critical judgement and allow untested and even damaging therapeutic regimes to operate in children's homes. 'Some of these treatments were at best frankly loopy, and at worst dangerous,' said Professor Phillip Bean of Loughborough University. 'Beck was a result of this culture of therapy and the lack of an orthodoxy – his claims to solve problems when no one else could solve them fit into that mould.'

Another important issue was the culture of secrecy inside Beck's homes, and their isolation from County Hall. Where some other Leicestershire children's homes co-operated and shared information and ideas, Beck refused and created an alternative network connecting the homes where he had worked, and where other abusers continued to work after he had left. At Ratcliffe Road, Fiddaman followed Beck as acting officer-in-charge, and Beck continued to visit. Another example is Rosehill, where Kenneth Scott – separately convicted as a child abuser – was appointed officer-in-charge by a panel of county council officers including Beck.

Paedophiles and child abusers thrive amidst secrecy. Beck was able to bully his workers, as well as the children in care, partially because they were cut off from the non-abusive world. Children's contact with their families was tightly controlled, and often discouraged. The homes were physically and socially isolated, and the children and workers had little life away from the home. Shift patterns meant that workers were isolated, even within the staff group. They seldom met and it was hard to build up the level of trust necessary to discuss serious issues like the suspicion of abuse. Supervision of homes was mainly conducted by appointment, giving plenty of time for anything embarrassing to he concealed. Similarly, visits by councillors often amounted to little more than cosy chats over a cup of tea with the officer-in-charge. Contact with the consumers, the children, tended to be minimal, especially in homes run by Beck.

If the system appeared cosy, this in itself warned off potential complainants. Without confidence that complaints will be taken seriously, concerns will not be raised. The culture of secrecy extended to the scrutiny of the homes as well. Whenever questions were raised about the homes, up went the ramparts and down came the verbal defences. A succession of senior officers and councillors failed to examine the conditions of their children's homes property, because they were so busy defending them. A series of internal investigations was conducted by Leicestershire County Council, but the results of most of them were kept highly confidential. We know that evidence of abuse was literally crying out to be heard – young people were already telling the police and others what was happening, but officials repeatedly failed to react. Nor did anyone seem to notice the poor quality of much of the investigation work. Time and again, managers investigating allegations failed to interview alleged victims of abuse, or even the main accusers.

The unwillingness of Leicestershire's senior managers to investigate problems in children's homes properly, suggests a lack of confidence and a sense of defensiveness. Why, for instance, were the findings of investigations kept secret? What was the public interest justification in refusing to publish results of internal inquiries, such as when Kenneth Scott was revealed as a paedophile?

Beck's managers bear a heavy responsibility for the failure to protect the children in their care. They failed to monitor Beck's activities and their repeated failure to investigate complaints effectively is one of the most striking features of the whole affair. They even failed to move against him when clear grounds for action were established. The lesson here is that ultimately, any set of safeguards depends upon the calibre of people operating it.

But if managers are to be blamed, the politicians who appointed them and kept them in office must also be criticised. Child care became a backwater area, where managers regarded as 'plodders' could safely be left to plod. A comfortable culture, focused on routine issues rather than the quality of the care, was allowed to develop. It is strange that, at a time when the very role and existence of children's homes was being questioned, the homes themselves were subjected to such minimal scrutiny. If Beck's political connections and his influence within Leicestershire had been weaker, this might not have been the case. Rogue empires cannot be tolerated in any organisation. Charismatic leaders must not be allowed to operate without supervision. In children's homes it is especially important that inspection procedures should not become cosy, uninformative rituals: children and staff should have several avenues through which to make complaints and senior managers need the skills to investigate allegations and concerns effectively. One of the most alarming aspects of the Leicestershire case is that complaints did reach Beck's managers, who seemed unable to act and perhaps shrank from the implications of the allegations.

A particularly distressing element of this is that, despite the creation of a children's rights officer and other monitoring systems in Leicestershire, social workers employed by the county council continued to say, as late as 1997, that the authority had no effective whistle-blowing system to receive and investigate anonymous allegations. Most local authorities take complaints from children in care or from staff much more seriously now, believes Bob Lewis. ' believe that authorities have gone some way down the road to giving residents a voice,' he said. 'I think that a young person who complains is more likely to be listened to than they were pre-Beck. I think a social worker who reports a concern is more likely to be taken notice of than pre-Beck. My feeling is that things probably have got better, but I am not yet convinced that we have reached the point where we can say that we can have a reasonable degree of confidence that a residential place is a safe place for a child or a young person to go to.'

Brian Waller, who was the Director of Leicestershire social services when the case came to light, is confident that the warning systems he put into place – more rigorous inspection procedures, a children's rights officer and a series of independent routes by which complaints could be made – would prevent systematic abuse, as opposed to one-off offences, from happening in Leicestershire children's homes in the future. 'Of course you can't help wondering what might come to light ten years on,' he added. 'There's nothing I know about that I thought 'I hope they never find out about that' as I retired, but you can't know about the things you don't know about.'

Unskilled staff

A key factor in Beck's survival as an abuser was the culture within the homes he ran. His personal and often sexual domination of his workers meant there were few complaints from that quarter. Most that did get through came from people who were attached to his homes on a temporary basis – such as students on placement. Few of the staff had professional qualifications, so they seldom questioned the activities of a man seen by their employer as an expert. He made the rules, and if they seemed unorthodox or damaging, who were they to argue?

Beck was their boss, he flaunted his 'untouchable' status. He could threaten, browbeat, cajole and reward his staff. This is underlined even by the events surrounding his eventual removal. There was widespread unhappiness amongst junior staff at the methods used at The Beeches, but it still took an outsider, the visiting psychiatrist Dr Chris Lewis, to bring their discontent into focus and mobilise them into action. If Beck had not allowed his staff to meet Lewis as a group, he might have continued in charge of the home for far longer.

The low skill base amongst social workers is a continuing and central problem in residential care. According to Allan Levy: 'There are still an enormous number of people whose hearts are in the right place, but they have not had enough training. Until relatively recently, 19 out of 20 residential care workers had no qualifications and no proper training either. And very few of the heads of homes are qualified. It is a pretty grim picture. From my experience in the courts, it seems that inexperienced social workers are being pushed into cases far beyond their experience or competence, and not receiving the support or supervision that they should.'

Many experts doubt that the Diploma in Social Work is the most appropriate basic qualification for staff working in residential settings. One social services director described the diploma and its predecessor, the Certificate of Qualification in Social Work, as 'not being worth the paper it is written on'. Some councils even prefer to appoint qualified social workers from elsewhere in Europe, where the training courses are better respected. Bob Lewis of the ADSS suggests a move towards a core qualification, followed by specific training to deal with the needs of particular client groups – the frail elderly, children, people with learning difficulties, etc. He believes that residential workers need special training for work in a field that is very pressured and intensive in comparison with much of community social work.

An Audit Commission report on young people and crime, *Misspent Youth* (November, 1996), highlighted the need for specially trained practitioners to work with young offenders, in order to try and change their behaviour. Beck's training for the therapy he conducted was minimal, and it was used indiscriminately on children with serious psychiatric problems, as well as on those who were repeat offenders. Yet he was accepted as qualified to treat them, and trained others in his methods. No wonder his unqualified and untrained junior staff hesitated to question his actions.

The disciplinary system

A vital safeguard is the disciplinary system used for social workers. One local authority social services Director says that there is a continued problem with the standard of proof required in internal disciplinary hearings. Where a criminal prosecution must prove 'beyond reasonable doubt' that a person is guilty, in theory an internal disciplinary hearing reaches its decision on the basis of evidence that makes the case only 'on the balance of probabilities'. In practice, though, says this director, the disciplinary hearings (made up of councillors, often untrained in their role,) actually exercise judgement on the basis of demanding proof 'beyond reasonable doubt'.

As we have seen, this was a feature of several investigations by officials at Leicestershire into complaints against Beck. While this problem has perhaps decreased since the Beck era, it remains true that the rights of social workers are often protected in preference to those of children and other vulnerable people in care. The 'precautionary principle' – that if in doubt you should err on the side of safety – seems to have been overlooked for residents in care.

Part of the problem is the priority given to workers' rights over children's rights. 'I think authorities all too easily think in terms of [alleged abuse] being an employment issue,' said Bob Lewis. 'It is also a child protection issue, and parallel to any employment process there must also be a child protection process, where quite clearly the rules of evidence are very different.' He admits, though, that officers are very aware of what action councillors will or will not support, and what burden of proof they, and industrial tribunals, are likely to require. These concerns mirror those of Leicestershire's, then senior assistant director of social services, Terence Nelson, at the time of Beck's resignation (*see Chapter 6*). He was clearly worried that some politicians might have given Beck 'the benefit of the doubt', allowing him to remain in post. Lewis concedes, however, that, in cases where there is insufficient evidence to justify dismissal, senior officers would often resort to moving staff accused of impropriety to other areas. In this way, staff are not sacked on flimsy evidence, but are placed where they can he supervised more closely.

Another important issue is the unwillingness of many social services professionals to give blunt and honest references. It was this that allowed Beck to be re-employed in care after leaving Leicestershire and to continue to have, at the very least, unprofessional relationships with people in local authority care – in one case an under-age youth. 'There is a tradition in social work that good references are written for people that are no good,' a social services Director said.

It is a concern echoed by Bob Lewis. He says that while references are generally more honest than in the past, they still often conceal important facts. Some applicants have avoided the rigours of the reference system by naming a friend in another council, who has given a positive character reference without having the authority to do so.

'I think things are tighter,' adds Lewis. 'The issue is whether they are tight enough; whether people are offered jobs verbally subject to references, which of course is the wrong way round; whether references are honest; and I think there is evidence to suggest there are still people within social services who have concerns about individuals, but don't explicitly refer to them within references. There is still, I think, the opportunity to avoid direct contact with former employers by giving a named person within that organisation, who may well be the individual's friend, rather than the formality of applying to the authority for a reference. I think that is an area of some concern.'

Lewis is also critical of existing safeguards. 'There clearly still are problems with the Department of Health list – who is on and who isn't – and also in some parts of the country there are real problems with police checks. It is still too easy to avoid them by silly things like putting up a different date of birth on the application form. Some checks would show no one on the list born on that date, when a more in-depth inquiry would show that there is somebody with the same name, the same address, but born on a different date. That checking system is still open to some question marks, as is the fact that the two checks by the Department of Health and the police aren't integrated. The sooner we have a common database the better.'

He believes the fear of compensation claims has meant that insurers are now pushing local authorities into a more diligent approach. Councils are now more likely to follow proper systems and procedures, so it is less likely that an abuser can gain access to children through an old-boy network. It is more likely that proper references and proper procedures will be invoked.

Concern is expressed too by Allan Levy QC, who regards the existing vetting system as sloppy and full of holes. He believed the elaborate safeguards recommended in the report by the former Director of Kent social services, Norman Warner, on the recruitment of people working with children, must he fully implemented as soon as possible: 'I feel instinctively that people are still insinuating themselves into the system, or they are there from a long time ago, and they have not been found out. I really don't believe it all happened in the '60s, '70s and '80s and it is not happening in the '90s. Human nature, I am afraid, is against that.'

Warner's report, *Choosing with Care*, was commissioned by the government in reaction to the Beck case. Its recommendations included a rigorous process of preliminary and final interviews, complete with written exercises. Applicants to work with children should be questioned in detail about their attitudes to control and punishment, about significant events in their childhood, their personal relationships and the issue of sexual attraction to children. References should always be checked and past employers questioned directly about disciplinary records and there should be a fast track system for checking police records and government blacklists. Warner said prospective employers should have 'no inhibitions' about making informal checks about a job applicant through personal contacts. Once employed, staff should be better supervised, with a system of annual appraisal to monitor performance and identify training needs. Eventually, a licensing system would be introduced preventing unlicensed care staff from working in children's homes.

Many of these points reflect weaknesses that emerged in the Leicestershire case. A more efficient blacklist of suspected sex offenders would not have prevented Beck's employment in Leicestershire – there was no evidence at the time that he was, or would become, an abuser. Such a system might, however, have stopped Colin Fiddaman. He might have been caught earlier, with more efficient police internal communication and cross-referencing, which should have logged his cautioning for cottaging, as well as his questioning about suspicious behaviour with a youth in a car. Police procedures have improved enormously since the time of Beck and Fiddaman. It is only quite recently that police forces have set up dedicated child protection units, staffed by trained officers who are trusted to deal sensitively with children. For many years there was a refusal by the police and the public to recognise the extent of abuse of children, either in the family home or in residential or foster care.

There is now considerable debate about how the system can be tightened, fuelled by Warner and more recently Sir William Utting's report on the safeguards for children living away from home, *People Like Us* (1997). The Utting report concluded that the widespread abuse of children in residential homes had occured up to 20 years ago, and was unlikely to be repeated on that scale, though the danger to children in care remained ever present. To prevent recurrence, the report made a series of detailed recommendations, which the government responded to by setting up a task force of ministers. Utting said that fostering is one of the worst areas of risk today, because children are too vulnerable and isolated to complain about abuse, with many children inappropriately allocated. Another major risk comes from small unregistered homes. Utting also found that school and health services for children in care are often neglected, with a third of children in residential care not receiving an education. One of the repeated problems pointed to by Utting was that recommendations of previous reports, and legislation designed to put right previously recognised problems, were often not implemented. He also found that the criminal justice system persistently let down victims of abuse, such as children and disabled people.

The ADSS supports the idea of a General Social Services Council modelled on existing professional bodies for doctors and nurses. But if this was confined to the relatively small body of professionally qualified social workers, it would miss the vast bulk of unqualified people who work in the care industry. An all embracing body, on the other hand, would be a vast undertaking which would require substantial public funding. The British Association of Social Workers wants to see a national register of qualified social workers, something that the government seems sympathetic to. This might help, believes the association, in improving standards within the profession, and might also help employers to log concerns before they reach the stage of suggested black-listing on the Department of Health register of wrong-doers.

Protection first?

One of the most complex and uncomfortable issues in child protection is that of dealing with workers who are suspected of abuse, but against whom nothing is proved. What standards of suspicion or certainty are necessary before someone is deprived of their job, has their career shattered, and is labelled as a possible child abuser? Or to put the problem the other way round, how much risk should children be exposed to before managers are prepared to act on their suspicions?

It is clear that the issue of standards of proof was an important factor in the Leicestershire case. Beck got away with abusing children, in part, because his managers decided that without a successful prosecution against him they had no grounds for disciplinary action. Then, of course, there was the bizarre decision to give Beck a reference for a post in social work – a prime example of the issue of misleading references.

The mood in the government may now be shifting towards a review of the standard of proof needed before action is taken in child abuse cases. But that may mean more cases will be brought before the courts by alleged abusers relying on the Human Rights Bill/Act 1998 – which incorporates the European Convention on Human Rights into domestic law – complaining of an interference with their civil liberties. 'I have never believed it is only in murder cases and terrorist cases where there are miscarriages of justice,' said Allan Levy. 'In the area which we are talking about, alleged child abuse, we suspect – more in the civil sphere than in the criminal sphere – things go wrong. And they go wrong both ways – you get people who are abusers who get away with it, so the children go back to abusing parents, or you get it the other way, parents get [wrongly] convicted or categorised in civil proceedings.'

Another difficult area is the supervision of convicted offenders. There is a strong argument that if someone has offended, and served a prison sentence, then they have paid their debt to society. But the difficulty is that, statistically, a significant proportion of the 100,000 convicted sex offenders in Britain will offend again. Allan Levy argues for retrospective legislation to require past offenders to be registered, despite the risk of this being contested under the European Convention on Human Rights.

'You have got to balance the interests of the offenders and the interests of protecting children,' says Levy. Existing precautions like the register of sex offenders will not prevent re-offending. There is now undeniable evidence from cases across the country, of networks of child abusers, often centred on children's homes, procuring victims – and with abusers protecting each other. Members of such networks show great mutual loyalty and protectiveness, so even if one individual is caught, it can be extremely difficult to prove the involvement of others even when there are strong grounds for suspicion.

These issues do not apply only to people working with children. It is now quite widely predicted that similar cases of physical and sexual abuse will emerge relating to elderly people and those with learning disabilities. The same issues of vulnerability and power occur, and very often they, like children, are disbelieved when they make allegations. One important safeguard, suggests one social services director, would be to extend the scope of the Sexual Offences Act. This Act made it illegal for people who had been convicted of rape and other sexual offences to work with children. The same protection needs to also be given to other people in care. It is still possible, the social services director explained, for a man with a conviction for rape to be given responsibility for giving a woman with learning disabilities a bath.

Learning lessons?

Andrew Kirkwood's meticulous inquiry revealed many alarming features of the Leicestershire case. But the sheer weight of detail in the Kirkwood report may blind its readers to its overall lack of perspective. 'Kirkwood's remit was wrong,' said one person who had been closely involved with The Beeches. 'It was about damage limitation. You have to ask yourself why? Kirkwood did not properly look at what happened, only at the management lessons. Leicestershire County Council was much keener to gloss over the problems than to learn from them.'

Kirkwood is also open to criticism on the grounds that he fell into Leicestershire's trap of talking about the 'Beck case' rather than the 'Leicestershire abuse cases'. Fiddaman was not properly investigated, even though he was a serious abuser on his own account. Kirkwood was surprisingly gentle about the role of the visiting psychiatrists at Beck's homes, who might have been expected to take a closer interest in the supposed psychotherapy treatments used there. He also failed to examine properly the links between a series of abusers who infiltrated Leicestershire's care service.

The decision to conduct the inquiry in closed session made it difficult for anyone who was not there to assess its conclusions. And Kirkwood's refusal to discuss or defend his findings publicly did not help. One of the purposes of such inquiries is to reassure the public and produce answers they can rely on. Kirkwood's findings were damning, especially on detailed examination – but they were poorly presented to a constituency accustomed to receiving information via two minute reports on the evening news, or a few hundred words in their daily paper. Each major child abuse case has brought its own inquiry. Each has found that much the same thing has happened, but the lessons are seldom applied beyond the local authority in question – if there.

Pressure from the insurers – worried that publication will lead to new compensation claims – has led to many reports being kept confidential, leaving little opportunity for their recommendations to be implemented outside the authority concerned.

Bill Upall, the solicitor for many of the Leicestershire compensation claimants, believes that the inquiry process is unlikely to reveal many new lessons about institutional child abuse. He says a Royal Commission is now needed, to overhaul the entire child care and child protection system. 'We need to move away from these sensational inquiries, which offer no justice to abuse victims and no protection for the potential victims within the system,' said Upall. 'We should be auditing the entire system, not just reacting to individual scandals. We need to move to a proper BMA-style professional body for social workers, which can establish proper professional standards and deal with misconduct. We are talking about a profession which can have a huge impact on people's lives, but which has nowhere near the kind of safeguards that are needed.'

Every time a new child abuse case surfaces, reassuring voices are heard saying that these are cases from the past, and that social services have now greatly improved their practice. Some experts, without vested interests, take a less complacent view. 'I have no doubt that there are continuing problems with sex abuse in children's homes,' says Levy. 'Research and anecdotal evidence demonstrates very considerable concerns still. In 1993, for example, the Social Services Inspectorate did a survey of 11 special and residential child care services, in 11 local authorities, and Herbert Laming [then head of the SSI] was quoted as saying 'conditions have improved since the Beck scandal, and the pin-down business in Staffordshire, but there is still much bad practice and there is no guarantee that such scandals cannot occur again'. And that really is the message, and the reports I have seen later have said that whilst there have been improvements in some areas, there are still major failings.'

Is the problem growing?

The steady accumulation of similar cases has begun to reveal the nature and extent of child abuse in care institutions. 'Until recently it was generally believed that sexual acts between adults and children were rare owing to the strong taboos against such behaviour,' wrote Matthew Colton and Maurice Vanstone in *Betrayal of Trust.* 'However, over the past 10 or 20 years it has become increasingly clear that child sexual abuse is fairly commonplace and exists at all levels of society.'

Colton and Vanstone quote a study in the United States that found a 600 per cent increase in reported cases of child sexual abuse between 1976 and 1982.

In Britain, the number registered by the NSPCC rose from seven in 1977 to 527 in 1986. This does not necessarily indicate any strong increase in the incidence of abuse, merely that the social climate has changed to allow children to complain and, to an extent, to be listened to.

Other researchers found that in the USA, the estimated level of child sexual abuse varied widely in different studies, ranging from six per cent to 62 per cent in females, and from three per cent to 31 per cent for males. This partly reflects differing research methodologies, and partly reflects different means of defining abuse in terms of activities and age.

Colton and Vanstone accept the true rate of abuse might be regarded as about 10 per cent – 12 per cent among girls, eight per cent of boys. They point out that the theory that abuse victims are more likely to become abusers has a limited validity; most victims are female, and most perpetrators are male. High proportions of male abusers had themselves been abused. Research indicates that abuse is most harmful where the abuser was a father figure.

Only a child abuser can understand the reasons for becoming a child abuser – and even then any person will only understand their own personal circumstances, which may offer little in the way of general lessons. It may be instructive, then, to listen to those abusers who have spoken of their own experiences.

Betrayal of Trust quotes many abusers talking about their experiences. It is possible that 'David', who used his position in the Church to gain access to children he abused, may contribute to our understanding of how abusers in a variety of institutions – which might include residential homes – can operate through unspoken mutual protection:

> *'There is definitely, I would think, a culture within the Church. It has a great deal to do, I think, with the fact that there are a lot of single clergy, a lot of clergy who are living on their own, in a situation where they can abuse. But they are not necessarily single clergy, because the first person I went to for help was a married man. There seems to be something within the system which encourages, if that's the word, almost gives permission for others to do it, and get away with it. Therefore you think 'why won't I?'. And I think that's a great mistake, and I think the Church has a responsibility for my offending and other people's offending, by not addressing what is a known problem. There is nowhere to go to. There is no one to speak to in confidence. There's no system of help set up. It's almost acknowledged by a nod and a wink, but no official action was ever taken.'*

If this is a fair description of at least parts of organised religion, there may be equally important lessons to be learnt about residential care work.

It is impossible to assess the impact of physical and sexual abuse on children in care. Even academic experts have been frustrated by the difficulty in proving the effects on later life. Research conducted in Britain and the United States has concluded that just being in care has a strong detrimental impact on later life – probably a worse impact than being with abusive parents. Interestingly, a study by Lee Robins and Michael Rutter found that institutional care had a much worse impact on males than females.

The problem for academics is that so much abuse is kept secret, making objective analysis very difficult. Jocelyn Jones is keen to conduct more research into the phenomenon of child abuse in institutional care, but says the problem is that so many inquiries from around the country are not published.

Almost by definition, social workers and care workers have access to vulnerable people – and the Leicestershire case highlighted the need for effective procedures to ensure that potential abusers are weeded out, before they can enter the profession.

Some observers suspect that the current torrent of child abuse scandals results from more than simply greater awareness of the problem. Allan Levy suspects itself is greater. 'Is there more abuse now, than there used to be? – who knows?' he said. 'I suspect there is, because the boundaries have been extended at all levels. I get involved in these horrific cases where you get grandparents as well as parents involved in abuse, so you are getting two generations involved, and three if there are siblings as well. Who knows whether this went on years ago? My own instinct is that there probably is more abuse. There is also more abuse disclosed and recorded.'

Levy predicts the next spate of abuse scandals will relate to foster care. He believes many foster placements are unsatisfactory, because local authorities have found it very difficult to find foster carers, particularly for adolescents. Councils have had difficulty in maintaining rigorous vetting procedures on foster parents, with too few potential fosterers coming forward to meet the demand.

Who should run child care?

Local government has hardly covered itself in glory in its stewardship of children's homes. Although there are undoubtedly many homes doing good work, with high professional standards, attention naturally focuses on the spectacular catalogue of failures. But it is also fair to point out that few other organisations – charities, Churches, the Home Office – have an unblemished record in providing residential care for vulnerable people. Today there are far fewer children in homes – about 8,000, compared to nearly 40,000 when Beck began his career, and they are accommodated in smaller homes which offer less potential for the kind of mass abuse committed by Beck.

Children's residential care has increasingly been transferred into the independent sector, run by businesses or charities. The government required councils to buy a proportion of their care services from the independent sector and few councils had the money to finance their own provision properly. But now equally serious abuse scandals are emerging from homes in the independent sector as well, notably in Clwyd and Edinburgh. Some experts believe that the level of supervision and regulation of privately owned homes leaves them even more open to abusers than council-run homes. Viewed in this light, the pressure for councils to use private and voluntary sector provision has alarming implications for the policing of children's homes.

Bob Lewis does not share the sense of complacency expressed by some social services departments about their children's homes' management. 'I think that rather than getting better at it, we are getting worse at it. My biggest concern is the huge expansion of private child care in recent years, and its relatively low level of regulation. I would like to think that things have improved after Beck and Staffordshire and so on. Maybe in some local authorities, if not every local authority, processes have improved enormously. But the issue now is, what is going on in the independent sector? And in fact we are actually distancing ourselves, and it is much more difficult to manage this.' A similar point was made by Allan Levy, who cannot be dismissed as the voice of local authority vested interest.

Perhaps the bleakest conclusion to be drawn from the Leicestershire case is that these things happen because care of the vulnerable – particularly when they are difficult, even unpleasant adolescents – is simply not a priority within our society. Experience has shown that without high quality management and rigorous policing, children's homes and other organisations concerned with child care, are easily infiltrated by abusers. Hopefully, under the weight of the growing number of scandals, the political will to address the problem now exists. But the evidence is that effective protection for children is still lacking in many areas. As a consequence, a new generation of Frank Becks may already have established itself close to those it will abuse.

Postscript

Frank Beck died on 31st May, 1994, two and a half years after he was given five life sentences – one of the most severe sentences awarded since the ending of the death penalty for murder. He collapsed while playing badminton at Whitemoor Jail in Cambridgeshire. Fellow prisoners, some of whom had been Beck's own sexual victims, soon began to talk about the real cause of Beck's apparent heart attack being speed, which they suggested other prisoners had surreptitiously added to his food over a period of months.

But in death as in life, secrecy continued to surround Beck. The verdict of the inquest was death by natural causes, citing his heart attack. The coroner, however, refused to release any papers relating to the case, or to disclose whether an autopsy was conducted to determine whether Beck had been dosed with speed or other drugs. Frank Beck was mourned by relatives and friends who continue to maintain his innocence, and Lord Longford sent a big bunch of flowers to the funeral. But his victims celebrated instead. One said: 'Hell is where he belongs.'

EPILOGUE
Greville Janner
by Paul Gosling

Throughout the Frank Beck trial there was a shadow in the court – a man named by the defence and who much private speculation centred around. That was Greville Janner MP. Just as Janner was an elusive figure in the Beck trial, so, for legal reasons, he was only mentioned, almost in passing, in the original version of *Abuse of Trust*. Now more can be reported – and very much more is known.

For nearly 30 years, Greville Janner was a senior figure in Leicester politics. He was MP for Leicester North West from 1970 to 1974 and then, after constituency reorganisation, for Leicester West from 1974 to 1997. It was a family affair – he inherited the position of Leicester North West MP from his father, Barnett.

Greville Janner was born on 11 July, 1928 in Cardiff, the son of Barnett and Elsie Janner. As with many Jewish settlers in Britain, both sides of the Janner family escaped from the Baltic region to avoid persecution from the Tsar. Greville Janner's paternal grandfather came from the Lithuanian village of Vitumjan and when he left he became known as Vitumjaner, or the 'man from Vitumjan'. The Vitumjaner surname became corrupted in Britain to Janner.

Barnett Janner was a solicitor, an Orthodox Jew, an executive member of the British Zionist Federation and president of the Board of Deputies of British Jews – the most senior lay role in British Jewish society. Barnett Janner joined the Liberal Party in 1924 and unsuccessfully stood for the Parliamentary seat of Cardiff Central in 1929. In 1932, he joined the Labour Party and was selected as its candidate for Leicester West. With the outbreak of the Second World War the next general election only took place in 1945, when he won the seat. It was reorganised as the Leicester North West seat in 1950, which Barnett again won and held for the next 20 years. Barnett Janner became seriously ill shortly before the 1970 general election. According to a mischievous story in the *Sunday Express*, he left his standing down as Parliamentary candidate until just two days before nominations closed in 1970, so that, with the 'Vote Janner' leaflets already printed, the Labour Party would have to approve his son as candidate.

Janner's version was that he attended a selection conference and won on the first ballot. As Janner himself reports, though, he was first anointed not just by the retiring MP, but also by national and local Labour Party officials. Working with his close colleagues (all now deceased) Janet Setchfield, George Billington and David Taylor, Janner junior took total control of the Leicester West Labour Party. Not only were Setchfield, Billington and Taylor all city councillors who served as lord mayors, they were county councillors too. They were also constituency party officers. Working together, they were famed for their ruthless control of the party machinery and for their capacity to 'lose' membership applications from potential members with different political beliefs.

It was a period of ruthless 'rotten borough' politics, with various allegations of corruption and other criminality.

One Labour Party member who was a member of the left wing 'opposition' within Leicester West recalled how naive Janner's opponents were. For years they had put forward resolutions at constituency party meetings but lost the vote. They told themselves they needed to recruit more Labour Party members.

Throughout those years George Billington as Leicester West party secretary had stood up, counted the votes with a flick of his forefinger and reported that the left had lost. Then one day the left doubted the result and asked for a recount – and found they had won. They instantly realised that they had probably been winning votes for years, but had never thought to challenge the accuracy – and honesty – of senior Labour Party figures.

Greville Janner himself appeared to have little interest in much of the day to day detail of political life. Janner was also a senior lawyer – he became a barrister in 1954 and a QC in 1971. He was a leading employment rights QC – and prolific author of books and articles on the subject. Janner had limited time to devote to local politics.

On one occasion, members of the Transport and General Workers' Union expressed outrage that a column by Janner in an employment magazine advised an employer on how to sack a trade union activist. Janner subsequently explained to an angry meeting of trade unionists that he should have simply told the employer not to do so.

Another reason for suspicion by Labour Party members was Greville Janner's active life in business. He was a non-executive director of the Ladbrokes betting group from 1986 to 1995 and a director of an asset management company, West Heath Road Seasons, from 1999 to April 2015. For several years in the 1970s, he was a director of the *Jewish Chronicle*, until he became President of the Board of Deputies of British Jews – which created a potential conflict of interest.

Janner was founding partner of JS Associates, a book publisher, and also a founding partner and former chairman of the JSB Group, providers of employment law training and events management. Janner wrote at least 19 books, several dealing with employment law.

Much of Janner's political time and energy was devoted to pro-Israel lobbying, including, it was reported, urging the Indian government to lift its arms embargo on Israel. Like his father, Greville Janner was a member of the Board of Deputies of British Jews, rising to the position of President – a role he held from 1978 to 1984. The son exceeded the influence of his father, though, and became vice president of the World Jewish Congress. Among his contributions, Greville Janner co-founded the Holocaust Educational Trust, which did important work in encouraging schools to teach about the horrors of the Holocaust. He was influential with the Israeli Labour Party, co-writing the book *One Hand Alone Cannot Clap*, with the former Israeli premier Shimon Peres, which urged Israeli Jews and Arabs to co-exist happily and peacefully.

Janner appears to have been a politician of significant international influence and connections. He was on good terms with political leaders in Israel, India, Egypt and Jordan, and was a regular guest in palaces across the Middle East; he attended funerals of world leaders.

One of Janner's strongest commitments was for tough action to be taken against war criminals – he was himself a war crimes investigator, following the Second World War. He was heavily involved in the enactment of the War Crimes Act in the UK Parliament. In Janner's view, legal action against perpetrators of war crimes should take precedence over the age or health of the accused. Szymon Serafinowicz was a police chief under in Nazi-occupied Belarus and was charged with committing war crimes during the Second World War. Serafinowicz denied the allegations, but was unable to answer questions or be tried because of his dementia. Janner complained: 'War criminals have managed to evade prosecution under our system of justice for decades. There were absolutely no reasons why he should have escaped charges for ever.' In an interview with the *Jewish Chronicle*, Janner said: 'I don't care what bloody age they are. These criminals should have been dealt with years ago.' When concentration camp guard John Demjanjuk was convicted of war crimes at the age of 91, Janner said: 'No concessions to age or the time that has passed can be made when it comes to justice for crimes of this magnitude.'

Janner otherwise played a relatively minor role in political life, though he actively supported racial tolerance, including strengthening Jewish-Muslim ties. Despite taking a fairly low profile in national Labour Party politics, the foreword to Janner's memoir, My Life! ('A record of a life of service to humanity and a chapter in the history of the post-war world'), was written by Tony Blair. Blair wrote: 'He had a distinguished career in the Commons, not least as Chair of the Select Committee on Employment, and now in the Lords, and he has been and remains tremendously influential and important, both in the parliamentary world and because of the work he does on behalf of the Jewish community and for charities up and down Britain.'

Within Leicester, Janner had one notable skill – an amazing memory. He could walk down a street in his constituency and seemingly remember the name not just of every constituent that he met, but also the names of all their family members. This feat helped generate genuine loyalty and affection from many people, who felt they had a connection with their MP.

Janner's fantastic memory might have been connected with one of his other famed abilities — as a magician and member of the Magic Circle. This was, though, one of the factors that counted against him in his later years when police investigated him for child abuse. By then the police were deeply sceptical about magicians, both in terms of how their skills might be used and about the often unsupervised access they had to young children.

A strong denial

During the Beck trial, the public heard allegations against Greville Janner for the first time. They heard of a supposed 'relationship' between Janner and Boy A and the explanation pleaded by Beck that he was an innocent person, who tried to stop the abuse of Boy A by Janner.

Prosecuting lawyer Peter Joyce dismissed the accusations as the 'great Janner diversion'. 'It is put forward as a great pretence that Mr Beck was the great protector,' Joyce told the jury. 'Greville Janner is not on trial here. The prosecution are not here to defend Greville Janner.' He added that early witness statements by Boy A had not mentioned Janner.

Shortly after the end of the Beck trial, Greville Janner had the opportunity to present his case at length, in a House of Commons debate on contempt of court rules that had prevented Janner arguing his innocence during the Beck case.

The then Leicester West MP said:

'Anyone involved in a trial can make any allegations they wish about anyone else — provided that the judge cannot disallow them as irrelevant — however harmful, horrendous and vile the lies may be. Those whose reputations are attacked are forbidden even to deny the allegations. To do so would be a criminal offence — contempt of court.

'As the House knows, Frank Beck of Leicester was convicted of a series of filthy and most serious crimes and received what must be a near record sentence — five life terms and a total of 24 years' imprisonment. He called [Boy A] as a witness. Long ago, when [Boy A] was a deprived youngster living in a Leicestershire children's home, my family and I tried, unsuccessfully, to help him. Soon after, he was placed in a home run by Beck. After 15 years of Beck's influence — including a period when [Boy A] lodged in Beck's private home — and after I had refused to provide Beck with references and shortly before Beck's trial was due to begin, they combined to make disgraceful, contemptible and totally untrue allegations of criminal conduct against me.

'Their motive was made blazingly clear by a letter that I received only yesterday [2 December 1991] from a former cellmate of Beck's. I do not know the man, but he took it on himself to communicate with me. He writes that Beck told him that he — Beck — was going to frame me. According to Beck, that would take the light off him. To that end, Beck had enlisted the help of [Boy A]. The former cellmate also wrote that the police knew that he was willing to give evidence to that effect if the Crown thought it necessary to call him. In the event, it did not, but the allegations against me were precisely as the prosecution alleged in Beck's trial — an attempted diversion from the reality of Beck's guilt. Both verdict and sentence showed — happily — that the attempt failed totally.

'However, is it not horrendous that Beck and [Boy A] were able to make such terrible and lying accusations against me in court and that the media could, and with honourable exceptions did, report these falsehoods, all under the cloak of absolute privilege? I had effectively no legal rights in the matter, and I was not allowed even to nail the lies. No wonder many people were mystified by my uncharacteristic silence — it was imposed by the cruel operation of the rules on contempt.

'Happily, I am a fairly tough character. I have been able to ride out the agony on this ordeal in good heart. But it has not been easy. As a Member of Parliament, I am now well placed to fight back.'

There was little, if any, observation in the media of the irony that Janner used the same principle of privilege to defend himself (and accuse Boy A) that he was charging others of misusing. Just as Janner had no opportunity to publicly defend himself against privileged comments made by Beck and Boy A in court, so Boy A – who was named in Parliament and then in the press – had scant opportunity to defend his character against the statements made (under privilege) in Parliament by Janner.

As far as the public were concerned, allegations had been made against a respectable and respected MP – with dirt thrown in a vain attempt at defending a psychopathic abuser who was found guilty of extremely serious criminal offences.

But the reality is far more complicated. It is only now, following Janner's death, that the full story can be told of the allegations, the police investigations and the failures to prosecute. This is not just because the libel laws prevented many things being said that were suspected but not provable – but also because so much was unknown until the time of writing, 2016.

The police investigate
Police first heard allegations of child sex abuse by Greville Janner in 1989 – during the investigations into Frank Beck, two years before Beck's trial.

During the Beck trial, defence witness Boy A claimed that he had a 'relationship' with Janner from the age of 13 to 15. He alleged that Janner gave Boy A a ten speed bike as a present and that Boy A slept at Janner's London flat, shared a room with him at Leicester's Holiday Inn hotel, had gone with him on a lecture tour in Scotland and visited the MP at the House of Commons. Boy A also told the court that Janner had bought him toys, clothes and concert tickets. He claimed that Janner had buggered him on several occasions. The 'relationship' ended when Janner caught Boy A stealing money from him, Boy A said.

In private, Boy A – identified in later inquiries as 'Complainant 1' – went very much further. During the Beck trial, the prosecution made much of the point that Boy A's official statements had not at first made any allegations against Janner. But what prosecution counsel failed to say – and may not have known – was that Boy A had told the police verbally about the allegations. Those allegations were not, though, included in Boy A's statement to the police.

According to the allegations made by Boy A, Janner had been engaged in oral sex and carried out indecent assault and buggery between the summer of 1974 and December 1975, while the boy was under the age of 16. These allegations by Boy A were very similar to the accusations Beck made in court and to the police.

That there was some sort of 'association' between Janner and Boy A became clear to the police when they conducted a search of Beck's home on 30 August, 1990. Letters from Janner to 'Boy A' were found there, which contained the sign-off 'love Greville'. The letters urged the boy to write to Janner, described the boy as Janner's 'right hand man' and offered for 'Boy A' to assist the then MP at his surgery for constituents.

In one of the letters, Janner wrote that any letter by Boy A 'which is private will be treated confidentially by me'. Janner continued that 'it seems strange not having you flipping around like a friendly flea! In fact I miss you.' The letter, on House of Commons notepaper, ended 'and my love to you, Greville. P.S. you were a super excellent and very helpful and thoughtful guest, I know the effort it sometimes took, well done! See you at the Holiday Inn on Tuesday. Jonathan will arrange for a bed for you in the sitting room... good night now, it's 10 and the division bell has just rung so I must vote.'

The letters did not prove there was a sexual relationship between Janner and the boy, Boy A. But they were highly suggestive of it. And they arranged for meetings between the two when Janner's wife and daughter were out of the country on a visit to Israel. Yet, despite the doubts about the nature of the relationship, it appears that the police took no action to resolve the obvious questions.

According to his complaint, Boy A first met Janner when the MP carried out a magic show at his school. At the time the boy was living at Station Road children's home in Wigston, on the edge of Leicester. Boy A told the police the correct details of Janner's car, a red Jaguar, and the full registration number. The description of Janner's home was also accurate.

Janner was in regular and frequent contact with Boy A. He phoned the boy at the children's homes most weeks, they wrote to each other most weeks and met at weekends. Janner took the boy with him to meetings at Labour Party offices, even taking him to meet constituents in surgeries, providing the constituent did not mind. The boy was described as 'a friend'. When Janner had private meetings that the boy could not sit in on, an aide of Janner would take the boy around the city, giving him money to buy sweets and toys.

The boy would often be collected from the children's home by Janner. On other occasions they would meet at the Holiday Inn, which Janner described in his autobiography as 'our Leicester base'. Despite being one of the city's MPs for many years, Janner never owned a home in Leicester, commuting to the city from his homes in London and Bournemouth.

Soon after this period of initial contact between Janner and Boy A, the boy received a large amount of money in the post from Janner and a rail ticket for him to visit the MP in London. He was met off the train at St Pancras station by Janner. The boy told the police that Janner had given him a cuddle at the station, which felt 'strange'. It was the first physical contact between them. In the car going to Janner's home, the MP went further and patted him twice on the knee.

When they arrived at Janner's home, the boy was shown to his accommodation – a box room. In his statement to the police, Boy A was able to accurately describe the house in detail, and correctly remembered the name of the cook.

Janner and the boy were left alone in Janner's house. Janner, said the boy, took advantage of the situation to kiss him, cuddle him and simulate sex upon him. The next day, said the boy, Janner took him to a friend's house where there was a swimming pool and the two were left alone by Janner's friend. The boy was told he could swim, he jumped in wearing just his underpants – which fell off when he hit the water. Janner responded by jumping into the pool, naked. Mutual cuddling and petting followed.

The police followed this up, but Janner's friend contradicted the story. He did not leave guests alone and could not recall Janner bringing a boy with him to his house. While Boy A said he had been taken by Janner to the wedding of the friend's daughter, the friend said he did not even have a child who got married at that time. The police accepted the statement as fact.

Years later a video was obtained by police. This not only proved that the wedding did take place – it also showed Boy A present at it, in the company of Janner.

There was a gap in contact between Janner and Boy A, but contact soon resumed. This time the boy stayed with Janner in a suite at the Holiday Inn. According to Boy A, following dinner they took a shower together and then cuddled and petted each other. Later, according to Boy A's evidence, the two went to bed together, where simulated sex took place, followed by oral sex. Boy A's statement said he did not want to participate in the oral sex.

Following this, Janner and the boy met infrequently, with oral – but not penetrative – sex taking place, according to Boy A's statement. The two swam naked together and shared a bed naked on occasions. Janner took the boy with him on a two week lecture tour, on employment law, of Scotland.

Shortly after this, Boy A moved children's homes. He had been living in the Station Road home in the Leicester suburb of Wigston. The boy then moved to the Radcliffe Road children's home, where Beck was the manager in charge.

Boy A told Beck about the alleged relationship with Janner and gave him letters from the MP that proved their close contact. Soon after Janner gave Boy A a racing bike as a present, but this was returned by Beck on the grounds that it showed favouritism to one boy and seemed to imply an unhealthy relationship between the boy and the MP.

There was no doubt that Janner and the boy knew each other very well. One of the Radcliffe Road social workers and a girl and a boy resident all made statements to the police about Janner, which confirmed that Janner knew Boy A. The social worker told the police that he had visited Janner and told him the association had to end as it was not in the boy's best interests. The social worker also wrote in the social work case notes that he was unhappy that 'the relationship with Greville Janner to continue' and that the boy was to go on a camping holiday with the MP.

In Beck's statements to the police, he claimed that Boy A had told him of sessions of joint masturbation with Janner, as well as oral sex. According to this account, almost every meeting between the boy and Janner involved sex.

Beck claimed that he reported the allegations to his head office at County Hall, where the response was 'oh no, not again'. However, some years later – after the boy had left care – Beck said that he had put Boy A and Janner back into contact with each other, in the hope that Janner would provide some assistance to Boy A. And after Beck was arrested, Boy A contacted Janner – who denied ever having known the boy. This was despite the now adult Boy A inviting Janner to his wedding and receiving a £50 gift in response, followed by money and clothes for his new baby.

Boy A made a formal complaint against Janner in January 1991, through the involvement of Ian Henning, on behalf of Beck's firm of solicitors, Greene d'Sa. At this point Boy A was aged 30 and made allegations relating to events of about 17 years earlier. He was only willing to make a statement to police in the presence of Beck. That statement ran to 30 pages.

At one point Boy A explained his discomfort about the interview. "I must tell you something else, which is very difficult for me.' He then alleged that while staying at the Holiday Inn, Janner had buggered him and that it hurt a lot. It injured him, requiring a doctor to treat him at the children's home. He was given some cream, but he did not explain to the doctor how the injury occurred.

Boy A also claimed that he was buggered by Janner on two occasions in Scotland and on two or three instances at the Holiday Inn. He said that while he did not object to their other sexual activity, he was very unhappy at being buggered.

The police interviewed the house mother of Station Road children's home. She confirmed that Janner and Boy A knew each other. She added that when she informed County Hall of this, officials responded calmly, saying they knew and approved of the connection. Social services records also reported that Janner invited Boy A to go on holiday to Israel with him. The house mother told the police that Janner had informed her that Boy A had stolen money from the MP while he was in the shower.

Despite the strength of these statements, the response from police and prosecutors was cautious. They met and agreed that some potential witnesses could be approached without this becoming public knowledge. A 1991 memorandum within the Crown Prosecution Service referred to the case. 'There is the possibility that other boys were taken out by the MP and the police are seeking to establish whether this is the case and if so what their identities are,' the memo stated.

A note in the police files from the time indicates scepticism by investigating officers about the allegations. 'I am of the opinion that something untoward happened in 1975 between [Boy A] and Janner. However, I am not convinced that the allegations made by [Boy A] are completely genuine. There is no direct corroboration and it could be that the allegation has been made to fit the letters recovered from Beck.'

When the police interviewed Janner, the MP appeared with his lawyer, Sir David Napley, and declined to answer any questions – which was perfectly within his rights and which, at that time, did not carry any legal inference of guilt. But Janner's behaviour did nothing to persuade the police that he was innocent.

At the time one of the key investigating officers into the Beck case, Detective Sergeant Mick Creedon, was worried about the allegations against Janner. He believed that the complaints against Janner were certainly 'credible' and warranted detailed inquiry. But Creedon was warned off taking the complaints against Janner seriously. One of Leicestershire's superintendants spoke to him and told him to back off.

Many years later Creedon, who became Chief Constable of Derbyshire, told *The Times*: 'The decision was clear, he will be interviewed by appointment and there won't be a search of his home, his constituency office or his office in the Commons. It was a decision made by people more senior than me.'

Creedon's recollection is backed up by the most senior police officer investigating Frank Beck, former Detective Inspector Kelvin Ashby. Many years later Ashby told the BBC that he was instructed not to arrest Janner. 'I would have preferred to arrest him because I felt we had enough evidence, but the powers that be just said that wouldn't be the case, this man's an MP, we've got to think of his character and his reputation,' said Ashby.

The implication was that the instruction came from the then chief constable, Michael Hirst (now dead). Hirst was a senior freemason (which his widow denies) – as were many police officers, council officials and politicians at the time. It has also been suggested that Janner was a mason, though there is no proof to support the claim.

In the Crown Prosecution Service in 1991 the feeling was that there were grounds for a further investigation into the allegations against Janner, with additional resources needed by the Leicestershire Chief Constable to continue inquiries. Further information was needed, suggested officials within the CPS, to determine Janner's room arrangements at the Holiday Inn and medical case notes obtained on the injuries to the boy's anus. This never happened.

One conversation between the leading counsel in the Beck case and the CPS articled clerk – a former police constable – provides a flavour of the discussion about the Janner allegations. Leading counsel asked, 'is there anything in it?', to which the articled clerk replied: 'Yes, undoubtedly, the police also think so.'

The CPS sought leading counsel advice on whether there were grounds for a prosecution. Its articled clerk noted that the

CPS's leading counsel 'had no hesitation in concluding that at present there was inadequate evidence to proceed against Mr Greville Janner in respect of the allegation made against him by [Boy A] and others'. The leading counsel added that he 'was satisfied that on the papers he had seen in respect of the Janner allegations, the police had discharged their duty to investigate the allegations impartially.'

The meeting considering possible further action involved the CPS articled clerk, two other clerks and the police. There was no one senior from the CPS present as the Chief Crown Prosecutor was abroad at the time. It was decided that a final decision would await the outcome of the Beck trial. But, crucially, the matter was not considered after the close of that trial. It was one of the key moments in the Janner case where the criminal justice system failed.

Instead, on 4 December 1991, three working days after the completion of the Beck trial, the Chief Crown Prosecutor – without conducting a full review of the evidence — told Leicestershire's chief superintendant that on the available evidence there was no realistic prospect of conviction in relation to Greville Janner MP. On the same day the assistant chief constable wrote to Janner's solicitors that the police did not intend to charge him.

Yet by the end of 1991, 10 civilian witnesses had made statements to the police about the allegations against Janner. When, years later, a proper effort was made by the police to pursue allegations against Janner some 32 witness statements supported the allegations made by Boy A — with 12 of these specifically relating to events at the Holiday Inn. All this evidence should have been available to the police in 1991 – and more. By the time the police actually looked for evidence some of the witnesses may have died, others might no longer have recalled events, while some would have become difficult to track down.

The 1992 Kirkwood Inquiry was intended to provide a sign-off on the Beck affair, providing clarity as to what happened, why it was allowed to happen, what institutional failings had taken place and the lessons for the future. Janner was clearly a central character, even if at the time assumed to be innocent of the allegations made against him. Janner gave both written and verbal evidence to Kirkwood. Yet Janner was permitted to give that verbal evidence in private and that evidence has never been revealed. The reasons for this secrecy also remain secret.

Janner's written statement to the Kirkwood Inquiry contradicted key evidence given by Boy A. Those contradictions included details of the type of room that Janner stayed in at the Holiday Inn and the length of the Scottish lecture tour. Had the police followed this up, they could easily have determined if Janner or Boy A had told the truth.

It became clear in later years that Janner had given factually wrong information to the Kirkwood Inquiry. Janner told Kirkwood that he did not know Beck and had no contact with him between 1975 and 1986. That was clearly untrue: there is substantial supporting evidence to show that Janner had been a regular visitor to children's homes in that period, including those managed by Beck.

Despite the lack of police and CPS action against Janner following the Beck trial, the rumours about Janner became more widespread.

Nigel O'Mara set-up the first charity to support male victims of sexual abuse – Survivors UK – in 1986. During the early 1990s he received calls alleging that Greville Janner was abusing children. 'We had a number of calls from different people in the same location,' he recalls. 'I wrote to the Home Secretary Kenneth Clarke and never even had a reply – I did not really expect to.'

Calls to Survivors UK alleged that Janner had taken boys out of children's homes and had then sexually abused them. Other callers made similar allegations about Liberal MP Cyril Smith.

O'Mara recorded two interviews in 1993 with Roger Cook for the *Cook Report* about the allegations he received about Janner and Smith. 'It seemed to be going ahead until the last couple of weeks,' he says. 'I did not hear from him again.' He never found out why the programme had been dropped.

Instead the following year O'Mara and his partner were beaten-up in their own home. While he was being beaten he was told that he was 'to stop what you are doing if you know what's good for you'. O'Mara interpreted this as a warning and a threat to stop his work on cases of abuse. The attack was reported to the police, but he says that no action was taken. O'Mara then moved to Italy and Belgium, where he was involved in establishing the White Flowers campaign against child abuse.

In 1992, a leaflet was published by a previously unknown group, 'Concerned Leicester Parents', which repeated allegations against Janner that had been raised in the trial and which highlighted his Jewish ethnicity. That leaflet was largely ignored by mainstream media and the political establishment, as it was assumed to have been published by supporters of the far right: the National Front was active in Leicester at that time.

A longer booklet containing the same allegations was published in 1995, titled: *Is Greville Janner QC, MP, above the law?: How people in high places covered-up for a Parliamentary paedophile*. Again the allegations were generally dismissed because the publication's provenance was false. The book was supposedly written by Dr A. Van Helsing – a pseudonym based on the character in Dracula – and was claimed to be published by LRD. This falsely implied that those behind it were the Labour Research Department, a legitimate body providing information for the trade union movement. The imprint even used the address of the Labour Research Department. The work was widely assumed to be the malicious product of members of far right organisations.

Within the Labour Party, though, there were concerns about the allegations. Backbench Labour MP and former actor Andrew Faulds – a strong critic of Israel — tried to have the complaints properly investigated. How far he got is unclear. He is now dead, but the two publications are contained in his personal papers which are archived at the London School of Economics.

Even if the allegations were treated with scepticism by the Labour Party hierarchy, there was a feeling that Janner's time was over as an MP. According to a then Labour Party official in Leicester, Janner was persuaded, against his wishes, to stand down and make way for a younger person. Janner's version has it that he decided to step down when his wife Myra became seriously ill – she died in 1996.

Janner was ennobled as a reward for stepping down. In October 1997, he entered the House of Lords as Baron Janner of Braunstone, taking the name from a large council estate in Leicester West. In Janner's autobiography, *To Life!*, he credited Peter Mandelson with playing a central role in persuading Tony Blair – soon after becoming Prime Minister — to appoint him to the House of Lords. The new candidate in Leicester West was Patricia Hewitt, one of the party's rising stars and a close confidante of Blair. She retained the seat in the general election and went on to become a senior Cabinet minister, holding the roles of secretary of state for health and for trade and industry.

In 2002, Janner's name arose again in another police investigation, Operation Magnolia, into allegations of abuse against children in two Leicestershire children's homes, Ratcliffe Road and the Holt. Janner was named as an alleged abuser, by another former child resident, Complainant 2, who claimed to have been buggered by Janner. The police, it seems, disbelieved the allegations, in part because of the criminal offences committed by the accuser after he left care.

Operation Dauntless began in 2006, investigating allegations raised by a former resident of The Beeches that Beck and Janner jointly sexually abused boys in care. The boy, Complainant 3, alleged that Janner had been guilty of offences involving oral sex and buggery. After one sex act, Janner was alleged to have turned to Beck, patted him on the back and commented to the effect 'well done, you groomed him well.' No charges came out of Operation Dauntless and Janner was probably unaware that he was even being investigated. CPS notes suggest that prosecutors regarded the evidence as insufficient to take the matter further.

In 2009, Janner was diagnosed with dementia. He continued to run his business and to sit in the House of Lords, where he voted on legislation and claimed expenses. He was, ostensibly at least, a respected and eminent peer.

But his status changed slowly from 2012 after the exposure of the TV presenter, Jimmy Savile, for being – in the words of the NSPCC – 'one of the most, if not the most, prolific sex offender that we at the NSPCC have ever come across.' Having failed to properly investigate Savile while he was alive, his death was followed by more than 300 credible allegations that the DJ had carried out rapes and other abuses of children. After the stories of Savile emerged, police attitudes changed: victims became more likely to be believed and the police were more willing to investigate those public figures that previously had been protected by their fame.

A new investigation was opened into Janner after a letter was sent to the Commissioner of the Metropolitan Police, which had investigated Savile after his death. As the allegations related to matters in Leicestershire, the Commissioner, Sir Bernard Hogan-Howe, referred the matter to Leicestershire's Chief Constable, Simon Cole. Given that allegations against the politician had already been investigated by his force three times, in 1991, 2002 and 2006, Cole decided it was sensible to conduct a review to confirm that those investigations had been diligent. A recently retired female detective sergeant with expertise in investigating sexual crime was asked to review the case papers. Her finding was that the past investigations had been inadequate: the case should be reopened.

This led to the launch of Operation Enamel, into allegations of historic sexual abuse of young people by Baron Janner of Braunstone. Operation Enamel had the largest resources of any investigation into Janner: a team of 20 officers, initially investigating 11 allegations, the earliest dating back to the 1950s and the most recent being in the 1980s. The police officers involved in Operation Enamel concluded the allegations were 'credible'. During this operation, Janner's House of Lords office was raided – in what is believed to be the first time a House of Lords office had been the subject of a police search warrant. Janner's London home was also raided.

Among the leads investigated by the police was one that reinforced previous suggestions of connections between Janner and Beck. Investigating officers took these allegations seriously. Police were told that some boys were abused jointly by Beck and Janner, at children's homes in Leicester and also in London. The BBC reported that residents of the homes, social workers, a former police officer and a former council official all stated that Beck and Janner were what the BBC described as 'associates'.

During Operation Enamel, the police moved from scepticism towards the allegations to cynicism about those who had been accused. They eventually had little doubt that Janner was guilty, nor that he and Frank Beck were partners in crime. They concluded that Beck had taken boys from his care to London, where the two, together, abused them.

Police also examined the possibility that Beck might have taken children to the Elm Guest House – amid a Metropolitan Police investigation into claims that children were sexually abused there by Establishment figures – but decided this was not the case. One investigating officer explained that Leicestershire Police had checked the angle with the assistance of the Met 'but there is no Elm-Janner connection that we are aware of.'

The officer explained: 'We didn't get any connection between Beck and Elm, but had multiple links between Beck and Janner. We do know that some of our victims were taken to London where Beck and Janner [were] present too.'

The strength and consistency of the allegations persuaded investigating officers that there was a strong link between Beck and Janner. The officer explained: 'Multiple independent witnesses linked Janner to Beck and Janner to the children's homes where Beck was in charge. As for Beck taking kids to London, there are accounts which say this, but not many.'

Off the back of Operation Enamel, Scottish police also launched their own investigation into the allegations of rape and other abuse on the lecture tour of Scotland.

A leading national campaigner against child abuse, the Labour MP Simon Danczuk, took up Janner's case. Danczuk, who had co-written a book revealing the scale of sexual and physical abuse by the former senior Liberal MP Sir Cyril Smith, had convened meetings in the House of Commons, in which abuse survivors could tell their stories and discuss future action. Danczuk was an obvious person for a police whistle-blower to contact to pass on allegations about Janner.

In October 2014, Danczuk wrote to the then Labour Party leader, Ed Miliband, saying he had been 'visited by three senior officers from Leicestershire police' and that the alleged abuse by Janner they had disclosed to him was 'stomach-churning'.

Danczuk urged Miliband to suspend Janner's party membership – and went public on his call for action.

A few days after the letter was sent, Janner took 'leave of absence' from the House of Lords and ceased attending sittings of the House of Lords. In the five years since his diagnosis of dementia, Janner had attended the House of Lords 634 times and voted 203 times. According to a report, during this period he was paid more than £100,000 in expenses as a working peer.

Janner's family responded angrily to accusations and consistently maintained his innocence. In a statement his family said: 'Lord Janner is a man of great integrity and high repute with a long and unblemished record of public service. He is entirely innocent of any wrongdoing.' In October 2014, his daughter, Rabbi Laura Janner-Klausner, told *Huffington Post UK* that the allegations against her father had led to 'putrid, toxic Anti-Semitism' against the family. She said: 'It is extreme stuff. It is beyond comprehension. Vile, vile fascist anti-Semitism.'

However, the police investigation was amassing evidence that the allegations were founded in fact. Thirty individuals made allegations against Janner to Operation Enamel. Most of them were residents in Leicestershire children's homes between 1970 and the mid to late 1980s.

Following the evidence gathering, Lord Janner was requested to attend a new police interview. As the result of what were described by the CPS as 'medical concerns' followed by an independent police neuropsychiatrist's report, no such police interview took place.

By the time files were passed to the CPS in 2015, a substantial body of allegations and evidence had been collected. These included the original allegations by Boy A (now termed Complainant 1), which comprised what was later described as 'grooming and sexual abuse of the alleged male victim between the ages of 13 and 15'.

But the file went far beyond that original set of allegations by Boy A. It also contained the allegations from Complainant 2, arising from Operation Magnolia in 2002, which did not lead to Janner being interviewed. The file further contained allegations arising from Operation Dauntless, when in 2006 Janner was again not questioned.

Of the 30 witnesses who had made allegations against Janner, 12 regarded as the strongest potential witnesses would have testified against him in a trial.

On 16 April 2015, the Crown Prosecution Service finally gave its decision on whether Janner should stand trial – and ruled that he shouldn't. In an unusually long statement, the Director of Public Prosecutions, Alison Saunders, said it would not be in the public interest to try him because he was suffering from severe dementia.

However, she said that but for Janner's ill-health he would have been tried because the allegations were 'extremely serious' and the evidence warranted bringing a case. Saunders said that Janner would have been charged with:

- 14 indecent assaults on a male under 16 between 1969 and 1988
- 2 indecent assaults between 1984 and 1988
- 4 counts of buggery of a male under 16 between 1972 and 1987
- 2 counts of buggery between 1977 and 1988.

Saunders explained: 'The CPS has concluded that Lord Greville Janner should not be prosecuted because of the severity of his dementia which means he is not fit to take part in any proceedings, there is no treatment for his condition, and there is no current or future risk of offending.'

Perhaps more revealingly, she said that the CPS now considered that Janner should have been charged during the previous police investigations. She said: 'It follows that the CPS judges that mistakes were made in the decision making at the time by both the Leicestershire police in 2002 and the CPS in 1991 and 2007. Lord Janner should have been prosecuted in relation to those complaints.'

One individual, the Director of Public Prosecutions added, had made allegations of 'serious sexual offending around 1981 by three individuals including Lord Janner.'

Factors influencing the previous directors of public prosecutions included concerns that witnesses – including alleged victims – were not regarded as sufficiently credible. They were regarded as likely to be dismissed in court as motivated by money or revenge, or because of their difficult life experiences.

Saunders said that had the cases been brought, Lord Janner would have had the opportunity to challenge the evidence and defend himself through the trial process, with a jury ultimately deciding on his guilt or innocence. Equally:

'Victims of the alleged offences have been denied the opportunity of criminal proceedings... It is of obvious and particular concern that such proceedings did not take place as a result of what the CPS now consider to be wrong decisions.'

Janner's diagnosis of Alzheimer's disease in 2009 had been confirmed by four medical experts, two of whom were instructed by Janner's legal team and two by the police and prosecutors. Saunders concluded: 'Lord Janner is suffering from a degenerative dementia which is rapidly becoming more severe. He requires continuous care both day and night. His evidence could not be relied upon in court and he could not have any meaningful engagement with the court process, and the court would find it impossible to proceed.'

Moreover, there was no prospect of recovery and the experts said there was no possibility that Janner was capable of 'manipulation' so that a false diagnosis had been made. Saunders decided there was also no risk of future offending.

The former children's home residents who made allegations against Janner, and the two police forces who had investigated those allegations, responded with fury.

Leicestershire Police took the unusual, perhaps unique, step of issuing a statement on behalf of one of the by now 25 complainants against Janner. The unnamed accuser said:

'This animal is still being protected because [of his status] and isn't able to stand trial. They say that it's not in the public interest, but isn't it in the public interest to know what his victims have gone through at the hands of this man? If he was an everyday person with a normal life and job, justice would [have] been served, but as it stands we victims are just being pushed to the ground again and walked over.

'Let someone feel the pain and suffering that I've endured and still going to endure for the rest of my life. It's not a case of being found guilty or going to prison — it's about being believed after so long being told that we were lying. Justice needs to be served.'

Leicestershire Police issued a strong statement of its own, pointing out – without naming Janner – that a person 'suspected of sexually abusing vulnerable children who were resident in Leicestershire care homes in the 1960s, 1970s and 1980s' was not to be prosecuted.

Assistant Chief Constable Roger Bannister of Leicestershire Police, who oversaw the investigation, said he believed the decision would discourage victims of abuse from coming forward. Bannister said:

'Thanks primarily to the courage of 25 victims who have made a complaint and the complete professionalism of the investigation team, we have built a case that the DPP has acknowledged is the result of a thorough investigation, evidentially sufficient and gives rise to a realistic chance of conviction.

'There is credible evidence that this man carried out some of the most serious sexual crimes imaginable over three decades against children who were highly vulnerable and the majority of whom were in care.

'I am extremely worried about the impact the decision not to prosecute him will have on those people, and more widely I am worried about the message this decision sends out to others, both past and present, who have suffered and are suffering sexual abuse.'

The true scale of Operation Enamel became apparent. Bannister described how in the course of the investigation, more than 2,000 individuals were seen 442 statements were taken, more than 2,700 lines of enquiry pursued and nearly 600 exhibits pulled together. Some of the exhibits were created, while others were seized — including cine film and videos. More than 6,000 pages of case file material were supplied to the CPS.

The police also revealed that Operation Enamel had not focused solely on Janner and that other individuals might yet be prosecuted. But the force was not content to let the matter drop with regard to Janner and Bannister said that the police were taking legal advice about the possibility of Janner being prosecuted, despite the CPS decision.

A few weeks later, on 26 May 2015, Leicestershire Police issued a third statement on Operation Enamel. This said that unless the Director of Public Prosecutions changed her decision not to prosecute, Leicestershire Police reserved its right to seek a judicial review of the decision in an effort to overturn it.

The neighbouring Northamptonshire Police were also angered by the decision not to prosecute. The force's Commissioner Adam Simmonds said: 'Greville Janner may not have been found guilty in court, but a man who has protested his innocence and accused victims of lying in my view has a lot of strong and compelling evidence against him. I believe in the right to a fair trial that underpins our justice system, and stand by the notion of 'innocent until proven guilty', but I for one will take the DPP's statement that 'but for medical considerations, it would undoubtedly have been in the public interest to prosecute' extremely seriously.

'Moving forward, the question remains how a person fit to stand trial can be brought to justice, yet where a perpetrator has died, as had Jimmy Savile, that a Metropolitan Police report can conclude 'Jimmy Savile was one of the UK's most prolific known sexual predators.' It is a sad and worrying state of affairs that although a potential perpetrator is still alive, the victims of his crimes are not able to seek justice for what he has done.'

Under the newly introduced CPS Victims' Right to Review scheme, which allows victims to have their cases looked at again, even after a decision not to prosecute, six people who made allegations against Janner requested the formal right to review.

In May at Alison Saunders' request, the decision was reviewed with the assistance of a leading criminal barrister, David Perry QC. The review concluded that it was in the public interest to bring proceedings before the court. In reaching that conclusion, the review agreed that Janner would inevitably be found unfit to plead but that the most likely outcome would be a 'trial of the facts' in which complainants and witnesses would give evidence. There could be neither conviction nor punishment – the court's options would be to order an absolute discharge, or impose either a supervision order or a hospital order. But the alleged victims would, it seemed, at least and at last have their day in court, with full publicity of their accusations.

Alison Saunders responded: 'I have always said that in my view this was an extremely difficult and borderline case because of the strong arguments on both sides.'

The first hearing took place at Westminster Magistrates' Court on 7 August 2015. Some 22 charges were listed against Janner, alleging various incidents of buggery and indecent assault against boys and men. The earliest alleged incident could have taken place in 1963, while the most recent could have been in 1988.

When Janner was due to appear at the Old Bailey, he did not turn up. His legal team requested the court allow him instead to appear through a video link from his home. The magistrate, Emma Arbuthnot, refused, threatening to have Janner arrested if he did not attend in the afternoon.

Janner turned up later that day — for just 59 seconds. He appeared confused, seemingly confirming medical reports that the 87 year old was suffering from advanced dementia. Looking around the court room, Janner said: 'Ooh, this is wonderful!' He then left, holding his daughter's hand, with the promise of an ice cream on the way home.

Greville Janner died on 19 December 2015, peacefully at home, aged 87. Despite the substantial evidence that he had sexually abused children, he had never been prosecuted. The 'trial of the facts' to consider allegations against him, which had been due to take place in April 2016, was cancelled.

In January 2016, a review of the failures to prosecute Janner was published by the CPS. Sir Richard Henriques, a retired judge, who had been commissioned to conduct the review in 2015, concluded that Janner should have been prosecuted in 1991 – 24 years before he died. He reported: 'The police investigation was incomplete and inadequate in 1991 and police officers failed to carry out enquiries advised by the CPS... I have concluded that the decision not to charge Janner in 1991 was wrong and that there was enough evidence against Janner, on the 4th December 1991, to provide a realistic prospect of conviction.'

What went so badly wrong with Greville Janner, time and time again, for decades?

The newly-instituted Independent Inquiry into Child Sexual Abuse will consider in detail the allegations against him as part of a wide-ranging investigation into allegations of institutional child abuse – and allegations that prominent politicians used their positions to abuse children. The inquiry is commonly called the Goddard Inquiry after its chair Dame Lowell Goddard, a judge from New Zealand deemed to be sufficiently independent of the English establishment. Her inquiry will carry out 13 detailed investigations into institutional child abuse cases. The first will be Janner's.

The Goddard Inquiry

The Goddard inquiry will consider the strength of the allegations and why they never led to Janner being prosecuted.

Ben Emmerson, Senior Counsel to the Inquiry, explained: 'The overall purpose of the investigation is to determine the extent to which public and private institutions may have failed in their duty to protect children from sexual abuse or failed in their duty to ensure accountability for offences allegedly committed by Greville Janner and others associated with him.'

The Janner aspect of the inquiry will allow victims a public hearing and develop public policy to ensure that people such as Janner and Cyril Smith do not avoid prosecution merely because of their status as senior politicians. However, the scale of the wider child abuse crisis dwarfs the Janner case.

According to Emmerson's opening remarks, 50,000 children in England and Wales were identified by statutory agencies as victims of sexual abuse in the period from April 2012 to March 2014, while the Children's Commissioner believes that by including unreported victims the real figure is probably 450,000 in that same period. The scale of this crime is staggering, as is the psychological damage done to victims.

Part of the Goddard inquiry's focus will be on the institutional failures – and how those were influenced by the status of some of the abusers. Why did Leicestershire County Council not properly protect children in its care? Why did the police not fully investigate allegations against a prominent politician? Why were prosecutors not objective when viewing allegations against a powerful person? Why did Parliament, the Labour Party and other politicians not intervene? What, if anything, did the security services know of the alleged abuse? And why did they not act on any knowledge they did have?

There are other questions, too, that Goddard will consider. What did the Home Office know? What happened to the complaints from Nigel O'Mara, and perhaps others, that went into the Home Office? And why did the Kirkwood Inquiry treat Janner so differently from other witnesses – and why was some of his evidence allowed to be kept secret?

All these questions, as yet unanswered, are central to the operations of the Goddard inquiry. A key challenge facing

Goddard is to choose between accident and conspiracy for why Janner avoided prosecution.

Goddard might even conclude that the case against Janner is unfounded – through that would be a considerable surprise.

We know from the cases of Jimmy Savile, Cyril Smith, Rolf Harris, and Stuart Hall that status protects abusers. This is probably especially so with politicians who abuse children. If one beneficial lesson can be taken from the Janner case it is that the voices of vulnerable children should be heard – and that the words of politicians should be treated with greater scepticism.

Bibliography

Audit Commission, *Misspent Youth*, London: Audit Commission, 1996.

Michael Balint, *The Basic Fault: Therapeutic Aspects of Regression*, Illinois: Northwestern University Press, 1992.

David Berridge and Isabelle Brodie, *Children's Homes Revisited*, London: Jessica Kingsley, 1998.

Bruno Bettelheim, *Love is Not Enough*, New York: Free Press., 1950.

Bruno Bettelheim, *The Empty Fortress*, New York: Free Press, 1967.

Mike Boyle, Mike Leadbetter and John Walters, *Enough is Enough*, London: private paper, 1997.

Marion Clayden, *Institutional Abuse: a counselling service for the survivors*, private paper, 1992.

Graham Coates and Jocelyn Jones (eds), *Institutional Abuse: Leadership, power and rights explored*, Leicester: Leicester University, 1997.

Matthew Colton and Maurice Vanstone, *Betrayal of Trust*, London: Free Association Books, 1996.

Barbara Dockar-Drysdale, *Therapy and Consultation in Child Care*, London: Free Association Books, 1993.

D. Foster, *Inquiry into police investigation of complaints of child and sexual abuse in Leicestershire children's homes*, London: Police Complaints Authority, 1993.

Sigmund Freud, *Introductory Lectures on Psychoanalysis* (translated by James Strachey), London: Penguin, 1973.

Sir Richard Henriques, *The Henriques Report*, http://www.cps.gov.uk/publications/reports/henriques_report_190116.pdf

Hunt, Geoffrey (ed.) *Whistleblowing in the Social Services*, London: Arnold, 1998

Jocelyn Jones, *Institutional Abuse: understanding domination from the inside looking out*, Leicester: Leicester University, 1995.

Jocelyn Jones and Jenny Myers, *The Future Detection and Prevention of Institutional Abuse: giving children a chance to participate in research*, Leicester: Leicester University, 1997.

Andrew Kirkwood, *The Leicestershire Inquiry 1992*, Leicestershire: Leicestershire County Council, 1991

Allan Levy (ed.), *Re-focus on Child Abuse*, London: Hawksmere, 1994.

The Earl of Longford, *Avowed Intent*, London: Warner Books, 1995.

M.B. Newell, *Report on Leicestershire social services*, private report, 1990.

Sir William Utting, *People Like Us*, London: The Stationery Office Ltd, 1997.

Sir Norman Warner, *Choosing with Care*, London: HMSO 1992

Helen Westcott, *Institutional Abuse of Children*, private paper, 1990. printed paper for case hardback

Index

A

B

C

Authors

Mark D'Arcy is a parliamentary correspondent for the BBC and presents BOOKTalk on the BBC Parliament television channel. When *Abuse of Trust* was first published, he was the BBC's local government and social affairs correspondent for the East Midlands, and a former political commentator for the *Leicester Mercury*.

Paul Gosling is an experienced journalist, author, researcher, lecturer, and broadcaster. He specialises in the economy, accountancy, the co-operative sector, public services and personal finances. A freelance journalist for 27 years, he has written for most quality UK and Irish national newspapers. He is a former Leicester City councillor.

www.canburypress.com

Also by Canbury Press: *Beyond Contempt: The Inside Story of the Phone Hacking Trial* by Peter Jukes (ISBN: 9780993040719)

16/08/16